BIRDING IN AN AGE OF EXTINCTIONS

Birding in an Age of Extinctions

MARTIN PAINTER

Whittles Publishing

Published by
Whittles Publishing,
Dunbeath,
Caithness KW6 6EG,
Scotland, UK

www.whittlespublishing.com

ISBN 978-184995-487-7

MIX
Paper from responsible sources
FSC® C004116

Printed using FSC® certified paper from sustainable sources

Printed in the UK by Cambrian Printers

CONTENTS

GLOSSARY

Accidental	A bird that turns up in a locality outside its normal species range (also called a vagrant)
Banding	See 'Ringing'
Bins	Shorthand for binoculars
Blind	See 'Hide'
Burley	A cocktail of fish oil, fish innards and so on, thrown over the stern of a boat into the water to attract seabirds
Clements	Shorthand for *Clements Checklist of Birds of the World*, named after its first author. It is now managed and regularly updated by the Cornell Lab of Ornithology.
Checklist	A reference list of species that may be seen in a particular location or on a particular birding trip ('trip checklist')
Dip	Birder's jargon for failing to see or to ID definitively a bird encountered on a trip
Eastern Flyway	The route taken by birds that migrate between North East Asia and Australasia
eBird	A worldwide online database of birders' daily observations of species and their locations: https://ebird.org/home
Endemic	A species that is only seen in a particular country or region
Endemism	A measure of the occurrence of endemic species in a particular country or region
Exotics	Species occurring in a locality that are introduced from some other part of the globe (see also 'Feral' and 'Invasive species')
Feeder	Any device that serves up bird food (for example, a hummingbird feeder) often placed to enable a close-up view by birders
Feral	Birds (or other creatures) that have been captive-bred and have escaped to form breeding populations (for example, pigeons, free-roaming domestic chickens)

Fieldscope	A single-lens optical instrument mounted on a tripod and designed to magnify the image (for example, ×20, ×50, ×90)
Habituated	Accustomed to human presence by means such as provision of food at feeders
Hide	A constructed shelter or screen with viewing holes or windows enabling birders to conceal themselves while observing birds
Intergradation	When two species with adjacent or overlapping ranges hybridize, creating intergrades, or birds that share characteristics of both species
Invasive species	Exotic species that intrude on and take over habitat occupied by indigenous species
IOC Checklist	International Ornithological Congress world list of all bird species
IUCN Red List	International Union for Conservation of Nature list of species categorized according to the degree of threat of extinction
Kettle	A group of birds wheeling upwards in the rising warm air or thermal updraft
Lazarus species	A species formerly considered extinct but rediscovered living in the wild
LBJ	'Little brown job' – any small bird that is dull and mostly brown
Lek	A place where male birds customarily assemble to display and attract females for mating
Life list	A birder's list of species they have seen
Lifer	A bird seen for the first time (see also 'Tick')
Lister	A birder who keeps a list or lists of species they have seen; often applied to one who treats this as the most important aspect of birding
Local patch	An area close to where a birder lives that they visit regularly to look for birds
Lumps and splits	Taxa that are newly identified as such by field ornithologists and taxonomists, either by 'lumping' two or more into one or by 'splitting' one into two or more
Mega	Birder's jargon for a species not yet on their life list that would be a very special addition due to, for example, its rarity, remoteness or spectacular plumage
Mist-netting	Putting up large, finely meshed 'mist-nets' to catch birds in flight. Used both by ornithologists for ringing and by trappers collecting birds for food or for the live bird market.
Morphology	The science of the structure and form of animals and plants
Murmuration	A mass gathering or flock of starlings in flight
Nominate	The subspecies that bears the subspecies Latin name identical to the species name, due to it being the first collected and identified as a new

species. For example, *Turdus poliocephalis poliocephalis* (the extinct, endemic Norfolk Island subspecies of Island Thrush).

Ornithology	The science of birds
Oology	The science of birds' eggs
Passerine	A taxonomic category referring to those families (comprising about half of all bird species) that are 'perching birds' by virtue of having a particular arrangement of toes
Patchwatcher	A birder who mainly watches birds in a local patch of habitat
Phylogeny	The history of the evolution of taxa, usually shown by drawing a family tree showing the lines of descent
Pishing	Making a variety of sounds designed to imitate bird calls, by pursing one's lips and expelling air, with a view to attracting birds to come closer
Playback	A bird song (or call) recording played back to attract the same species of bird. Best results are sometimes obtained by first recording a bird's song and immediately playing it back to the same bird. The word is often used as a noun – 'let's try playback'. See also 'Pishing' and 'Tooting'.
Red List	See 'IUCN'
Ringing	A small ring or band attached to the leg of a captured bird, which is released. The ring contains numbers and letters that identify the time and place of ringing. When a ringed bird is captured, or spotted through a fieldscope, the numbers can be used to track its movements. Ringing is also termed 'banding'.
Roost	A place, such as a coppice, tree or bush, where birds choose to rest and sleep overnight, often communally
Scope	See 'Fieldscope'
Sonogram	A graph-like representation of birdsong, showing peaks and troughs of volume, pitch, rhythms and other features
Speciation	The emergence of new species in the process of evolution
Splits	See 'Lumps and splits'
Taxon, pl. taxa	A unit of classification used in biological study, for example 'species.' Hence 'taxonomy', the science of the classification and naming of taxa.
Tick	A bird is said to be a 'tick' if it is a birder's first sight of a species (see also 'Lifer')
Tooting	Imitating the call of an owl to attract small birds, which fly in to mob the supposed intruder
Trash bird	A mildly derogatory term used for a bird that is so common that the birder has little, if any, interest in noting its presence
Twitcher	A birder who devotes energy to seeing rarities, especially accidentals or vagrants, within a particular locality or country. A 'twitch' is a twitching event.

Type specimen	The preserved and catalogued skin (or DNA sample) of the bird that was shot or trapped at the time the first claim was made to identify it as a member of a species new to science. Type specimens are normally housed in museum and university collections.
Vagrant	See 'Accidental'

Introduction

I happily confess to being a mad birder. Birders, birdwatchers, bird lovers, call us what you may, come in many different forms and guises. There are millions of us, encompassing the many who put out food on the garden bird table and watch for the familiar visitors, and the far smaller number (me included) who have travelled all over the world in order to see as many new birds as is humanly possible. Hardcore, globetrotting world birders show a dedication, determination, energy and utter madness that sets us somewhat apart. But for the moment, I don't want to draw too sharp a distinction, we'll get to such matters later. In my experience, the vast majority of us share the same innocent enthusiasm and the same sense of wonderment and affection that draws all bird lovers to enjoy birds. At home, many of us have bird feeders in the garden and like to stroll through the local woodlands with binoculars around our necks, taking note of the familiar sights and sounds. It's just that some of us also like to travel to see a lot of new birds.

I haven't been a birder for very long, but I have packed a lot in. I have spent a great deal of time, money and energy searching out new birds and accumulating a life list (to date) of around 6,000 species. For a hardcore world birder, a life list of 6,000 species is just a start (there are nearly 11,000 to be ticked off in total). I have some traveller's tales to tell. But in writing about this experience, I first of all wanted to share some of the joys of just being a birdwatcher. So, this book is in no small part a celebration of the joys of loving birds, told through the lens of my own experiences. Its trajectory is autobiographical, but not strictly chronological, tracing my personal awakening of enchantment and wonderment as I looked for and encountered new and amazing birds, experienced their diverse habitats and enjoyed all of this in the company of other enthusiasts. The chapters describe different episodes in this personal journey and encompass different types of discovery – of birds, places and people.

But the traveller's tales are only one part of the story. As a relative latecomer to the birding community, I found much of the behaviour of the groups of birders I mixed with to be an object of occasional amazement and frequent puzzlement. They do some pretty odd things – and I don't exclude myself from this observation! This is not so much because, as individuals, we are a particularly odd bunch (OK, that's debatable), but more because birding as an activity is, in many of its aspects, itself a bit odd. World birding shows this in the extreme. And these aspects of birding turn out to be particularly instructive about and relevant to wider issues in the modern world, especially concerning our relations with nature. So, I found myself wanting to dig into the origins of some taken-for-granted (by birders) features of the world of birding.

Underlying the whole enterprise of birding is just one question: 'What bird is that?' (the title of one of my favourite bird books).[1] We don't just look, watch and enjoy; we have to know as well. We want to be able to label each bird correctly. Some threshold level of expertise is necessary to take satisfaction from birding. The knowledge you need is just like the curriculum of any discipline and is based mostly on science, enriched through practice and experience. In this respect, birding with its challenges often seems to be more like work than leisure. And it brings similar rewards, material as well as non-material. It satisfies and rewards a desire to acquire and accumulate and, for many, it becomes a vocation. Our list of the birds we have seen and our collection of the images we have captured are our measures of success and achievement.

For many, it's the competitive element that is the attraction, the urge to be the first to offer a correct identification in the field, to have the longest life list and to collect the most trophies by seeing or photographing the rarest or most spectacular birds. For others, in contrast, it is the satisfaction of observing and recording behaviour such as nesting and breeding, comings and goings on the local patch and, in particular, unusual arrivals. For all of us, it is the indescribable lure of being in the presence of birds, observing them, learning about them and simply appreciating them.

So, birding is an activity that not only takes us into nature and its wonders for their own sakes, but also uses nature as a vehicle for our expression of other, more mundane, desires and ambitions. It took me a while to work all this out – when you are having such fun, there is little reason for reflection. And this growing realisation was, in some respects, a journey of disenchantment. Some hints of this are in my traveller's tales, which describe the fun I was having but also record some more negative thoughts and encounters. The second part of the book probes these doubts and looks to unravel or even to resolve some of them.

The backdrop was my growing exposure to a world of nature that was in decline under the relentless pressures of human activities. My career as a birder has coincided with the awakening of a public consciousness – mine as well – about the dire state of crisis in which the natural world finds itself. I have seen it for myself, wherever I have been on my birding adventures. My own awareness and understanding of nature's decline and our species' role in it have been sharpened by my observation of what birders do, and why – and how, when faced with the results, we carry on birding, as if it were all just normal.

All of my birding has been conducted in the presence of accelerating habitat loss and looming extinctions. Aside from encountering some magnificent near-wilderness remnants and precious protected sanctuaries, my experience as a world birder exploring the natural world has been of trashed habitats and shrinking wildlife populations. Nearly all of this is human induced – it is our doing. My traveller's tales of encounters with nature are both tales of discovery and celebration and also, in some cases, tales of loss and grief.

In saying this, I am not just putting a somewhat gloomy spin on things based on a one-eyed personal experience: solid evidence of the growing threats to wildlife posed by human activity has mounted alarmingly. One study has concluded that in the period 1970–2014, population sizes of wildlife in all its forms decreased globally by 60%.[2] I can't read or re-read that sentence without a sense of shock: nature took millennia to get to where it was by its

1 Neville W. Cayley, *What Bird is That?* Sydney: Angus & Robertson, 1931.

2 Monique Grooten and Rosamunde Almond (eds), *Living Planet Report – 2018: Aiming Higher*, Gland, Switzerland: WWF, 2018.

own momentum, and it only needed decades for us to eradicate 60% of it. What happens next? Another study has found that the total population of birds measured annually in the USA and Canada declined by 29% (or 3 billion birds) between 1970 and 2017.[3] Such a decline is leading inexorably to extinctions.

Statistics about extinctions can be mind-numbing, but they all point in the same direction.[4] Up to 1 million of the Earth's 8 million animal and plant species are threatened with extinction, representing an extinction rate that is certainly tens of times (but perhaps hundreds of times) the normal 'background' rate of extinctions (a summary of some of the facts and figures can be found on the UN Sustainable Development Goals website). One study proposes that the rate of extinctions today is actually over 1,000 times the background extinction rate, and future rates are likely to be 10,000 times higher.[5] There is an accelerating loss of biodiversity – that is, a diminution of the variety and richness of all kinds of living forms across large swathes of the Earth. We are in the midst of what many scientists have labelled the 'sixth mass extinction', this one distinguished by the prominent role played by humans in bringing it on.[6]

Many scientists describe the planetary scale and scope of the impacts of modern human society on the planet as a new geological era – the 'Anthropocene'.[7] Mass extinctions are only one sign of this, but a crucial one. Some scientists have coined another term – the 'Great Acceleration' – to describe the evidence they see about our dramatically escalating impacts since 1945. A recent headline in *National Geographic* summed it up well: 'Human-made materials now equal weight of all life on Earth'.[8] These materials include concrete, plastics, asphalt and metals. Scientists have dug up sediments from the ocean floor off California showing rapidly increasing traces of plastic, beginning in the 1950s and accelerating each decade thereafter.[9] To future geologists, all this stuff will be seen as a clearly defined layer in the Earth's crust.

There is a lively argument within the geological community about whether the Anthropocene should really be proclaimed a new geological era.[10] Leaving that aside, the important point is that the idea signifies a shocking fact: in the past few hundred years our industrial and post-industrial economies and societies have wrought changes on a scale and of a kind that formerly it took planetary processes and events to bring about, some of them unfolding over millennia, others of a one-off, catastrophic kind (a plunging asteroid, for example). Just by carrying on with our modern lifestyles, as if this were normal, we have had effects of a similar scale.

3 Catherine Offord, 'North America Has 3 Billion Fewer Birds Than It Did in 1970', *The Scientist*, September 2019.

4 Intergovernmental Science-Policy Platform on Biodiversity and Ecosystem Services (IPBES), *The Global Assessment Report on Biodiversity and Ecosystem Services: Summary for Policymakers*, Bonn, Germany: IPBES Secretariat, 6 May 2019.

5 Jurriaan M. De Vos *et al.*, 'Estimating the normal background rate of species extinction', *Conservation Biology*, vol. 29, no. 2, 2015, pp.452–462.

6 Gerardo Ceballos, Paul R. Ehrlich, and Rodolfo Dirzo, 'Biological annihilation via the ongoing sixth mass extinction signaled by vertebrate population losses and declines', *Proceedings of the National Academy of Sciences of the United States of America*, 25 July 2017.

7 George Dvorsky, 'New evidence suggests human beings are a geological force of nature', *Gizmodo*, 1 July 2016.

8 Maddie Stone, 'Human-made materials now equal weight of all life on Earth', *National Geographic*, 9 December 2020.

9 Jennifer A. Braddon *et al.*, 'Multidecadal increases in plastic particles in coastal ocean sediments', *Science Advances*, vol. 5, no. 9, eaax0587, 2019.

10 International Commission on Stratigraphy, Subcommission on Quaternary Stratigraphy, Working Group on the 'Anthropocene', *Results of Binding Vote by AWG*, released 21 May 2019.

Modern birding is in some ways directly shaped by the extinction crisis. For a start, it makes many birds harder to find. Birders are also made acutely aware of shrinking and increasingly degraded natural habitats. We very often bird in small fragments of protected havens for wildlife, getting to them by passing through miles and miles of mono-cultivated agricultural landscapes, where a few well-adapted species like crows and starlings, often introduced from elsewhere on the globe by humans, monotonously dominate the bird count. We revel in successful quests for remnant populations of species on the edge of extinction. Indeed, the deeper the extinction crisis, the more such quests beckon the intrepid birder. A looming extinction gives an extra exciting edge to an expedition to see a rare bird, even as we may bewail its fate when the thrill has faded. Then we head for the next rarity.

But it is also the case that an ethic of conservation is very much in evidence in the mind of most birders. This book records that I saw plenty to encourage me to think that we birders were not only having a good time but also trying to do some good. Most of us belong to national and local birding clubs or to societies and organisations that do a lot of conservation work. Many participate in bird surveys as an act of citizen science, hoping to contribute to the knowledge needed for conservation measures. Birders who travel to poor and developing countries in search of new birds for their list are supporting and encouraging the efforts being taken to preserve what remains of precious habitats. Well-managed nature reserves and ecolodges cater for our interests and help hold back the tide of habitat loss. From Colombia to Cambodia, and in many places in between, I encountered dedicated and brave people seeking to preserve their natural heritage and to celebrate it with visitors such as myself. All the birding trips described in this book brought me into contact with many such people and communities, and their stories figure prominently.

And yet, as we look more closely at what birders do and why, we also get a hint of some of the technologies and modes of thinking that define the Anthropocene as an era of nature-in-decline. The desire of a growing number of world birders to see new birds has spawned an industry devoted to making nature, particularly rare and remote habitats, more accessible, meaning more intruded upon. We travel great distances and, in the process, emit large quantities of harmful emissions and consume scarce resources as we demand quick, relatively easy access to pristine habitats. We tend to think about these side effects in the same way as we think about pollution more broadly: unfortunate, hopefully to be mitigated at some point in the future, but for the time being somewhat unavoidable.

In this respect, birding is not just some small, seemingly innocuous corner of recreational activity sheltered from the wider forces that are driving human societies to make such an impact on the Earth's life support systems. Birding in many ways echoes and replicates modes of thought and behaviour that result in these outcomes. It seems clear that we are all implicated, one way or another. And seeing how this is so in the case of birders turns out to be instructive – and much more so than I am comfortable with.

But as I have already said, I was having a really good time. I am in no place to preach, and this is far from my intention here. Rather, I want to record, reflect and perhaps gently provoke. As well as seeing loss and destruction, I visited some fabulous birding destinations and enjoyed every minute. When the destinations were tropical forests, wild windblown mountain passes, beautiful remote islands and sunny alpine meadows, the enticements of world birding were irresistible. They regularly reminded me of my passion for nature and sometimes raised my hopes for arresting its decline. I was uplifted and encouraged, just as often as those times when I was depressed and dismayed.

I was visiting destinations that were straight out of David Attenborough's wildlife TV series. Nothing in my previous life compared with the spectacular, magical, unforgettable experiences that the world of birding was affording me: watching a Wilson's Bird-of-Paradise on its display grounds; being in the close, immediate presence of an albatross in the Tasman Sea; seeing the last remaining male Gurney's Pitta in Thailand singing and defending its territory (both a birder's triumphal 'trophy moment' and also a tragic witnessing of an iconic species' extirpation due to human impacts); and much, much more. I was hooked and I couldn't get enough of it. I took countless photos and videos to record these experiences. The book contains a number of illustrations, mostly of photographs from my own collection that I have accumulated during my travels. When I go birding, I don't haul around a long lens but rely on a smaller, digital 'bridge' camera. These days, they have amazing zoom lenses that allow for close-ups.

So, what made me into a birder in the first place? I trace the origins back to a youthful interest in nature generally, growing up in a small town in the English countryside of East Anglia in the 1950s. I netted Sticklebacks in the local stream and butterflies in the surrounding meadows. I bought a fishing rod and lazed about on riverbanks. I owned an *Observer's Book of Birds*. I enjoyed studying biology but disliked my biology teacher (I am sure the feeling was mutual). But instead of going all-in on birdwatching, I took up trainspotting (at a time when steam engines were still on the rails) and dabbled in stamp collecting (an uncle gifted me his collection).

I had friends who were trainspotters, but none who were birdwatchers. Aged 11, I bought a weekly rail pass and, along with a group of like-minded friends, lived on trains for a week across the length and breadth of the United Kingdom, running the gauntlet of the Railway Police to visit locomotive sheds. Probably, my life list of birds and my international travels are a late-life substitute for my youthful, adventurous ticking-off of engine numbers; and perhaps also a way of compensating for the tragic near-disappearance of the steam locomotive. Sadly, many birds seem to be going the same way. Come to think of it, so are postage stamps.

As my career in its early years took me to Australia, I recall vividly the delight of my first encounter with Crimson Rosellas, impossibly vivid, feeding *en masse* on bushes in the gardens outside my office window. I was more used to being a bit irritated by the incessant cheeping of the humble House Sparrow. I laughed at the unfamiliar, rusty mangle calls of Australian Magpies, and dodged their dive-bombing as I walked to work. In my Sydney garden, I admired the brilliance of the Rainbow Lorikeets flashing by overhead.

But I only took up serious birding much later in life, not long after I moved from Sydney to Hong Kong in 2001. My first exposure to birders was through the Hong Kong Birdwatching Society. I moved out of the teeming city and ended up in rural Hong Kong, in the Lam Tsuen Valley (a local birding hotspot) where, in a somewhat desultory fashion, I cultivated a local birding patch. My village house had a flat roof, and I kept a 'rooftop list' of local birds, some seen with glass in hand as the day wound down (the highlight, among many memorable moments, was a flock of at least 30 wintering Chinese Grosbeaks in the nearby Feng Shui trees).

Untypically, I was an international birder from the start, largely because my job took me all over the place to conferences and such like and I found time on each trip to add on a day (or more) of birding. Also, my closest relatives were scattered across the globe and my visits offered new birding opportunities. Soon, I was also joining organized birding tours during vacation time to Rwanda, Argentina, Israel and so on. At first, the itineraries were as much governed by my curiosity about the destinations as by any underlying strategy to see particular birds or to build up a list. But I soon began to think more systematically about these destinations. Serendipity was fun but, by now, I was hooked: my life list, and where the gaps were (that is, where I would see the largest number of new birds) began to loom larger in my travel plans.

Hong Kong was a perfect hub for these global travels, but I left the city in 2018. I now consider myself to have two homes, one with my partner in Vancouver and the other in Canberra, closer to grandchildren. This places in context my several references in these chapters to my 'local' birding experiences in Australia and in Canada, as well as Hong Kong.

Something about birding that struck me, as I got deeper into it, was that although birders may enjoy going to wild and remote places, they are actually not very fussed about where they go, so long as they can find birds. But why be a birder other than to see and enjoy birds in their natural settings, in the wild? I soon found out that I had missed the main point. Birders are first of all looking for birds, not nature: if they are to be found at a rubbish tip, that's a good place to go birding. A feeding station in the hotel garden can be better than meandering down a forest trail, taking pleasure in the sights and sounds of the natural world, hoping something turns up.

Later, I got used to this and learnt to live more or less comfortably with the ambiguities of being both a birder and a nature lover. But gradually, I have reverted to my original instincts. I write about some of the growing frustrations and discomforts of single-mindedly chasing after new birds to add to my list, as against the pleasures of taking in the sights and sounds of nature, much of it in familiar places in the company of familiar birds.

I was prompted by some of these observations and reflections to delve into the origins of birding and how it has evolved. Where did it all come from? Nineteenth century poets and other romantics loved nature and keenly observed it. But technology and science, not poetry, have shaped the way birders look at birds and at nature more broadly. By the early 20th century, the science of species-naming and the technology of optics had come together to give birding its meaning and also to make it possible. Birding is all about identifying and naming the species we see in the field. Taxonomy produced the objects of our quest (species); Ornithology taught us what to look for, and where; and Optics gave us the means to find what we sought.

Birding experiences nature in a mediated form, 'at a distance', through binoculars or through the camera lens, and birders' field guides represent the world of nature in the same manner.[11] Underlying the point of view of the modern birder is that their object of view is not nature in the round, but species of birds, each one an abstracted object in itself and valued for its novelty or rarity – or, if we are on our local patch, perhaps for its comforting familiarity – as much as if not more than for its beauty. Ornithologists doing fieldwork have a similar view, but they have different purposes and go much deeper, using many other observational techniques.

There are multiple origins and forbears of birding. We use some of the language of hunters – on our travels, for example, we have 'target' birds. Like 19th century explorers,

11 Spencer Schaffner, *Binocular Vision: The Politics of Representation in Birdwatching Field Guides*, Amherst, MA: University of Massachusetts Press, 2011.

collectors and hunters, many of us are avid, busy travellers and accumulators. We venture out, we look, we take, and we move on. Some birders take this to extraordinary extremes. The birders who most come to the attention of the general public are the ones who are the maddest accumulators, the Big Year listers who frenetically travel around the world to see the most bird species anyone has ever seen in a year, or the twitchers who make cross-country, all-night dashes to catch sight of a stray bird in some remote corner of the territory, just because it has never been seen there before (even though it may be one of the most common birds somewhere else).

Of course, these are the extremes, but they are only exaggerations and extensions of more general features of birding. The kind of experience of and relationship to nature they demonstrate is a reflection of how most people in modern, post-industrial societies also interact with it. In some ways, birding is a metaphor for humanity's way of relating to the natural world, a quintessentially modern way of dealing with it. Modern humans draw a line between us and nature, often with the help of technology to erect a barrier, sometimes seeing the wild as alien or threatening, other times viewing wild beings as objects of entertainment, gratification, consumption and accumulation.

In our contemporary age of extinctions, science and technology have influenced birding in new ways. Conservation science shapes and regulates many of the habitats in which birders look for birds and, in some cases, ensures the very existence of the ones we see. Ecologists have performed heroics to rescue and safeguard endangered species. One such local hero, among many, is Don Merton, a prime mover in saving the Black Robin from extinction in New Zealand.[12] Birders are grateful that species may be saved from extinction by relocations or by sophisticated techniques of captive breeding, followed by release into safe havens, such as on islands or in fenced reserves, where they may be rescued from our depredations and those of the invasive species we bring with us.

But in this way, we accept piecemeal and 'last resort' remedies to the harm we see being done, not arrest or reversal of the underlying causes. Moreover, as a result, many rare birds, thus corralled, are more accessible to be enjoyed and (for a birder) to be ticked off with greater ease and comfort. We go 'extinction birding'. We put nature into sealed, hermetic containers, like specimens on a laboratory shelf or decorative stuffed bird skins under a glass dome, to admire and inspect for our benefit as much as for nature's.

So, fundamentally and unsurprisingly, modern birding is a reflection of the human societies in which it takes place and of the state of nature that has resulted from human behaviour. Although on the one hand this is accepting and submissive in the face of the extinction crisis, on the other hand birders are also participating in a wider awakening consciousness of the harm our human societies have done as they have accumulated wealth from exploiting the Earth's resources – its soils, its minerals, its forests, its oceans – without conserving or (where possible) renewing them. There is some hope.

Looking back on my birding adventures and writing about them, I have mixed feelings. There is no neat and tidy conclusion, no single message, no startling revelation. I struggle with contradictions and paradoxes between, on the one hand, my desire to travel, to experience different natural wonders and to see new birds and, on the other, my sense of dismay and unease over some of the damage to the natural environment that I have seen. And I have a nagging sense that I am implicated in it, however peripherally and indirectly, by pur-

12 David Butler and Don Merton, *The Black Robin: Saving the World's Most Endangered Bird*, Auckland: Oxford University Press, 1992.

suing these kinds of adventures. You will not find a consistent thread of diagnosis or advocacy in this book, but a story of personal awakening, mixed emotions and growing doubts.

The sources for this book are of many kinds. Most obviously, they are from memories of my own birding experiences and from my personal knowledge store. I apologise in advance for any mis-remembering and obvious inaccuracies. I also draw on other writers, news sources and online databases and, where I do so explicitly, I provide citations in the footnotes. But this is not an academic text. The citations are deliberately sparse in most chapters, although they are more numerous where I am making claims based on scientific or historical facts or interpretations. Most of the sources were accessed online, particularly those from newspapers and organizations with websites. I do not provide the Internet addresses in most cases because it is easier for the reader to type a few key words into a search engine.

Species names and other taxonomic details are based on the latest International Ornithological Congress (IOC) world checklist. This list is constantly being updated, so the one used for this publication will already be out of date by the time the book appears. Where I go into details about individual bird species, their distribution, their behaviour and their habitats, I am drawing on the species accounts provided in the *Handbook of Birds of the World Alive (HBW Alive)*, an online version of the multi-volume book publication *Handbook of Birds of the World*, published in Barcelona by Lynx Edicions. In May 2020, *HBW Alive* was merged with other online resources under the umbrella of the Cornell Lab of Ornithology in a new resource called simply *Birds of the World* (birdsoftheworld.org). The species accounts (which are regularly updated) have been migrated to the new website to supplement others already there. On the many occasions I have relied on them, rather than citing each one individually I am leaving it up to the reader to follow up if desired, unless I am using a direct quotation in my text. The home page of the *Birds of the World* website has a simple search engine, where you can type in a species name and be taken to the appropriate page. To access this publication in full, an annual subscription is required.

Birders have their own language and jargon and we also become familiar with some of the scientific jargon of ornithologist and taxonomists. I have already thrown some of it about in this Introduction. And I may be using some terms in a way that other birders understand differently. The Glossary should help.

I want to mention a few folks to whom I owe some words of thanks. First to Angel, who didn't complain (much) about my long and frequent absences while away birding. To Guy, who encouraged me and accompanied me on several pre- and post-conference birding excursions in my early birding years. To Graeme, who urged me to put my barroom ramblings down in more coherent, written form. To Doug, who added his voice to Graeme's and who supported me in other ways while I was sitting in my apartment in Canberra, typing away at my desk in the second half of 2018 and beyond. To Frank, with whom I walked the dogs on his local patch as we kept our eyes open for sparrows and bluebirds. And to a host of birding companions with whom I travelled to distant places and shared many moments of joy and many hours of discomfort, especially John, Ken, Les, Nick, Ron and Sue.

I wish also to acknowledge the permission granted to reproduce some of the photographs from others' personal collections appearing on these pages: first, Rob Hutchison of BirdTour Asia for his image of the Invisible Rail in Chapter 3; second, Punjapa Phetsri for her photo of the disappearing Gurney's Pitta in Chapter 16; and third, Jainy Kuriakose for her photo of the Western Tragopan in Chapter 4. Permission was also sought from and granted by the London Transport Museum to reproduce the London Transport poster in Chapter 12. Thanks also to Sam Painter, who drafted the maps, and to birding companion Dick Byrne, who tried to bring me up to speed on the species concept. Of course, any remaining errors on that topic and others are all mine.

Finally, and most importantly, I must thank all those who made my birding trips possible – the birding guides, the local agents and lodge managers, the backroom staff, drivers, boatmen and caterers and, above all, the enthusiasts, rangers and other nature-loving community members across the world who welcomed me to their local patches and who are having to fight hard to preserve them. I hope, more than anything, that I and other birders have helped.

CHAPTER 1

Memories of Birds

How patient is he as he puts out his wings for the blue:
He is an old guest of the sunlight – a child of the dew.
The bird is a noble, he turns to the sky for a theme,
And the waves are thoughts coming out to the edge of a dream.

From: John Shaw Neilson, *The Crane is my Neighbour* **(1938)**[13]

There is something about encounters with wild birds that strikes a chord in everybody. Perhaps it is because we so envy their seemingly effortless, boundless freedom of the skies compared with our Earth-bound stolidity. Maybe it is because birds invade all the senses in a unique combination – the elegance of shape and form, the subtleties of flight and movement, the beauties of plumage and colouration, and the amazing diversities of call and song. Perhaps it's because they have been on the Earth for so long; it's as if they've seen it all. Or perhaps it's because so recently and so rapidly on their timescale, so many of them have become part of our human landscapes, integrating into our gardens and cities and accepting us as part of their scenery, as neighbours.

We watch their life dramas in our streets, parks and gardens. Their generosity in revealing themselves to us in our familiar places is unlike the response of some other wild creatures to the presence of humans. Many mammals, in response to the ever-presence of humans, have evolved nocturnal lifestyles out of our sight. But birds are always likely to be in view and in earshot, so much so that for much of the time, they are an unnoticed part of our scenery. They are often our companions, at least judging by the ubiquity of bird feeders in so many different cultures across the globe.[14] It could easily be imagined that we live in harmony.

13 Margaret Roberts (ed.), *Collected Verse of John Shaw Neilson*, Crawley, WA: UWA Publishing, 2012, p.412. The 'Crane' in the poem is most probably a White-faced Heron.

14 Darryl Jones, *The Birds at My Table. Why We Feed Wild Birds and Why It Matters*, Ithaca, NY: Cornell University Press, 2018.

It seems as if I have always been attracted to birds, so a good place to begin is with my first memory. Actually, I have to confess, it is so old and so fleeting that sometimes I doubt its authenticity, wondering if it is an imagined reconstruction. Never mind, that's the way with memory. I could have been no more than 5 or 6 years old, but the image I have in my mind's eye is still sharp and vivid. Our house looked across a road on the edge of town onto a piece of waste ground, and thence into the Suffolk landscape, flat and wide to the horizon. There on this day in the mid-distance was a huge flock of small birds seemingly filling the sky. Like a swarm of insects, the individual birds formed a unified mass, shivering and shifting, twisting and reforming into new shapes, as they whirled through the sky. I ran inside and dragged my mother out of the house to share my discovery. We were looking at a distant murmuration of starlings, in the days when such sightings were more commonplace than they are in England today. Knowledge of the phenomenon and its name came much later, but such knowledge was not necessary to imprint the memory of the image itself, and the sense of wonder.

I remember more clearly another episode, this time when I was maybe 11 years old, which unwittingly presaged my later-life career as a birder. My father, whose job sometimes took him driving around the Suffolk lanes, came home one evening with the tale of a mystery bird that he had spotted from the car. It was quite big, like a thrush, and bright yellow, unlike any other bird he had ever seen. I dived for my *Observer's Book of Birds* and came up with the conjecture that it was a Golden Oriole. This, as it turns out, was quite likely, for these rare visitors to the UK are known to breed in parts of Norfolk and Suffolk. At the time, I was unaware of this, just curious. I insisted that, come Sunday, we should all bundle into the car and go and look for it. Of course, we didn't find the bird, but it was still a good day out: my first twitch, with a now-familiar ending.

Memories of birds I have seen since I took up birding flood into the mind. I remember very well an encounter that helped get me hooked, when I was just a beginner. Visiting South Wales in 2005, I was out for the afternoon with my recently acquired binoculars, scanning the reeds and the water in a hide at the protected Kenfig Wetlands, near Bridgend. I had ticked a few ducks, including two wintering vagrants which had been previously recorded by twitchers (a Canvasback and a Redhead, both blown off-course, far from their homes in North America). But this was not what I remember most. It was the unexpected appearance of a Eurasian Bittern, all subtle brown and black streaks with those long legs and a long, sharp yellow bill, that suddenly appeared out from the reeds to cross a channel less than 20 m away.

In the UK, bitterns were endangered due to the loss of habitat, but had made a comeback, thanks to places like Kenfig. The population has now stabilized. Even so, there are probably no more than 80 breeding males across the country and the wintering population is around 600 at the time of writing (according to the Royal Society for the Protection of Birds (RSPB) website). I had heard the tell-tale boom of a bittern in Norfolk, but never before seen one; now, not only was it close in front of me, but it was also about to perform: it waded across the channel into the reeds and emerged at the far edge, slowly and awkwardly clambering nearly to the top, perching precariously and swaying as the reeds bent under its weight. It suddenly took to flight. Its deep, slow wingbeats lifted it slowly but surely onto a gracefully arching trajectory to the far shore, a hundred or so metres distant. As it landed, I could breathe normally again. I had experienced something of an epiphany, the excitement of

Hoatzins, Peru

seeing a very special, rare and spectacular bird, close-up in all its detail, in its natural state, for the first time.

Since that day, I have accumulated many memories of special birds seen when out birding: the privileged, trembling excitement of seeing a much-prized rarity, such as a Geomalia in Sulawesi, on the Anaso Trail, giving access to a diminishing forest remnant; the triumph of success after a seemingly endless and futile quest for a Western Tragopan, finally seen in all its glory after seven days of dawn excursions, from tents clinging to an alpine meadow in the foothills of the Himalayas; and awe and wonder at an encounter with a living fossil in a South American swamp – bizarre, prehistoric-looking Hoatzins, evolutionary leftovers, blundering through the foliage.

One of the most dramatic of these birding memories was my first close encounter with a Hornbill (an Oriental Pied), on a birding trip to Kaeng Krachan in Thailand. We were peering across the valley at a distant fruiting tree containing some feeding Pink-necked Green Pigeons, when I became aware of a vibration in the air, indeed in my whole body, a deep beating rhythm that was accompanied by a crescendo of rushing air and wingbeats. Trepidation was my first reaction. Then, from behind and 20 feet over my head appeared a hornbill, its huge yellow casqued bill stretched out in front,

Oriental Pied Hornbill, Thailand

propelled by the beating claps of its black and white wing feathers. It was heading for a nearby tree where, after blundering onto its chosen branch, it hopped about a bit, nonchalantly peered down at us for a few seconds, and then proceeded with some preening on its perch. Striking was the contrast between the majestic, awesome entry on the wing and the almost comical appearance at rest – incongruous beak and huge eyes on cocked head, the whole bird teetering and balancing uncertainly.

Spectacular birds like the hornbill can leave indelible memories, especially when seen close-up. And for the birder, these memories are of course enhanced if the species in question is a rarity, a special target. A striking case in point was my encounter with the Helmet Vanga in Madagascar. On our trip, the chance to find the Helmet Vanga and one or two other locally endemic birds involved a post-tour 'extension', an optional add-on of a few days to the main tour, to a remote spot in the north-east of the country. It helped that the setting was idyllic – a quiet lodge in a small village, right on the beach and accessible only by a long boat ride. The forest was extensive and largely intact (rare for Madagascar) and the birds were plentiful. We found the Helmet Vanga down a trail with relative ease, as the locals knew where to find a nest.

Most birding field guides use fairly cool, scientific language in offering descriptions of each species but in this case, the authors go to town: 'Spectacular large Vanga (distinguished) from all other birds by ***outrageous blue bill***….'[15] Indeed, the extravagance of this bill has to be seen to be believed, and on this viewing, it also showed off its utility, clutching firmly in its grasp a fat beetle destined for fledglings in the nearby nest.

Altogether different, but equally spectacular, was one unforgettable encounter with a hunting Peregrine Falcon. This is a memory that is all movement and moment, vivid in its dramatic clarity but in other ways indeterminate. I cannot with certainty pin down the time or place – we were on a road in open country with distant forest edge on both sides, looking across the fields for storks, or herons, or whatever. But the action we witnessed is vivid in my mind. Someone called out and I looked up to see a pigeon desperately tearing across the sky right above our heads, pursued by a Peregrine at full pelt, straight and direct. In an instant, both had crossed our line of sight. The two of them disappeared into the shadows of the distant trees with a final swerve. Breathless, we all looked at each other. Did that really happen? It was all over and done in a few seconds. I still wonder about the fate of that fleeing pigeon.

Helmet Vanga, Madagascar

15 Frank Hawkins *et al.*, *Birds of Madagascar and the Indian Ocean Islands*, London: Christopher Helm, 2015, p.172. The italicized, bold font is in the original.

Greater Flamingos

Awe and amazement are common reactions to encounters with wild birds in nature: the splendour and beauty of plumage and song and in some cases, spectacular display (birds-of-paradise, most memorably); the invisible shadow of a night owl ghosting through the trees above one's head, sensed rather than seen; or the sheer volume of numbers in the flock, as countless waders spring from the Mai Po mudflats in Hong Kong's Deep Bay and fill the sky after being disturbed by an eagle; in particular, the sight of the whirling, flashing, black and white wingbeats of a thousand and more Pied Avocets, rising in unison, panicking and circling, then landing again.[16]

Individual species with their distinctive, identifying markers, such as an outrageous blue bill, are what birders look for and want to see. Pied Avocets are individually memorable as graceful, elegant birds when feeding or at rest. But my memories of birds are also formed from aesthetic, emotional and other responses to them as a collective presence in the landscape. We don't need to know what a Pied Avocet looks like, or even know its name, in order to stand and watch in amazement and appreciate the spectacle of a startled flock of them rising from the mudflats. My Mai Po memory, like that of my murmuration, is of a multitude of birds filling the sky and the mind with a sense of the wonder of the whole world of nature as a spectacle. A similar memory, this one from Romania, is of a kettle of dozens of storks, circling and rising in the warm air currents far above our heads, disappearing as dots towards the scattered white clouds in a blue sky. Another is from Lake Abiata in Ethiopia, where feeding Flamingos in their hundreds are splashed pink across the water's surface. Such sights arrest the mind and leave an indelible impression.

These encounters with a multitude of birds in their natural element, doing what succeeding populations of them have done for millennia, affirm a sense that the natural world as a collective, living system is a constant, and is something to be relied upon to nurture us. But that reliability, that reassurance, is fast disappearing. Many of my memories are reminders of this. The number of migrating birds, including Pied Avocets, that are using the Eastern Flyway, along which Mai Po is a major staging point, has been in dramatic decline as coastal mudflats were drained and as more and more concrete was laid. You might even be able to find people who remember the time when there were tens of thousands of Avocets in Deep

16 David Diskin, *Mai Po: The Seasons. A Photographic Essay*, Hong Kong: Accipiter Press, 2014.

Bay. Today's thousands may in the not-too-distant future be only hundreds. In an age of extinctions, our memories evoke regret and loss as well as wonder and delight. Grief as well as joy accompany them.

Witnessing the impact of harm to birds from human actions provides the stuff of a number of dark memories, ones that evoke anger as well as loss. Sometimes, that harm is intentional and immediate, a direct instance rather than just a by-product of our wider assaults on nature. One such case that springs to mind stemmed from a time we were birding along the coast of Fujian Province in China. On this day, we were not birding the mudflats for migrating waders but visiting a nearby area of turf farms and adjoining paddocks, which served as a magnet for migratory birds looking to recharge their batteries.

Walking through these fields looking for pipits, wagtails, buntings and others, it became apparent that of the many that were scattered across the ploughed areas and grassy patches around us, most were dead or dying. The reason became clear as we looked more closely – they had eaten poisoned corn that had been scattered on the ground. Caught up in the slaughter were some migrating waders, such as Little Curlews. Battery-operated tape recorders were continuously playing the songs of Yellow Wagtails in order to attract the birds to settle. In the next field, a man got off a motorcycle with a sack and began collecting bodies. One of our number, enraged, chased after him. He fled.

Migrating birds are a traditional source of food in China. Mist-netting in the rice fields has generally been the main method of catching them, but modern technology has afforded new ways. The growing conservation movement in China has had some effect on curbing these practices, but the laws are weakly enforced. We took photos and later that day shared the images with some birders from Beijing, who were keen to follow up and report the matter to the police. The sight of these hundreds of small, brightly coloured or brown corpses scattered across the ground and the grass, against the backdrop of their endlessly recycled tinny songs from the trapper's speakers, is a dark memory, rather forgotten but still in my mind. Unable to apprehend the perpetrator but still caught up in the heat of the moment, we ground his speakers into the dirt with our heels. We left that bit out when we passed on the evidence.

Then there are memories that are entirely innocent, recalling delight and amusement at the unexpected. In the case of my quest for the Tragopan in Northern India (Chapter 4), it was not my complete and final encounter that left the most lasting memory when I saw enough of the bird and its splendour in plain sight to identify it for sure and add it to my list; it was my first encounter, when a wisp of spiralling steam in the frosty air slowly floated up from a momentarily opened beak as a pheasant-like bird appeared briefly in silhouette, on a branch in the morning gloom, and called across the valley. This moment is imprinted not because I was looking at the dim shape of a rare Tragopan, the object of my quest, but because this curl of steamy breath was surprising and incongruous, as if on that branch I was seeing a gently bubbling kettle steaming on the hob.

It's no accident that birds are favourite cartoon characters – they have tonnes of personality and often provide comic relief. From our house in rural Hong Kong, we often walked a leisurely trail of an evening up the valley through the village of Ng Tung Chai into the lower slopes of Tai Mo Shan, past hillside graves, orchards and a Daoist monastery, where it began to get a bit muddy and steep (which usually prompted a retracing of the steps). Birds and birdsong – bulbuls, minivets, thrushes, babblers and others – accompanied us.

The call of one diminutive member of the babbler family, the Rufous-capped Babbler, was prominent in the chorus. A feature of its call is its ease of imitation: repetitive, monotonic, within the normal range of the human whistle. The temptation to call it out was irresistible. On this occasion, the bird was responsive. The Babbler called very close, then shot out of the foliage, head-height and straight at us. It whizzed by inches from our faces, the rush of air from its wings fanning our cheeks, disappearing in a flash into the opposite bushes, from where it continued to agitate. Our response was shouts of unanimous and spontaneous surprise, delight and laughter. We had shared an Angry Bird moment.

My mother, in her final few years, went partially blind. As she described it, familiar objects and faces became vague shapes and blurs, overlaid with flashes and whorls. During my visits, we sometimes went for a drive up into the hills and valleys behind Swansea. On one such excursion, driving along a narrow road across the sheep-dotted moors, with the steep valley on one side, she suddenly cried out 'Oh! Look!'. I glanced across her out of the car window and there, no more than 20 m away, tracking us as it glided in the breeze, was a Red Kite. It kept in direct view at eye-level for some seconds, its plumage glowing in the afternoon sun, its yellow eyes sizing us up as it glided alongside us, wings trembling in the breeze, until it veered suddenly out of sight down into the valley below.

'What a beautiful bird! I saw it, plain as could be,' she said, thrilled.

Of course, this thrill had a special significance for her, as she no longer saw things plainly – except, miraculously, on this occasion. In the days that followed, she would recount the incident to friends and relatives, and describe it in detail: 'I saw it first!' she would say. On subsequent visits, the topic would come up in conversation between us and we would relive the memory together.

For a birder, such a close-up flight view of a Red Kite, a majestic and graceful raptor with a 2-m wingspan, is very special. The bird is iconic as a conservation success story, having been brought back quite recently from the brink of extirpation in the UK. But my excitement as a birder at such a view was overwhelmed by sharing my mother's pleasure at her sight of the bird, so special to her with her failing eyes, and our common appreciation of its beauty. And the memory of that bird is indelibly associated with our fleeting times together in her last years. There are many reasons why I love birds. But none is more important than that they can harbour such memories, with such associations.

CHAPTER 2

An Odd Bird Out in the Ecuadorian Chocó

In Ecuador in 2014, our bus was heading down a bumpy road that would bring us close to a place renowned for its fabulous forest birding – Playa de Oro on the Santiago River in Esmeraldas, in the north-west corner of the country. As we drove through a tropical lowland landscape heavily impacted by logging and human settlement, I was thinking of our quest to see as many as possible of the 60 or so endemic bird species of the Chocó forests. What I was not expecting, but turned out to be even more extraordinary, was the slice of human history that I was about to encounter.

The Chocó ecological region (not to be confused with the Chocó Department of Colombia, which is located within this region, on the border with Panama) is a globally significant biodiversity hotspot. It extends northwards from the Magdalena Valley in Northern

Peru through coastal Ecuador and Colombia to the Darien region of Panama. Squeezed between the Andes, which separates it from the Amazonian Basin, and the Pacific Ocean, it harbours a rich array of endemic species of flora and fauna. In the Ecuadorian Chocó, 25% of mammals and 60% of amphibians are endemic.

However, in the part of the region we were visiting, approximately 90% of the original moist lowland forest habitat has been destroyed or transformed through logging, mining, industrial-scale plantation development and other agricultural uses. The remaining fragments depend on continued protection and vigilance by local communities and governments.

One bird in particular among the endemics was on my mind: the Sapayoa, *Sapayoa aenigma*. The Latin of the scientific name says a lot. This is a small, rather plain-looking bird that for years defied taxonomic classification – some thought it a manakin, *Pipridae*, others a tyrant flycatcher, *Tyrannidae*. More recently, it was placed on the taxonomic list and, in some field guides, in the category *incertae sedis* (of uncertain placement), along with a few other species whose exact place in the avian family tree was unknown.

These days, thanks to DNA analysis, taxonomists class it as belonging to its own monotypic family, *Sapayoidae*. And analysis of its genetic make-up shows that the Sapayoa is more closely related to two so-called 'Old World' families – broadbills and asities – rather than to those look-alike 'New World' species surrounding it in South America, with which taxonomists had first grouped it. This may all sound unremarkable, but remember, the Sapayoa lives on the western fringes of South America, while asities are endemic to Madagascar and broadbills are split between Africa and Southeast Asia. And just going on appearances, it would seem unlikely that the Sapayoa is a closer relative to the asities than it is to the tyrant flycatchers.

'Old World' and 'New World' are commonly used terms to divide the world into major ecozones. The origin of the terms lies in events in 15th

Sapayoa, Ecuador

Schlegel's Asity, Madagascar

Yellow-crowned Elaenia, Ecuador

and 16th century Europe, when explorers were discovering new lands across the oceans. The Old World was the then known continents of Europe, Africa and Asia. The New World was the newly discovered Americas (Australasia and the Pacific are somewhat left out, but never mind for now). The idea of a 'New World' has lasting resonance in the history of European (or 'western') civilization, signifying newly discovered lands of conquest and empire to the west, as the Americas were invaded and colonised by the major European powers. The modern legacies of this are many and far-reaching. Of more relevance in the current context, the terms themselves have continued to be used to apply to groups of similar species that have evolved independently in the different ecozones – for example, 'New World Parrots' as distinct from 'Old World Parrots'.

So how did the Sapayoa end up in distant Ecuador, in the New World, when its closest cousins are in the Old World? Actually, we are not quite sure, the story is a bit speculative. Currently, there are two competing theories.[17] In order to tell these stories, we must begin with a bit more taxonomy. The Sapayoa and its close relatives are members of the suboscine group of bird families. Suboscines are distinguished from oscines (often referred to as 'songbirds') by the more primitive structure of their vocal cords. The oscines arrived later on the avian family tree and have more complex song patterns. But suboscines also continued to proliferate into new species (or 'radiate', as the jargon has it) and to spread into new habitats. As well as the Old World suboscines already mentioned, there are also many hundreds of New World suboscine species. Among them are some 450 members of the *Tyrannidae* flycatcher family (including the Elaenia in the accompanying image, not to be mistaken for a Sapayoa), as well as many manakins, antbirds and others.

Sixty-four million years ago, the ancient avian ancestors of all the suboscines originated in Gondwana (the great southern continent that began splitting up some 180 million years ago to form Africa, Australasia, South America, Arabia, India and Antarctica). One story has it that this group split into three branches on the family tree, with one entering what is now South America across a continental shelf, while the rest headed north and east into what is now Asia and Africa. Broadbills and asities, along with close relatives the pittas, are the surviving descendants of one of the groups that headed into Asia and Africa (descendants of the other group survive today as the New Zealand wrens, of which there are four species). There are 15 extant species of broadbill, 11 of them in East Asia and the rest in Africa; in Madagascar, there are four species of asity; and there are 42 species of pitta in both Africa and Asia.

If we continue with this storyline, the Sapayoa is an offshoot of ancestors of the broadbills, separating within that group (probably in what is now Africa) some 50 million years ago. Around then, the climate of the whole of the northern landmass of Eurasia was mild, allowing creatures such as alligators to thrive in what is now the Canadian Arctic. The

17 John Reilly, *The Ascent of Birds*, Exeter: Pelagic Publishing, 2018, Chapter 16, 'The Sapayoa's Story: Odd One Out'; Jon Fjeldså, Les Christidis and Per G.P. Ericson (eds), *The Largest Avian Radiation. The Evolution of Perching Birds, or the Order Passeriformes*, Barcelona: Lynx Edicions, 2020, p.71.

Borneo: Black-and-Yellow Broadbill

ancestors of the Sapayoa found their way north and reached the New World to the west by the land bridge that then existed across the North Atlantic. With climate change, the warm zones shrunk southward, taking the Sapayoa with it. This Old World suboscine arrived in what is now called South America from the far north, through the back door as it were, and joined the already established New World suboscines as the odd one out.

The second story is just as likely (or unlikely, if you prefer). It agrees that the Old World suboscines are an offshoot of the New World's suboscine ancestors, but that the latter had already arrived in what is now South America from Gondwana before the Old World suboscines split off. By this account, the ancestors of broadbills, asities and pittas parted with their cousins and dispersed eastwards from their ancient stronghold to Africa and Asia, across a chain of islands that (it is speculated) then existed in the South Atlantic. Sea mounts remaining on the Atlantic Ocean bed today are consistent with this story. The Sapayoa's direct ancestors remained behind in South America and the Sapayoa is the lone survivor.

I have no idea which of these stories is correct, but I lean somewhat to the first one. So, let's proceed (for the moment) as if it were more or less true. Whatever is the case, evidently the Sapayoa is right at home among its New World suboscine companions, leading a placid existence in the sub-storey of the forest. It has found its niche in Chocó habitats from Panama to North Ecuador and is not considered to be endangered or threatened, notwithstanding the shrinking forests.

Despite its rather drab appearance, the Sapayoa is a special bird, one that many birders have on their 'must-see' list. Some visiting birders leave disappointed – birding in this kind of forest can be tough. The terrain is craggy, the treetops can be many hundreds of feet up, mist drifts through and it rains a lot. Flocks shoot by above your head, giving brief glimpses through the mist in the distant canopy. In the case of the Sapayoa, its elusiveness is more due to its stolid habits and cryptic colouration than to its swiftness of movement in the treetops. It generally doesn't perch high and, if not unduly disturbed, it tends to stay put, unless it spies an insect passing by and dashes out to snatch it – after which it normally returns to the same perch or to a nearby one to resume its quiet watch. We came across one next to the trail exactly in this manner, the bird catching our eye as it darted out and back, then obliging by sitting still, in plain sight.

Santiago River

But the Sapayoa wasn't the only highlight of my trip to the Santiago River. Even more rewarding was to encounter and learn about the people who helped me see this bird, and many others. Their origins and their history are just as extraordinary as the Sapayoa's. I suppose I should have been better prepared and done my homework before I began the trip, but I was too busy swotting up on all those new bird species to have time to delve into the history of the place and its people. I only began to ask the right questions and to get some of the answers as I looked around me at the people, as well as the birds.

Playa de Oro is a village of some 400 people and the last one you come to as you head up the Santiago River. The people of Playa de Oro are different from their neighbours downriver in at least one major respect: they have decided to keep their forest intact and to make it their livelihood, rather than log it and convert it all to alternative uses. Perhaps it was their relative remoteness and the lack of roads in the vicinity of Playa de Oro that was part of the reason for this. Whatever the case, they now see an opportunity to make their living by looking after these unique habitats, and our arrival was one among others that now helps sustain them. The community holds title to some 10,500 hectares of forest, adjacent to the Cotacachi-Cayapas National Park, which is poorly protected from loggers and settlers by a small band of overstretched rangers. The Playa de Oro forest is perhaps the best protected of the lot.

Getting there required boarding a boat to take us up-river, having arrived down the end of that bumpy road in the small town of Selva Alegre at a jetty surrounded by logs and cut timber. Along this road we passed through a number of settlements, and it soon became obvious that we were in an area populated in large part by Afro-American people. We were a bit early at the jetty and we did a bit of desultory birding in the dusty bushes and trees amidst the shacks.

Our boats finally arrived, and we clambered aboard. They were steered by Playa de Oro boatmen, also Afro-Americans. At intervals along the river, we spotted signs of industry, including heavy machinery and floating logs. The further we went, the fewer these signs became. We stopped at a riverside settlement – Playa de Oro – to pick up supplies and

Tigrillo Lodge

headed further upriver through undisturbed forest to Tigrillo Lodge, which was to be our base for the next three days.

The lodge was originally built as a camp for goldminers, but its Playa de Oro owners now use it for accommodating visiting birders and other ecotourists. Some visitors are shown how to pan for gold, but we were on a different quest. Basic but comfortable and welcoming, the lodge provides access to a series of trails that offer some of the best Chocó birding available. The trails take you into the heart of some fabulous unspoilt habitat.

As we got to know our hosts better, I became more and more curious about their story. Having watched on TV the Ecuadorian national football team in the World Cup, it was no surprise to me that the country's population is composed of different ethnicities. But I had not bothered to look into why, where they came from or where they now live. I now know that close to 10% of Ecuadorians are of Afro-American origin and, in Esmeraldas Province in north-western Ecuador, it is nearer to 50%.

Their origin is the traffic of African slaves during the Spanish colonial era. Their presence in Esmeraldas owes its earliest origins to a shipwrecked slave ship, *en route* from Panama to Peru sometime in the middle of the 16th century. The stranded slaves revolted, settled down, conquered the local Amerindians and, within a generation, had established themselves as a more or less autonomous community, beyond the immediate reach of Spanish colonial power in Quito, which lies across the mountains to the east. By the beginning of the 17th century, they had made peace with and paid their tribute to Spain, and in return were pretty much left alone. Such free communities attracted further so-called 'maroons' (freed or escaped slaves) in subsequent centuries. Slavery was abolished in Ecuador in 1852 after the country asserted its independence from Spain. Our boatmen and their fellow villagers in Playa de Oro were the descendants of some of these ex-slaves: their ancestors (like the Sapayoa's) were, without design but by circumstance, from the Old World.

In Ecuador, the Afro-Ecuadorian population has long experienced discrimination. They were first counted in the census only in 2001. They finally received formal recognition

of their identity and rights in the Constitution in 2008. Stereotypically, they are celebrated mostly for their music – *marimba* – and their footballing prowess. In Esmeraldas, they are the largest ethnic group, but not the dominant one economically or socially. Most of them are poor and their land rights are precarious. In the second half of the 20th century, colonists from other parts of Ecuador were encouraged to settle on forest lands in the Chocó by government land grants. Accelerating land clearance and deforestation accompanied this re-settlement. Many Afro-Ecuadorians participated in these economic activities, including logging; others were displaced or left the region in search of work in the cities.

As I described earlier, along the Santiago River we saw evidence both of deforestation and, in Playa de Oro, of conservation. This Afro-American community has chosen to express their long-standing connection to the river and the land through seeking harmony with the natural environment. They pursue a lifestyle and livelihoods that depend on preserving large tracts of the forest intact. The river also helps sustain them. They continue some of their traditional pursuits such as hunting, fishing and small-scale agriculture. In addition, they have planted cacao groves to make chocolate and they promote tourism and welcome visitors.

The leaders of the community have made connections between their situation and the wider environmental movement. They were given support by California-based non-governmental organisation (NGO) Earthways Foundation from 1998 to 2007 and they have also partnered with the Maquipucuna Foundation, an Ecuadorian non-profit organization devoted to conservation and sustainable development, to bring external funding for local livelihood projects such as sustainable cacao growing and chocolate production.[18] Whether these efforts provide a viable long-term future for the community and the forests they protect, in the face of externally driven pressures of development that have seen the destruction of most of the Chocó forests around them, is a moot point.

You can now understand, after reading all the above, why I prefer the first story about the Sapayoa's origins. If it is correct, the Sapayoa's presence in Playa de Oro represents one

18 Vanessa Ratten, 'Fundacion Maquipucuna: an entrepreneurial Ecuadorian non-profit organization', *International Journal of Business and Globalisation*, vol. 6, no. 2, pp.271–224, 2011.

half of an unlikely symmetry between an ancient dispersal of Old World birds and a more recent diaspora of Old World people, coming together in the New World in Playa de Oro's magnificent forests. There is a kind of poetic symmetry between the ancient origin story of the Sapayoa and the more tragic troubled one of their modern-day guardians. Both are singular in their status as inhabitants among their kind in this part of the globe, but they are also a mirror image of each other. The conjunction of the two is a happy ending for both, a good way to wrap up a story. The very different processes by which this conjunction came about are, to me, equal sources of wonder and amazement. The result is a shared and interdependent existence where they are living together, for the time being at least, in harmony.

And if science in the end proves the second story is much more likely to be the case – that the Sapayoa and the broadbills, asities and pittas are cousins who separated millennia ago from the same group of ancestors in what is still the Sapayoa's New World ancient homeland – then so be it. For the time being, I'm not going to let some awkward facts spoil a good story.

CHAPTER 3

An Invisible Rail

Rails are chicken-like birds, some of them flightless and most of them loth to fly in normal circumstances. All of them are pretty hard to observe because they skulk in reed beds, often in impenetrable swamps, or (in the case of forest rails) in the undergrowth. Many have long legs and beaks, adapted to feeding in muddy hollows and swamps, and laterally compressed bodies, allowing them to slip unheard and unseen through the vegetation. Dawn and dusk, when they feel most emboldened to venture out, are good times for birders to spot them. Otherwise, they are more often heard than seen, advertising themselves deep in the ground cover or reeds with an occasional series of loud, raucous squawks and other odd noises. So, when a member of this family of birds is named 'Invisible Rail', the birder knows they are in for a tough time.

Among all bird families, rails have been one of the most adversely impacted by humans, for a number of reasons. Speciation of rails has been in large part due to isolation on islands. The ancient ancestors of modern rails were not flightless, and some were migratory. But being somewhat weak flyers, they were readily blown off course, landing on many remote islands where they were stranded, survived, settled down and evolved further. In the absence of predators, many became flightless (flight consumes a lot of energy and so, without the need for wings to escape predators, it's a good strategy to do away with them). Islands all over the Pacific, for example, acquired their own endemic rail species, many of them flightless.

But with the spread of human foraging and settlement to such islands, rails were vulnerable to extinction both from human hunting and also from predation by introduced invasive species, like rats and snakes. Being unable to flee on the wing was now a fatal vulnerability. The International Union for the Conservation of Nature (IUCN), in compiling its Red List of threatened species, as of May 2020 accounts for 168 species of rail, including 24 that are already extinct (others, unrecorded, must also have gone extinct). Of the remainder, six are Critically Endangered, ten are Endangered, 19 are Vulnerable, 13 are Near Threatened and 94 are of Least Concern; two are 'data deficient' – that is, we just don't know.

For a birder, rails have a special allure. They are not only, in some cases, vanishing as species, but they are also a big challenge to whoever wants to see one. Many are found in remote locations and finding them may involve ending up in a sweaty swamp. And, as already indicated, they are hard to see even when you know they are there. With all that effort required, adding an island rail to the life list is an irresistible challenge for the most hardened and intrepid of birders. If you are one for whom the length of their life list is the most important thing, it is pretty certain that your diminishing 'wanted' list will contain a disproportionate number of species of remote island rails, making them even more desirable.

Invisible Rail

The Invisible Rail is normally observed (more often, only heard) in sago swamps adjacent to forest in remote parts of Halmahera, one of Indonesia's many islands. These swamps are harvested for their sago and some are disappearing as people find more profitable uses for them. Trapping the rails for food is not that hard, especially because they are flightless. Birdlife International describes the species as 'enigmatic' and 'poorly known'.[19] On the IUCN Red List, the Invisible Rail is considered 'Vulnerable' and in decline. There are maybe between 3,000 and 15,000 individuals in the wild. Much remains to be discovered – diet, breeding habits, the exact distribution and size of remaining populations and so on.

Looking at one of the few really good images available online, the Invisible Rail's supposed invisibility might be doubted. While its appearance overall is a uniformly brownish-black and it inhabits dark, swampy places, its beak is long and strikingly red. In this image, it glows at you out of the reedbed like a beacon.[20] Its eyes and long legs are also red. And, for good measure, it is quite a large bird. But still, in my experience at least, its name is apt. When I was in Halmahera birding in 2014, I was that close, heard a scuttle in the reeds and saw a movement, but not a glimpse of the bird and its splendid beak. To me, it remains an Invisible Rail in the vanishing swamps.

The scientific name for the Invisible Rail is either *Gallirallus wallacii* or *Habroptila wallacii*, depending on which taxonomic list you consult. Regardless of the disagreement, the association in both scientific names with the 19th century biologist and explorer Alfred Russell Wallace is the significant point. Wallace was the first to collect the bird for the sake of science on Halmahera in 1858 (just by-the-by, no doubt he, like the locals, probably considered his rail well suited to the dinner table). It was officially proclaimed a new species to science by ornithologist George Robert Gray in a report to the Zoological Society in 1860. But this wasn't Wallace's only discovery on Halmahera. On the same trip, he struck, independently of Charles Darwin, on his version of the Theory of Evolution by Natural Selection.

Wallace had earlier published papers outlining other elements of the theory, but the crucial missing piece was the mechanism of natural selection, by which traits that are passed on through succeeding generations are selected according to the extent to which they contribute to fitness, eventually producing population-wide changes that can lead to the emergence of new species. By his own later account, he formulated this idea during a feverish bout of speculation while laid low with malaria. Returning to his base in nearby

19 Birdlife International species factsheet, *Habroptila wallacii*, available online.

20 The image is reproduced with permission from Rob Hutchison/BirdTour Asia.

Ternate in February 1858, Wallace boxed up his specimens for dispatch to London and also mailed off his paper on natural selection to Darwin for his opinion.

Darwin had penned his own version of the theory some 20 years earlier but had put it away in a drawer while he collected more evidence, fearful of the controversies it would invoke if published and the consequences for his reputation (as well as for his domestic harmony – his wife was a devout Christian). Wallace's discovery forced Darwin to put out his own version, and Wallace's and Darwin's papers were read simultaneously to the Linnaean Society on 1 July 1858. Shortly after, Darwin rushed to print with his *Origin of the Species*.

But I digress, we have gone off the rails. The common name for the bird that I have used to this point has not always been adopted. Just as the experts can't agree on the family name, they don't always agree on the common English name. It is sometimes named Drummer Rail after its call, which resembles a drumming noise. This is not the place to embark on a discourse on one of the most favourite topics for argument among birders – the 'correct' name for a species (another favourite being 'is it a full species or not'?). Let me just say that Invisible Rail is quite obviously a better name and leave it there (Wallace's Rail – which is also OK in my book – has sometimes been used as well, but it has gone out of fashion). A separate species it most certainly is – it occupies a distinctive ecological niche in its specialized habitat, it has long been isolated on Halmahera, and is recognized by its big, red schnoz (if you are lucky enough to see it) and (for the rest of us) by its distinctive call.

That swamp, where I heard but didn't see *Habroptila wallacii*, was near a resort on the eastern coast of Halmahera increasingly popular for its birding as well as for its diving. We visited the swamp and the adjoining forest on two occasions. On the first of these, we unsuccessfully played the call at a good roadside viewing spot adjacent to the swamp. Later, we walked in single file down a short, winding trail through the sago palms, trying to avoid their sharp spines. As our leader turned a corner, there was a scurry and he alone saw two juvenile rails disappear forever (so far as we were concerned) into the undergrowth. The rest of us cursed our luck.

On the second occasion, full of optimism, we entered another area of the swamp, where the ground underfoot was far wetter, and where we were surrounded by vividly green reed beds. Insects buzzed and things went 'plop' in the mud. A rail called from some distance, answering the playback on our iPod, and we stayed still and silent, listening, leaving the circling mosquitos unmolested for the moment. This montage was repeated several times as we squelched further into the swamp, the bird occasionally responding. Finally, at our last stop, we heard approaching sounds of scuttling and saw a brief movement of the reeds. Then came sounds of fleeing as the bird caught sight of us, turned and ran. One of our number saw a brief shape, but scrupulously declined to enter a tick because he could not be certain of the ID. I might have been tempted in his shoes, but as it was, to all of us the rail remained invisible.

That was it, three hours of typical birding in the tropics at considerable effort, with a familiar outcome – a dip. I will never go back; life is too short and there are so many other places to go and birds to see. But no matter, the allure of this Invisible Rail and of birds like it on my target list, some of which I have seen but most I never will, is one of the reasons I am a birder. And in retrospect, the quest for a glimpse of this iconic bird in that swamp was no less exciting (and only a bit less rewarding) for not succeeding. The memory of the moment,

The Sago Swamp

including the discomforts, once they were in the past, is hardly less pleasurable than the reliving of more successful quests. This is not to deny that the best thing would have been actually to see the bird. The disappointment was heartfelt at the time. But the second-best turns out to have been almost as good.

Indeed, perhaps my failure to see the rail is a more authentic experience of this elusive species than if our efforts to attract it with a sound recording had been successful. Such artifice with the aid of digital playback devices, essential to the modern birder, were not available until relatively recently. Previous adventurers into the forests and swamps of Halmahera had a much tougher time of it. One such was the zoologist Gerd Heinrich, who led an expedition to Sulawesi and Halmahera in the early 1930s and, *apropos* the Invisible Rail, later wrote, with characteristic immodesty:

> I am solidly confident no European has ever seen this rail alive, for that requires such a degree of toughening and such demands on oneself as I

cannot so easily attribute to others. *Habroptila* is shielded by the awful thorns of the sago swamps.... In this thorn wilderness, I walked barefoot and half-naked for weeks.[21]

It is quite possible, indeed, that even its original discoverer Wallace never saw his rail alive and in the wild, but that his specimen was taken in a snare set by a local hunter (especially as Wallace spent so much time on his sickbed). All such explorers and collectors relied primarily on local hunters not only for information about where in the forest to find what, but also for many of the dead specimens they collected.

But the intrepid Heinrich did indeed see and catch his own Invisible Rail. A family photograph published in his biography shows him emerging grinning from the swamp, clad only in shorts, his torso and legs scored with scratches and bites, grasping his rail by the legs and waving it triumphantly over his head.[22] My own experience of the swamp – including the bites and scratches – was only a weak, pale replication, but true to life nonetheless; and I take some solace for my dip in the fact that it took even Gerd Heinrich several weeks to find his target.

Not far down the road from the swamp, we enjoyed 100% success on another day, in far more comfortable circumstances, in our quest for a different mega target with a similar aura, Wallace's Standardwing (yes, the same Wallace, who first collected this bird for science on Halmahera, along with the rail). The Standardwing is a member of the bird-of-paradise family and is endemic to Halmahera (plus two offshore islands). From a specially built hide down a short trail from where we parked the car, our eyes feasted on a number of displaying males and at least one watching female.

This was a very different experience – hardly a pursuit through a barely penetrable swamp, but still we had arrived at a birder's nirvana. We just had to turn up at the right time of the day, take a short walk and sit quietly on a bench. The Standardwing, unlike the Invisible Rail, is on my life list; but it is the Invisible Rail that brings back the most vivid and rewarding memories.

For both birds, I owe a very special thanks to the owners of the resort. Through the Sawai Ecotourism Foundation, they have purchased large areas of nearby forest and they provide employment for local people to help protect it. They built the hide where I observed the Standardwing and they watch over the site to prevent disturbance. They found a second lek and bought that bit of forest as well. The Foundation works with neighbouring communities and landowners and runs education programmes to spread the conservation message. We stayed at the resort for several days and nights, saw a number of top birds, and in our small way when paying the bill, we contributed to improving the chance that the Invisible Rail does not become forever invisible by going extinct.

That photograph of the Invisible Rail peering from the reeds was taken in the same swamp in 2012. A more recent photo, taken in January 2018, is of a bird seen much closer to the resort and to surrounding human settlement.[23] This one was in plain sight on a track. Herein lies a different story. In a context of the shrinking swampland where the bird

21 Nigel J. Collar, 'Pioneer of Asian Ornithology: Gerd Heinrich', *Birding Asia*, vol. 11, 2009, p.36.

22 The photo is reproduced in Collar (op. cit.) and taken from Bernd Heinrich, *The Snoring Bird: My Family's Journey through a Century of Biology*, New York, NY: Harper Collins, 2007.

23 The image can be found (as of May 2020) in the photos stored online in the Internet Bird Collection (IBC) in the Cornell Lab of Ornithology Macaulay Library.

Weda Resort, Halmahera

has traditionally been observed, its adaptability to other habitats, including those close to human habitation, is one of many unknowns about the species. In the absence of trapping by local people, perhaps the Invisible Rail is not so limited by habitat specialization as might have been thought. In those all-too-rare and wonderful places like Weda, where efforts are made to protect wildlife, including this edible rail, it and some other vulnerable species may yet show new signs of life in a changing environment that is more and more impacted by humans.

I have already described my conflicting feelings in comparing my experience of the Standardwing, handed to us on a plate in full view thanks to the local guardians, with the Invisible Rail, scuttling unseen into the swamp as we looked in vain, hot and exhausted. The photo of the rail out in the open presents me with a teasing hypothetical: would I really prefer to dip on a rail in a steaming swamp, where the bird is supposedly in its element, and where I must sweat and get bitten alive for the privilege of trying to see it, rather than come across one in passing that is just walking across the village road like a chicken? To be honest, if I had experienced the latter first, I would most likely not have ventured so far into that swamp. But in that event, I would also have missed out on something very special.

So, let us first and foremost keep the swamps and forests that would allow us to observe (or not, as the case may be) birds in their ancient, natural settings. But supposing, in this age of extinctions as the sago swamps shrink and disappear, this other 'bird in the hand' thrives on village scraps and even fearlessly shares the chickenfeed, so much the better for all of us. A distant second-best is better than nothing. And no doubt, for many birders, the ease and comfort of the tick would be a definite plus.

CHAPTER 4

The Tragopan Trek

Birding trips to distant parts of the world are not always all about the birds. The Tragopan trek was memorable in good part for the human dramas, although this is not to play down how good the birds were as well. Most of those dramas grew out of the fears and tensions of the quest, which was focused on finding just one bird, the Western Tragopan. I mean (no spoilers allowed), what if we had gone all that way to the far north-west of India, trekked up into the foothills of the Himalayas, camped out for a week and, after all, not seen it…?

The Western Tragopan, *Tragopan melanocephalus*, is one of five species of the genus and is found in the Western Himalayas. Male tragopans are big, startlingly brightly plumaged members of the pheasant family, *Phasianidae*. The Western tragopan is less brightly coloured than some of its namesakes, but it is no less striking for that, as the illustration shows. The species is listed as 'Vulnerable' on the IUCN Red List and there is a captive breeding project to help it out. One estimate is that there are around 5,000 left in the wild. Much of this bird's habitat is remote and relatively inaccessible. The places it is found are not especially good for travelling birders. Only a few other species that inhabit the lower

Western Tragopan

slopes and foothill valleys of the Himalayas are not found in other regions further east. These latter regions are more accessible and also offer a better chance of seeing a bigger list of other sought-after species. So, this expedition was, to say the least, a bit off the birders' beaten track.

The party was an interesting mixed bunch – two French, one Belgian, one English and me (an expat Brit with an Australian passport at that time living in Hong Kong). Not forgetting, of course, our leader, a birding guide with just as strong a desire as the rest of us (if not stronger) to see the Tragopan, a lifer for him as well. Our trip took us to the Great Himalayan National Park, which is in the northern part of India in the Kullu region of the state of Himachal Pradesh, bordering Jammu and Kashmir. We met up in Delhi, flew to Chandigarh and drove north for eight hours, passing close to Shimla, the old hill station of the British Raj, and arriving in the Tirthan Valley with the Himalayas in our sights.

Here, we stopped for two nights to make final preparations for the trek, and also to find a Cheer Pheasant, which was known to frequent the upper slopes of the valley. As with so many rare birds whose populations are in decline due to pressures from human activity, it was reliably accessible here only because a local hill farmer had decided to provide it with a safe haven on his property. To get there in time to see it in the early morning, we set off from our hotel at 3 am, climbing up the hillside in the dark. As dawn broke, the views of the valley and the far mountains took the breath away (not that there was much breath left in our lungs after the climb). The pheasant called from the hillside as the sun rose, and gave us good, if distant, views. Calling Upland Pipits were visible on several closer outcrops. We enjoyed a simple breakfast in the farmhouse and headed back down.

This excursion was just a taste of what was to come. Our trek into the Great Himalayan National Park began the next day. We were accompanied by a very impressive support team: the chief guide of the local ecotour company who had looked after most of the ground logistics; two ex-Tragopan hunters-turned-trekking guides; the cook and his assistants; and

a shifting team of up to eight porters, some of whom kept us supplied from the local village down the mountain every day, others of whom joined the camp for the duration.

The first leg of the trek took us to 'base camp' at Rolla at 2,190 m, a collection of huts and tents on a campground next to the rushing river. Our destination was Khorli Pohi, a part of the park that was off-limits to most trekkers, but which we were able to access with special permits. The second leg was a climb of another 1,000 m or so, via a knife-edged ridge in the forest, and thence down to an alpine meadow and our camp site laid out next to a stone hut that was to house the kitchen and the porters' sleeping quarters. The stragglers among us barely made it, but it was well worth it. The setting was spectacular: a backdrop of snow-clad mountains, fronted at the edge of our meadow by steepling conifers, and above and below us, tree-clad, rocky slopes. A glacial stream provided fresh water, filtered (just in case) by our equipment at the camp site.

Our leader was in his element. Impressively, he treated every part of the journey as an explorer might, keeping a record, noting the exact route and recording the journey for posterity. From the starting point at Chandigarh Airport, he had entered every turn of the road in his black pocketbook with precise readings from the vehicle's odometer and his GPS gizmo. On the trek up, we stopped at regular intervals as he took GPS readings and recorded them.

He was leaving no stone unturned, no eventuality unanticipated. We were instructed strictly in a set of protocols for the birding and, in particular, for the Tragopan search. This was to commence before first light the next morning. The first evening in camp, two spotters were sent out to search for a Tragopan roost in the nearby forest, while we were given our marching orders: a minimum of bags and no spotting scopes to clutter us up or make a noise; an oath of complete silence; an absence of any piece of bright clothing to scare the bird; and, if we were staking it out, no sudden movements and, in particular, *absolutely no pointing.*

I had been lectured the day before about my cap, which was pale cream and apparently too bright for a Tragopan (the birding tour company that had given it to me on a previous trip should have known better; although, in mitigation, it was a trip in the African bush, not in a forest of conifers). That night we turned in fully briefed and ready for anything, and I dug out another piece of headgear. We were left in no doubt that our leader was desperately serious about seeing this bird. I, for one, was impressed with his military-style demeanour, which surely would guarantee our success.

There may have been a communication problem, or maybe just some Gallic stubbornness, as next morning Serge emerged from his tent carrying a spotting scope and tripod. As the days passed it became apparent to those of us who didn't already know him that he was an accomplished professional artist specializing in drawing birds from nature, as he spent a good part of the trip perched with his scope on the hillside, sketching birds that came into view in his powerful lens. Optimistically, he hoped to do this with the Tragopan. But the 'no scope rule' was not to be denied. He passionately stated his case but was delivered an ultimatum: 'If you insist on bringing the scope, you can stay behind'. True to his artistic integrity, he duly spent the morning at the campsite sketching grosbeaks and redstarts.

With that matter dispatched, the rest of us set off with high hopes, as the spotters had found a roost tree on their evening recce. It was still dark, but the tree was not far. We crept up silently, and took our places on the ground, expectantly. The spotters, who had brought a rug, adjourned to a nearby clearing and lit up, passing the time of day with small talk. Our leader called for silence, but when it was not forthcoming, they were sent packing, back to camp. That was the last we saw of one of them, who must have taken umbrage and immediately set off down the mountain. He had been hunting and trapping all his life and obviously thought he knew a thing or two about how to behave around a Tragopan.

As the first rays of the sun appeared, there was a stirring in the tree and we all heard the call: 'kuwaaah, kuwaaah' (described by one authority as a 'nasal goat-like bleating'). No one saw a thing at first. The call was repeated, and this time, looking up into the tree I saw a dim, pheasant-like shape slowly come into view on a branch. The sun was hardly up, and all I got was the silhouette against the brightening sky. As it called one more time, magically its breath rose from its beak in the cold morning air in a wisp of vapour. It retreated, still only a dark shape, and that was that. Shortly after, we heard it clumsily flap away down the mountain, out of our line of sight.

I was the only one to get a look. Not believing in the moment that I was so uniquely positioned to see it, and so well drilled was I, that I had sat motionless and said nothing. I definitely didn't point. In the aftermath, there was a certain grumpiness in the air. As one in the party said: 'We should have lamped it' (he was referring to shining a torch into the tree, not knocking it out). In contrition, I affirmed that my view was not good enough for a positive ID, so I wasn't going to tick it. Indeed, although this was a magical moment and, with hindsight, there could be no doubt about what I saw, a silhouette and a wisp of breath was not enough for me. I still needed to see it in full view, red upper breast, white spots and all.

By now the sun was up, and we headed down in the direction of the bird's flight. We found a viewing spot, a log overlooking a long slope dotted with trees, down which the bird had flown. We took our seats in a line, our leader down one end of the log, and he played the call. Each of us peered down the slope, views partly obscured by the intervening trees. An excited whisper from Alain, at the far end of the log, indicated that the bird had stepped into his line of sight, as well as that of the lucky birder sat next to him. The rest of us bent our necks and peered in vain down the slope:

'Voila! Voila!'

'Where? Where?'

'Sit still! Shut up!', came the fierce instructions from the other end of the log, as the rest of us shuffled about, desperate for a view. By now the excited whispers were accompanied by frantic gesticulations as it became evident to Alain that we couldn't see the bird.

'Shut up! Don't point!'

As Alain and everyone else became more agitated, the bird in full view to his eyes but not to ours, so came the final, explosive admonition from down the end of the log, as unprintable as it was dramatic. We froze in astonishment, but the bird had already flown.

'It went that way,' I said helpfully, pointing.

'Martin!! Don't!!! Point!!!!' was my reward.

Nerves frayed, we headed back to camp. At least, we knew the birds were in our neighbourhood. Over the next five days, we spent some early mornings searching, playing the call and listening, trying to get a response. Serge went on with his sketching. Our leader quietly brooded but went about his business like the professional he is. We heard the Tragopan on several occasions, but not close by. We did some general birding (the diminutive and elusive White-throated Bushtit was a highlight) and on some mornings or afternoons, each of us went our separate ways. Two of us briefly saw a Black-headed Jay around the campsite while the leader was off on an expedition. He was sceptical ("We saw a Black-headed Jay" – "No you didn't!") because supposedly our altitude was well above its normal range. We saw it later in the trip at a lower altitude, but I had already ticked it anyway.

It had been pointed out to us that this was not a normal birding trip, but an 'expedition', and we were all free to explore on our own, including the leader. Tour leaders have been sacked in other circumstances for wandering off on their own to find a bird, because being alone gives them a better chance, leaving the clients to fend for themselves. But some of the normal 'rules of the road' that prevailed on birding tours did not apply – in particular, the cardinal rule that the main purpose of the trip was, first and foremost, to make every feasible effort to show every bird to every member of the group. In advance, we had been told that one reason this trip was put on was to add the bird to the tour company's 'life list'. For that purpose, the leader had to see it to confirm the sighting, and this was the first priority. We all knew what the score was, and we took our place in the queue. One member of the party claimed to have seen the Tragopan briefly, but none of us were with him at the time to share the viewing. It rained one day and snowed another. It all seemed to be going nowhere.

One morning, our leader and a couple of others who chose to accompany him, set off along an overgrown, disused trail. The shepherds who had formerly used it were not allowed in this part of the National Park anymore in order to protect the habitat from the ravages of flocks of grazing sheep. As we followed the disappearing trail amidst the encroaching undergrowth, our leader had an uncanny knack of picking out the right way. He fastidiously snapped branches at every turn as we went, so as to leave a trace for our return. His spirits lifted as he realized the trail headed up the mountain into unknown territory.

Leaving us behind, the adventurer set out to explore. It began raining, and it was late afternoon before he returned from his excursion into the wilds with an air of satisfaction, having heard the Tragopan close by the trail on the way down. Very early next morning, he was off again, up the same trail. He reappeared after breakfast, exultant, having seen the Tragopan a short way up the mountain, not far past the spot where he had left us the day before. There were sighs of relief all round. But what about our turn?

Next day we were mostly confined to our tents by the rain and snow, but a plan was hatched to save our bacon on the final morning (we were heading down that day). The two of us who had not seen the bird (other than Serge, who still was having none of it) would set off very early and follow the leader up the mountain to the spot where he had seen it. I was up and ready in the pitch black at the time appointed, but (true to form) he had already left, and my fellow-birder was not in view: groans from his tent in response to my whispered calls indicated that Delhi belly had laid him low, so I set out alone.

I had only taken ten steps in the pitch dark when I fell in a hole (I still bear the scar). Staggering onward, and after going down a number of blind alleys along the half-invisible trail, I reached a landmark, the point where the trail emerged from the trees, crossed a small ice-patch in a gully and headed up the mountain. Encouragingly, I heard the Tragopan up ahead. By now, the day was dawning. As I climbed, I turned a corner to see a crouched figure, waving at me frantically to get down and keep quiet. I crept up and huddled down just behind him. There, down the trail in plain view, appeared a male Tragopan, strutting in all his glory. I watched it, spellbound, for several minutes. It charged down the track towards us and disappeared into the trees. When I got back to the camp, I must have acted unbearably smug, although I did try hard to hide my elation from my ailing fellow birder who had come all that way but dipped at the last hurdle.

Aside from the dramas of seeing (or not seeing) the Tragopan, there were many other things about the trip that made it an unforgettable experience. One I haven't so far mentioned was the catering. Our cook was a culinary genius, conjuring up a series of gourmet soups and curries from a smoky, leaking hellhole of a kitchen, over a wood fire. The porters were also amazing, skipping effortlessly up and down the trail to base camp and beyond in relays, bringing up supplies of fresh trout, chicken, vegetables and beer.

The landscape and the forest were stunning. It was a bonus that it snowed briefly, making the mountain tops shine with new white snow – although at the time it was not welcomed, being unseasonal and catching us unprepared. I left no item of clothing off when I climbed into my sleeping bag that night. But we had our share of sunshine as well, when the air was clear and crisp, and the mountain tops glistened. During our camp-out on that alpine meadow, aside from our team we saw nobody at our campsite. It seemed we were in sole occupation of this wild place, with only faint traces of a previous human presence. Even the stone hut, collapsing into just another pile of stones in the landscape, seemed to be giving up the attempt to leave a human mark.

But only the strict enforcement of prohibitions by the park authorities, in part to assist in preserving the habitat of the Tragopan, can keep people at bay. On one of our daily excursions, we did see signs of human intrusions other than ours, namely holes dug at the base of trees to extract truffles and, on one occasion, a shadowy figure with a sack disappearing between the trees. These black truffles are worth their weight in gold in the restaurants of Paris. But the shepherds and their sheep and goats have been banished and the bird poachers have mostly been frightened off or lured away with a different source of income as trekking guides.

But tradition demands that men in the area wear the tiny, vivid blue crest feather of the Himalayan Monal in their round caps as a sign of their status. Hunting of the Monal was banned in 1982 in Himachal Pradesh, but the feathers are still to be seen in a lot of caps in the nearby towns and villages. Thankfully the Monal, a brilliantly plumaged blue-green pheasant, was quite common around our campsite – we regularly disturbed them, sending them clattering down the mountain in alarm.

Down in the valley, below base camp at Rolla and outside the park boundaries, there are a number of settlements where families of herders and farmers lead a tough life in the idyllic landscape, supplementing their income when they can with what the mountain forests have to offer. We camped in one such settlement on the way down the valley, seeing a new set of birds and celebrating our safe return from the mountains with the porters around our campfire.

It was ironic but perhaps entirely fitting that, at the conclusion of the Tragopan Expedition several days later, the 'bird of the trip' voted on by the paying customers was not the Tragopan, but the Cheer Pheasant. Our leader was not impressed. All being said and done, I have no doubt we needed his kind of dedication and single-mindedness to see a Western Tragopan. The two of us who didn't share in this achievement no doubt have their own stories to tell. Mine, at least, had a happy ending.

CHAPTER 5

Hotel Birding and Other Unlikely Hotspots

While staying for a few weeks in 2017 in Bermondsey, an inner suburb of East London on the South Bank of the River Thames, I looked for House Sparrows. I had read that they were disappearing in the capital. Feeders on the balcony attracted Great Tits and lumbering Common Woodpigeons. In the nearby park, a Eurasian Wren sang, European Goldfinches visited, and Common Starlings hopped about. Crows were also common as, of course, were feral pigeons. A Common Blackbird could be heard singing somewhere. But no Sparrows, until I roamed further afield. On a piece of waste ground, I found a small party in the long grass. Later, I came across another group in a secluded corner of a public housing block. That was all.

The Common Woodpigeon is a woodland bird and is a relatively new arrival in inner cities where it hangs around parks and large gardens. Unlike most woodland birds in Britain, it is thriving. Eurasian Wrens also seem to be doing OK in the Bermondsey Spa local park. Signs in the park point out how the local authorities have been making it more 'bird-friendly' – it seems to be working. But not, it seems, for the House Sparrow. As their name suggests, they have a long association with built-up areas and people. They typically nest in cavities in the walls and in the roof spaces of buildings. The notion that the 'Cockney Sparrow' might be hard to find in London would have been unthinkable only a few decades ago. How such population changes happen and why is often a mystery. Falling insect numbers is one possible cause in the case of House Sparrows. A recently advanced theory pinpoints the effects of air pollution from diesel vehicles.[24]

All this shows that what we do in and to our cities provides both opportunities and threats to birds, to which they respond, often in a short space of time. Birders, as well as birds, are opportunists. While we mostly head for birding spots away from cities, we can

24 Will Peach *et al.*, 'Depleted suburban House Sparrow *Passer Domesticus* population not limited by food availability', *Urban Ecosystems*, vol. 21, 2018, pp.1053–1065.

Bull-headed Shrike

also find good birding in urban parks, hotel gardens and urban waste ground (not forgetting sewage farms and drainage channels). I have visited my fair share. One reason the birder likes these spots is that they are, by nature, refuges for wildlife in an otherwise crowded, built-up landscape. You can mark them on the map and know that they'll hold birds before you get there. Conveniently, rather than wandering the streets of the urban jungle, you can just get in a taxi or catch a bus.

Such refuges often have quite surprising residents and visitors. Birders who visit Taiwan often make their first birding stop the Taipei Botanical Gardens, slap in the centre of the city, where a secluded pond holds a population of Malayan Night-Herons (at least, that was so on my visit some years ago). This species, uncommon but widely distributed across Eastern and Southern Asia, is normally hard to find and elusive, as it inhabits dark, wet forests and hides quietly amidst the foliage. In the Botanical Gardens, the suitably muddy forest patch is tiny, but obviously cosy to a Night-Heron. There they are, relaxing in the park, lazily eyeing the passers-by. Around the time I was there, birders knew that if you wanted to see a Malayan Night-Heron, this was one of the best places to go.

Kowloon Park in Hong Kong, a small patch of green in the midst of one of the most densely populated places on Earth, is home to a close cousin of the Malayan Night-Heron, the Black-crowned Night-Heron – and much else besides. The Night-Herons roost in plain sight up in the park's trees. Hong Kong annually records a large number of passage migrants and winter visitors, and many of them (especially the passerines) turn up in this urban park, which is surrounded on all sides by tower blocks, shopping malls and highways. The park itself is never quiet, people are everywhere. Even so, since 2016, over 20 species of migrants have been recorded here on eBird, including some that are eagerly sought by keen Hong Kong birders each year, such as Bull-headed Shrike, Fujian Niltava and Orange-headed Thrush.

The Bull-headed Shrike was a rooftop tick in my Hong Kong village on the urban fringe. The other two are on my Hong Kong office-window list, spotted while I rested my eyes from the computer screen (only briefly, of course). They were stopping over on migration in a small ornamental Chinese Garden, carved out between towering office blocks about 3 km north of Kowloon Park. Migrating birds in particular enjoy patches of refuge habitat in the midst of the concrete and bitumen, but others also benefit. Up to December 2020, 151 species have been recorded on eBird at the Kowloon Park 'Hotspot' – the number keeps rising as the years pass and as more observers submit their lists.

The value to birds of these oases makes a good case for deliberately making green areas in cities more than just human playgrounds, quiet lunch spots and exercise trails. Parks should have bird-friendly trees and shrubs and quiet nooks and crannies away from the paths, as well as green swards for young lovers and bouncy castles for the kids. Visiting an urban park with my bins, I usually make a beeline for the less manicured bits, or the sections that seem to contain predominantly native vegetation. Few such parks are laid out with this in mind, although, as mentioned earlier, in some places (such as Bermondsey) this is beginning to happen. Little Lenin Park in the centre of Hanoi, just by the Lenin Statue and across the road from the Military Museum, is bustling with exercisers and children on bikes but has some quiet corners and scruffy bits; it offers decent birding in the migration season. While visiting Hanoi for work, between meetings I would pull my bins out of my bag and look for a green patch, often with excellent results.

Botanic Gardens in our larger cities are often among the more welcoming patches of green, especially if they reserve places for native vegetation. Singapore's Botanic Gardens, for example (with an eBird list of 213 species), contains a small, deliberately preserved rainforest section, where an assortment of woodpeckers, owls, flycatchers and other indigenous birds can be found. Right next to the forest patch is a small lake, which attracts a decent number of wetland birds. In Australia, the Botanic Gardens in Sydney, a mere 5-minute stroll from the Sydney Opera House, is sometimes home to a Powerful Owl, which finds the exotic trees (where fruit bats roost) just as good a hunting ground as the native ones.

In Australia's capital city, Canberra's Botanic Gardens celebrate Australian flora and are laid out to show off different forms of native vegetation, which attract different birds. A small patch of well-tended rainforest in a gully is home to Bassian Thrush, a forest floor

Yucatan Jay, Cancún

skulker that had frustrated me for years, successfully evading my attempts to see it until I visited this spot in 2018. As is so often the case, a human-created piece of nature, there mainly to put on a show for our benefit, also helps the birds – and the birders. That is, until the busload of children on their school outing arrives on the scene.

City hotel gardens are another type of refuge that can be a good location for birders. My first encounter with birding in Mexico was in the gardens of a hotel in Cancún, where we found Hooded Orioles and my first endemic, the Yucatan Jay. Even hotels without gardens sometimes provide excellent vantage points for surprise birding encounters.

In Addis Ababa, the capital of Ethiopia, I stayed in a modern hotel for a couple of nights in a mainly residential area undergoing redevelopment. The surrounding streets were busy with people and traffic and, one morning, a large herd of sheep caused chaos. From my balcony on the 10th floor, I overlooked an abandoned building site, fast becoming overgrown by weeds, fringed by a few trees and shrubs. From my vantage point, I had a dozen ticks, including three Horn of Africa endemics (a Seedeater, a Flycatcher and a Pigeon). But I should perhaps have stayed at the Ghion Hotel, popular among Addis visitors as a green oasis in a hot and very dusty city. It is surrounded by grounds that were formerly part of an Imperial Palace. Indeed, that was the starting point for our guided tour of Ethiopia, where I ticked off a dozen more lifers.

But perhaps my most notable hotel garden birding adventure was in an actual oasis in the desert. This oasis was purely artificial, created and nurtured for the sake of the hotel guests and visitors. And it was on an island that was similarly artificially 'greened': Sir Bani Yas in the United Arab Emirates (UAE). I visited in 2015 with my partner for a vacation. Sir Bani Yas is some 75 km^2 in size and has no natural water supply. Originally, it was rocky desert. This all changed in the 1970s, when the founder of the UAE, Sheikh Zayed bin Sultan Al Nahyan, commenced a project to 'green the desert' and created an animal sanctuary on the island. He installed a desalination plant and laid thousands of kilometres of irrigation pipes. Three and a half million trees and shrubs were planted – they now cover 70% of the island. Most of them were not indigenous but imported from other African countries. They grow, somewhat incongruously, in long straight lines stretching across the landscape, planted in rows following the black irrigation hoses.

As well as importing desert plants, the authority running the project imported animals, including some (from zoos) that were native to the UAE but had gone extinct in the wild. Oryxes, gazelles, antelopes, goats, hyenas, Giraffes and Cheetahs from all over Africa and the Middle East now roam the animal reserve, behind a tall fence (the precious Arabian Oryxes are in their own enclosure for safety, while the wildlife managers let the Cheetahs feast on the gazelles). Arabian Oryx were hunted to extinction in the wild in the mid-20th century. They have since been reintroduced to their customary habitats from captive populations, as well as still being preserved in reserves such as Sir Bani Yas. A selection of birds was also introduced, including Ostrich, Black and Grey Francolins, Helmeted Guinea Fowl, Grey crowned-Crane and Indian Peafowl. In 2015, a small flock of Houbara Bustards (in danger of extinction in the wild under pressure of hunting) was released in an enclosure. Island visitors get guided 'safari tours' to inspect the wildlife.

The resort hotel where we stayed is on the seashore and is surrounded by lush, cultivated lawns and shrubberies, with palms and other trees dotting the area. Semi-cultivated native grasses and shrubs fringe the heavily irrigated greenery. A lagoon behind the hotel is a magnet for migrating waders. Saunders's Terns breed on the hotel's dirt landing strip.

Grey crowned-Crane

Saunders's Tern on the runway

Socotra Cormorant doing laps

Rufous-tailed Scrub-Robin

Egyptian Geese perch on the hotel roof, a Kestrel keeps watch on the gardens from the same vantage point and an Osprey sits on the low clifftops nearby.

We visited in early April, during the migration season. As always, I packed my bins, although I expected to make more use of my swimming gear. However, the only time I was particularly attracted to the swimming pool was when a Socotra Cormorant waddled up from the beach and went for a swim in the pool. My first swimming pool lifer! Most of the rest of the time, when not touring the island or walking around the lagoon looking at the waders, I was hanging out in the gardens checking out the migrants.

The gardens were like a magnet for birds, at this time of year attracting migrants on passage to northern breeding sites from their southern wintering grounds in Africa. The lawns were teeming with pipits, wagtails, warblers and at least a dozen Eurasian Hoopoe, stocking up for the next leg. There were five species of shrike (Isabelline, Red-tailed, Woodchat, Masked and Great Southern Grey), a Wryneck and a Rufous-tailed Scrub-Robin, two species of rock thrush (Common and Blue) and three of wheatear (Isabelline, Northern and Pied). A Song Thrush and a Bluethroat turned up one day, while Ortolan Bunting and Pale Rockfinch hung out in the stony fringes of the gardens. In a lagoon behind the resort that had been created during construction, there were around 20 species of waders and gulls. I had expected some birds, of course, but not such riches. What had started as a nice poolside holiday had ended as something of a tick-fest.

The hotel made a point of stressing its green credentials, including shutting down a popular guest attraction – windsurfing behind a light plane – because of the nesting terns. They were conscious of the benefits of the hotel grounds as a staging point for migrating birds and the hotel staff and sunbathing guests even tolerated the Cormorant, waiting patiently for it to finish its lengths in the pool and head back to the ocean. Excursions to see the safari wildlife were part of the attractions on daily offer – the stars were the Cheetahs and the Giraffes. Professional conservationists, who were employed by the authority that ran the reserve, acted as guides and showed us around in their safari jeeps. When not doing this, they tended the wildlife and monitored the introduced populations.

Wildlife park, open zoo, accidental haven, nature reserve…? The boundaries are fuzzy, but so are all the boundaries between people and nature. Human-made habitats for wildlife are now the norm as much as the exception, whether it is agricultural land, plantations, reservoirs, urban or semi-urban landscapes and so on. A very small number of these habitats are specifically designed to be bird-friendly, but most welcoming habitats in cities are accidental rather than deliberate havens for birds. Wasteland is always of this kind, as it is often in transition from one urban use to another. Parks and gardens are not accidental in the same sense, but their purposes are most often to do with the tastes of human recreation rather than the needs of wildlife. But the two purposes can coincide, and a little tweaking can do a lot for the birds, while also letting people have a good time. Some urban parks, such as New York's Central Park, are famous birding hotspots and parts of them are deliberately tended as such. Sometimes, as in the case of the resort hotel on Sir Bani Yas, the interests of the proprietors of land with a commercial purpose are seemingly well-served by welcoming and nurturing the wildlife, in addition to pleasing the guests with a well-manicured garden.

Not all urban landscapes completely dichotomize between the concreted bits, fit mostly for humans and their machines, and the waste ground and green bits that either incidentally or purposely welcome wildlife. I now live in a planned city, Canberra – Australia's capital – that was designed in the early 20th century with the 'Garden City' idea in mind. Of course, this is not the same as a 'wild' city, but still, green spaces that at least mimic the wild are part of the city fabric. The overall plan has remained pretty constant for a hundred years: wide avenues and expansive ceremonial spaces; a central precinct for government use with scattered office blocks and public buildings around an artificially created lake, with green surrounds and trees; lots of parks, broad nature strips on tree-lined streets in artfully laid-out leafy suburbs; and a growth policy under which satellite 'new towns' connected by green transport corridors, rather than uncontrolled urban sprawl, cater for the growing population. Artificial lakes and wetlands are found all over the suburbs, playing their role in regulating stormwater runoff while harbouring lots of wildlife.

Some tastes have changed since the early 20th century, when the concept began to crystallize under the guidance of founding designer and planner, Walter Burley Griffin. Griffin experimented with planting exotic trees and shrubs – for example, imagining that one of the nearby hilltops at one end of a key axis for the layout of the centre of the city would be planted with red-flowering trees and shrubs, and another, at the other end of the axis, with yellow (this didn't work out, unsurprisingly). There are many exotic trees and shrubs in Canberra, as in any city worldwide. But in the last 50 years or so, the vogue has favoured native plants. As a result, there are more mature gum trees, wattles and bottlebrushes in Canberra than in much of the surrounding countryside which, apart from the higher hills and more distant mountain ranges, are given over to grazing. As a result, the whole urban landscape of Canberra is effectively a refuge for native birds. And it has to be said, they don't mind feeding on the exotics either.

From the balcony of my apartment in 2018, I looked out from the third floor onto a recreational-cum-decorative open space, which contained a number of large, mature eucalypts and a collection of smaller, decorative plum and cherry trees. The latter flowered spectacularly in the spring and so, too, did the gum trees. One of these, a big red-flowering eucalyptus, was just opposite my balcony and was home to a changing population of parrots during the year. In this tree, seven species of parrot squabbled, socialized and fed (variously

Rainbow Lorikeet in the red-flowering gum

of nectar, seeds and shoots): Eastern and Crimson Rosella, Galah, Rainbow Lorikeet, Sulphur-crested, Gang-gang Cockatoo and Superb Parrot. Oh, and a pair of Yellow-tailed Black-Cockatoos flew over one morning but didn't stop by. All of these birds are more or less common in Canberra (the Superb Parrot is regularly recorded but in relatively small numbers – it was a very pleasant surprise when three of them turned up in my tree).

All this in a suburb of a city of half a million people. Out of town, there are nearby National Parks in the higher altitudes that also preserve precious habitat, although the catastrophic 2019–2020 bush fires razed a lot of the forest within their boundaries. Red Hill, which was close to my apartment, contains an important remnant of Yellow Box/Red Gum woodland, formerly the dominant habitat in the surrounding countryside (as well as much further afield in New South Wales and Victoria), but was severely disrupted by European settler agricultural development beginning in the 19th century. This particular patch in the city has been declared a 'critically endangered ecological community'. It is seriously degraded but being slowly restored. About 80 Eastern Grey Kangaroos live on the hill and they sometimes wander down into the surrounding suburbs, where they face the risk of being run over. Kangaroos are a common sight in a number of Canberra suburbs. Across the city, there are numerous other patches of remnant forest and new plantings of native vegetation that are reserved and protected in varying degrees.

So, urban spaces can be birding hotspots: not just the non-built bits of the city like parks, but in some cases the whole urban fabric. But in Canberra and in the surrounding countryside, introduced invasive species such as cats and foxes are thriving. Marsupials such as the Eastern Quoll continue to suffer depredations. However, the civic authorities and conservation-minded residents can still do something. At Mulligan's Flat in northern Canberra, a fenced reserve has been created. The fence is predator proof, electrified and 11.5

km in length. The Eastern Bettong (formerly locally extinct) has been reintroduced, as has the Bush Thick-knee, a ground-dwelling bird last seen in Canberra in the 1970s. Mulligan's Flat is one of the best places in Canberra to see Superb Parrots and endangered, migrating Swift Parrots have also been recorded there. A local committee of volunteers helps manage the reserve.

The Australian Capital Territory Government has declared 17 suburbs as 'cat containment areas', including those next to Mulligan's Flat. A cat owner letting their cat roam free is liable to a fine of up to $1,500. The accompanying image of a street sign designating the suburb of Forde, which adjoins Mulligan's Flat, as a cat containment area includes, as a backdrop, an installation representing the presence in the adjoining wetlands of Latham's Snipe. This bird is a summer non-breeding visitor that migrates from Northern Japan. The wetlands have been deliberately preserved and are used to regulate stormwater drainage from the surrounding streets.

Very few cities have started from scratch in the middle of the bush, like Canberra did, in the era when conservation and a wish to bring green spaces close to everyone was a priority in urban planning. But there are lessons for all cities from Canberra, just as there are from Sir Bani Yas and Kowloon Park. The common thread is that urban spaces and all built environments where people congregate can be made more friendly to wildlife, birds included, with a bit of effort and forethought. In the Anthropocene, the destruction and transformation of habitat that is driving so many species to the brink of extinction is mostly taking place in non-urban spaces through damaging forms of unmanaged human settlement, agriculture and natural resource exploitation. In that context, city dwellers have a bigger role to play in preserving biodiversity than they might think.

CHAPTER 6

Pelagic Birding

Pelagic birding involves trips to the open ocean – the term pelagic loosely means 'open seas'. Ocean cruises offer great opportunities for pelagic birding but (with one exception), my few pelagic trips have been day excursions in smaller vessels. In this case, the best sites are those where the continental shelf is close to shore, or where strong ocean currents come close to land. Either way, out there you find birds that spend their life riding the waves and traversing the oceans, only coming to land to breed – birds such as albatross with their huge wingspan, both a bird of myth and also something of a mystery to science – although some scientists believe they have cracked the puzzle of how they can travel hundreds of miles across the waves with only a few flaps of those giant wings.[25]

I haven't done as much pelagic birding as I would have preferred, partly by circumstance but also because I don't take too kindly to seagoing in a small boat. That aside, there is something enticing about pelagic birding that sets it apart. The habitat looks timeless and unspoilt and the birds don't all treat humans as mortal threats. Humans mainly hunt fish, not birds, when at sea. Their boats are treated as feeding opportunities, as fishermen often chuck edible waste overboard, especially from fishing boats. So, take a boat out and the birds will often come by for a look. Release a suitably stinky burley over the back of the boat (often called 'chumming') – a mixture of fish oil and rotten innards for example – and the birds will sniff it out, land on the surface and hang about for a feed off the stern. Never mind that's when I get most queasy, at that point in time there's plenty to concentrate on to take the mind off the heaving stomach.

Actually, my first venture into birding on the high seas is perhaps not best described as 'pelagic', as we never got beyond the sight of land into open waters. Birders in Hong Kong regularly organize boat trips into the Southern Waters of Hong Kong, where there are deep ocean channels between strings of islands. The farthest islands are over the border outside Hong Kong, but these trips were organized with the purpose of exploring the variety of seabirds that entered 'Hong Kong Waters', that is, birds that could be counted on the Hong Kong list. Most of the excitement came not from braving the ocean swells, as the islands provided shelter, but from dodging between the giant ocean-going vessels crowding some

25 'Engineers identify key to Albatross' marathon flight', *MIT News*, 10 October 2017.

of the busiest sea lanes in the world. And we came across some good ocean birds, including Pomarine, Parasitic and Long-tailed Jaeger; Streaked and Short-tailed Shearwater; Ancient Murrelet; a number of species of tern; and once only, in my six trips, a Great Frigatebird. We also encountered migrating passerines flying by, sometimes landing on the boat, exhausted.

Pelagics that take you out of sight of land, to the edge of the shelf and into the ocean swell, are the real thing. One of my first really memorable birding experiences was a pelagic trip from Wollongong Harbour in New South Wales in 2006, run by the Southern Ocean Seabirds Study Association (SOSSA). We set off at about 7.30 in the morning and got back around 4 pm. I didn't really know what to expect beforehand, including how small the boat seemed at the jetty. The continental shelf is about 20 nautical miles offshore and the trip out was relatively uneventful.

The bird count posted by SOSSA on that day was pretty good, and some of the birds were spectacular. When we let go the burley, several albatrosses flew in, gliding majestically over the waves on their huge wings, and alighted on the ocean just astern of the boat. These were my first close-up sightings of albatross – we encountered Wandering, Black-browed, Shy, Buller's, Grey-headed and Yellow-nosed Albatross. I 'dipped' on the Buller's and Grey-headed (it was all new to me in those days), but never mind.

When I say I 'dipped', this does not mean I didn't 'see' them – after all, you can't miss seeing a passing albatross, can you? But in the process, I did not identify them, I didn't see the field marks that said: 'This is a Buller's', or 'This is a Grey-headed', so I didn't tick them, even after I was told they had crossed my line of sight. 'Seeing' a bird, for a birder, has its own meaning. But any albatross is an albatross, whatever identifying label you add on in front of it, and it was for me enough that day just to be in their presence, close-up.

The real highlight was when the SOSSA members started ringing some of the birds. The Kelp Gull dragged over the stern was impressive enough, and I marvelled at how the ringers were able to dodge its lunging beak. When I saw them netting an albatross and grabbing it over the stern, I was not sure I could believe my eyes. Once on board, it tried to spread it wings before they could fully restrain it, at which point it submitted and eyed us with its fierce look, although with some degree of equanimity. When they put it back on the ocean, it looked more affronted than anything else.

Shy Albatross

A few years later I took a trip to Peru and joined a 'pre-trip' pelagic that was separate from the main itinerary. This was memorable for several reasons. The organizer was a well-known local expatriate birder and tour organizer, affectionately known by many birders as 'Captain Chaos'. The nickname (and the affection) is probably due to his uncanny knack of leaving so many of his customers with a war story to tell. On this occasion, we arrived at the jetty at the appointed hour – but no boat. Sometime later, a phone call informed us the boat and our Captain were on the way, or rather, a replacement boat was, after the first one was deemed unsuited to the purpose. When it arrived, there were already passengers aboard, a group of young hipsters lounging on the deck – evidently not birders. Fortunately, the label on the can said it was a pelagic birding trip (I've no idea what they were told).

We settled in and soon drove them into a corner as we crowded into the best vantage points with our birders' gear and small talk. One of our number regaled us with the tale of another Lima Pelagic, when the boat returned with one fewer birder on deck than had first boarded, a fact discovered only after a headcount upon landing. A tall story, no doubt – I didn't believe a word of it. Having convinced myself of this, the rest of the trip was brilliant. The hipsters no doubt took away their own war stories about sharing a boat with a bunch of crazy birders.

Head out to sea from Lima and you soon encounter the Humboldt Current flowing south to north up the coast of South America, a veritable conveyer belt of seafood, including sardines, anchovies and jack mackerel, attracting a multitude of birds. The sheer quantity of albatross, shearwaters, gulls, petrels and storm petrels out there is astonishing. Not to forget the aptly named Inca Terns, Peruvian Boobies, Peruvian Pelicans and Humboldt Penguins. Our leader was the first to spot a rare Markham's Storm Petrel, endemic to the Humboldt Current. They spend most of the year on the ocean, never venturing to land until it is time to breed, when they burrow into the ground in deposits of saltpetre, which provide ideal crevices and easy digging, while having a hard surface to deter predators. Some of these sites are in Chile's Atacama Desert, one of the world's driest places. So far as being near water is concerned, it seems to be all or nothing for Markham's Storm Petrel.

A highlight on the way back to harbour was the diminutive Peruvian Seaside Cinclodes, pottering about on the stony seashore as we neared safety. The fact that I saw this LBJ on the same pelagic excursion when we had seen two species of albatross, and many other deep-sea wanderers, struck me at the time as so incongruous that it seemed hilarious – perhaps that had something to do with my safe return. Undoubtedly, this was the bird of the day, especially with that name.

Actually, the sea was pretty calm that day and there was nothing whatsoever to fear. On my next pelagic, in New Zealand out into the Hauraki Gulf in 2011, things were very different. I had just come from visiting Tiritiri Matangi Island on the outer edge of Auckland harbour, one of those offshore wildlife havens that New Zealanders have created by freeing them of invasive species, planting native flora and introducing native birds and other fauna once the coast is clear of rats, cats and other mortal threats. The Little Spotted Kiwi was the big attraction. I had booked an overnight stay, specifically to get a good look at the Kiwi, which is nocturnal. You bring your own sleeping bag and food, and bunk down in a cottage, returning to Auckland next morning. But on this occasion, the wind got up overnight and the swell was too heavy for the boat to land at the jetty. We were stuck for another night. Great! More nocturnal encounters with the Kiwi!

Fortunately, the swell had subsided enough to allow a landing the next day, getting me back to Auckland well in time for my planned pelagic. But the day following, when I set out and headed for another boat jetty, the sea was still rough, and the wind was blowing mightily. The boat looked the size of a dinghy, with a giant outboard motor hanging off the back. Out at sea, it tossed like a bucket as it ploughed into the waves. There was a small cabin which offered a modicum of shelter, but on the tiny deck area at the front of the boat where you could get a view, the spray and the wind were fearsome. My terror was enough to subdue my churning stomach, and the birding out there was good. In particular, we succeeded in finding our target, the New Zealand Storm Petrel. My view was of the bird dancing over the waves at some distance, but that was good enough. It is a distinctive storm petrel, with a white rump band and a lot of white on the underparts, including big white underwing patches.

The New Zealand Storm Petrel is a classic 'Lazarus species', having been presumed extinct. It was only known from 19th century museum specimens until 2003, when it was rediscovered off the coast of New Zealand by a group of birders, who fortunately got photographic evidence.[26] Capture and genetic analysis later confirmed its identity. For several years after, its breeding site remained a mystery until it was found in 2013 (thanks to radio tagging). The petrels nest in burrows in tall forests on Little Barrier Island in the outer Hauraki Gulf. This island was only freed of rats in 2011, so it is indeed astonishing that the species survived the 20th century. The bird is still listed as 'Critically Endangered' by IUCN, although its future is now much brighter and New Zealand authorities have upgraded it to 'Vulnerable'. The size of the population cannot be more than a few thousand. It's not just me that has miraculously survived in the Hauraki Gulf.

A trip to the Galapagos Islands in 2014 had us board a very different kind of vessel, a well-appointed cruise boat that took about 30 of us around the islands for ten days. I'm not sure if this really counts as a pelagic, but I suppose so, although the degree of comfort was unlike any others I have taken. Most of the seagoing as we island-hopped was done by night,

Magnificent Frigatebird, cruising aboard the SS Isabella

26 Species entry for New Zealand Storm Petrel, *New Zealand Birds Online*.

but there were quite a few daytime hours of quiet cruising on calm seas, when a number of seabirds were seen, some of them close-up as they cruised with the boat.

The Galapagos Shearwater was a nice tick, but the frigatebirds most caught the eye. Elliot's Storm Petrels were a regular companion of the boat, dancing to pick up morsels in the ship's wake. Like Markham's, which we had seen on the Lima Pelagic, Elliot's is a Humboldt Current species, ranging from Galapagos south to the tip of South America and breeding on the coast of Chile. For good measure, I'm going to throw in my favourite seagoing bird of the trip, the Galapagos Penguin, although this was seen just offshore from a rubber dinghy, not in the deep ocean. Never mind, I was still on the water.

Another of my pelagic trips was in 2017, out into the Tasman Sea from a jetty on Pirate's Bay near Eaglehawk Neck, not far from Hobart, Tasmania. The swell was sloppy enough to produce that queasy feeling, but not rough enough to get in the way of good viewing. Here, I remedied my earlier 'dip' on Buller's Albatross, but on this occasion, what caught my eye most were the Wilson's and White-faced Storm Petrels, ever-present in good numbers. Storm petrels are diminutive, dainty birds fluttering, hovering and dancing on the surface. They look frail and vulnerable, but such is far from the truth. Apart from a brief breeding season spent on rocky islands and shores, they spend their life roaming the oceans.

The White-faced Storm Petrel is a southern oceans bird, many breeding in southern parts of Australia, but not venturing too far south into colder waters. Wilson's Storm Petrels are trans-equatorial migrants, breeding in the southern hemisphere, many of them in Antarctica, and spending the non-breeding season further north. In the Atlantic, they are found as far north as Labrador. It's hard to write that in just a matter-of-fact way – that's a lot of fluttering and dancing, there and back. Both Wilson's and White-faced Storm Petrels are abundant, with total populations in their millions. But for sheer numbers, they get nowhere near the Fairy Prion (which we also saw in the Tasman Sea) with 20 million; or the Antarctic Prion (which I have yet to see), with 50 million or so.

Storm petrels are clearly tough little birds. They are great survivors, as the New Zealand species demonstrates. They are split into two families, Northern and Southern. There are 18 species in the first family, of which six are labelled by IUCN as 'Near Threatened', while there are nine in the Southern family, of which one is 'Critically Endangered' and another is

White-faced Storm Petrel, Tasman Sea

Indian Yellow-nosed Albatross, Tasman Sea

'Endangered'. The rest seem to be doing OK, relatively speaking. But species of albatross are in a more precarious state. Nine out of the 22 are 'Endangered' or 'Critically Endangered'. Numbers have crashed for a number of reasons. Long-line fishing is a major cause, while disturbance at breeding grounds, including introduced diseases, is another. Ingestion of plastic waste floating in the world's oceans is also a growing threat.

My pelagic trips took me to the edges of what still has the appearance of being a wonder-world of nature's abundance and species diversity: the world's oceans. There are still huge populations of some seabirds, and good news stories, such as the New Zealand Storm Petrel, can still be found out there. But the appearance of clean, pristine habitats that a day on the Tasman Sea or riding the Humboldt Current can produce is not to be taken at face value. For now, we can take a pelagic and leave behind much of the evidence of human depredation of wild places that birding on land so often shoves in our faces. Out at sea, most of the evidence is hidden or indirect. It still smells and feels clean and pristine, timeless and undisturbed.

But life in and on the oceans is in deep trouble. Overfishing, dispersal of human waste (especially plastics) and climate change are beginning to take a heavy toll. Such is the magnitude of the effects of climate change that vast, seemingly permanent oceanic features are in transition, such as the extent of the northern and southern polar ice caps and the predictability of continental-scale currents, such as the Humboldt. As southern oceans warm, plankton and other micro-scale life forms are adversely affected, threatening a key food source for a multitude of other creatures, including birds. Acidification due to absorption of atmospheric carbon is another threat to ocean life forms. Overfishing interacts with these changes to produce sometimes catastrophic collapses of fish populations. Most seabird species are feeling the effects.

Of the sea-birding trips described in this chapter, only in Hong Kong's busy shipping channels at the mouth the Pearl River Delta, one of the world's most polluted waterways, did some of the obvious evidence of human-induced harm present itself, in the form of flotsam and jetsam as far as the eye can see, oil slicks around the boat and a brown fog of pollution on the horizon. Elsewhere, it looked and felt unspoilt, timeless. But things are not quite what they seem on the surface. The lack of such obvious evidence of our impact offers only an illusion that all is more or less well with the natural world.

CHAPTER 7

Birds and Beasts in the Pantanal

The Pantanal is a vast floodplain in the south-west of Brazil, extending into eastern parts of Paraguay and Bolivia. The wetlands stretch some 600 km from north to south and are subject to seasonal flooding, with huge inland lakes appearing during the wettest parts of the year. In the dry season, the wetlands shrink, creating huge expanses of pastureland for the cattle industry. The region is a magnet for adventurous ecotourists, although less famous than the Amazon as a destination. On my visit, we accessed the northern part, setting out from Cuiabá and heading south to join the Transpantanal

Yacare Caiman

Highway just south of Poconé. We traversed its length, with two stops on the way south, the first in Piuval, the second on the banks of the Pixaim River, to our final destination, the end of the road, Porto Jofre.

On most birding trips, I tend to be single-minded. I view other creatures that cross our path as worth a good look, but basically as a bit of a distraction, or a nice photo opportunity (particularly the primates). I have enough trouble getting on to the birds and sorting out what is what in that part of the animal kingdom, without having to do the same with the rest of it. But the Pantanal is different. Such is the abundance of wildlife of all kinds that this, in itself, is a matter of wonder. Mammals, birds, snakes, crocodiles, insects and other creatures are everywhere in huge number, many of them in plain view. The mammal list was one of the longest I've had on any trip. And (at least, from appearances) so vast are the wetlands and so forbidding the task of taming them for human exploitation that our impact on this abundance of wildlife seems slight.

Many of the mammals and reptiles, like the birds, are individually spectacular, forcing themselves on the attention, however much one may be trying to focus on a fleeting sight of a parrot in the distance, or a woodcreeper working its way up a nearby tree. Most obviously, crocodiles – more accurately Yacare Caiman – are everywhere and they are amazing. It is estimated there are around 10 million in the Pantanal, supposedly the largest single population of *Crocodilia* on Earth. Crocodiles have been around as long as birds, and in fact are their closest living relatives (another good reason, aside from their teeth, to show them respect).

Crocodiles do look prehistoric, just like some of the birds living in their vicinity, each being species that belong to families that have a very ancient lineage. We found Red-legged Seriema at Piuval, one of two surviving species of the *Cariamidia*e family, of the order *Cariamiformes*, a large group of flightless birds that were around over 60 million years ago, when they included the family *Phorusrhacidae*, or 'terror birds'. Some of them were gigantic,

Red-legged Seriema

Jabiru

the apex predators of their time. They went extinct aeons ago. Look at the Seriema, magnify it 10 or 20 times, and it does begin to look a bit scary.

One of the most striking things is that this multitude of creatures, big and small, mammals, birds and reptiles, carry on seemingly oblivious of each other in close proximity, even though it must be the case that some of them regularly eat each other. Perhaps the very plenitude of meals all around makes each possible victim, chancing the odds, complacent.

More likely, they know exactly how far away is safe; or perhaps they can tell immediately that the Caimans in their pond are already sated – and why wouldn't they be?

Fish of course are abundant, but mostly they are seen by birders only when they are being eaten by various species of waterbird or raptor. Herons, kingfishers and raptors such as Snail Kites and Black-collared Hawks are, like everything else, astonishingly abundant. Good sport is to be had on the river at Pixaim by tossing dead fish off the boat to attract a swooping hawk from its riverside perch. Leftovers from this spectacle go to a near-tame Jabiru on the riverbank.

The highway – the Transpanteneira – that connects the lodges that cater for birders is a dirt road, 147 km from start to finish, elevated above the floodplain and dotted with 122 more or less intact wooden bridges. Their planks rattle under the wheels to jolt one awake at regular intervals. Side-tracks snake off into the surrounding grasslands, where there are cattle ranches. Traffic is regular, including herds of dust-raising stock driven by whip-cracking gaúchos. Wild creatures are often encountered crossing the dirt, in one case an enormous Yellow Anaconda. As the road penetrates further south, green wetlands stretch as far as the eye can see – at this time of year (July) relatively dry, but still very soggy in places, channels of water visible everywhere.

The final destination down the highway is Porto Jofre, where the road ends on the banks of the Cuiabá River. Here, the main attraction is another famous beast of the Pantanal, the Jaguar. Our birding trip timetabled three days to make sure we saw it. Having found it on the first afternoon, close-up and prolonged as we followed it along the bank of the river in our boat, we were consigned to cruising around on the river and its tributaries for the next two days, looking lazily at (by now) familiar avian fare. My lister's antennae recalled a few dips earlier in the trip, which combined destinations other than the Pantanal, but I was not so churlish as to raise the matter. It was absolutely right that we should be given the fullest possible chance to catch up with a Jaguar. We succeeded and it was awesome (and I use the word in its full and proper meaning).

Jaguar, Porto Jofre

So how did we get so close? The Jaguar paid not the slightest attention to our presence, nor to the six or so other boats clustered alongside us in the narrow reach, full of people with their long lenses. Was this the arrogance of a top predator in its element, or the tameness of a habituated local favourite? Both, perhaps. Separated by a few metres of water, watching such a lethal creature seemingly oblivious of our existence, was unsettling. It sauntered about its normal business, at one point diving into the shallows after something it fancied as a meal. It was as if it was playing to the crowd in the circus tent.

The sense that this was all a spectacle, with entertainment the primary goal, had already been suggested before we arrived at the scene. The boat ride that afternoon had begun with a slow meander along the channels. The boatman's radio crackled at frequent intervals and he spoke into it on several occasions. Following one such interchange, his demeanour was transformed. The slow meander became a harum-scarum, grip-your-seat roller-coaster ride, engine roaring, swooping around bends, white water streaming and crashing. The boatman had got wind of a Jaguar sighting from one of his compatriots. Whether out loud or just in our minds, we whooped and screamed. Rounding a bend, we saw a cluster of boats; we slowed, and sure enough there was the beast, nonchalantly strolling in the grass, displaying to the crowd. The boat ride was clearly part of the show and, indeed, it was the perfect overture.

Fittingly, among the spectators was a film crew, there to record the spectacle, accompanied by one of those bare-chested, bandana-clad, fearless faux-adventurers so popular on daytime Cable TV wildlife shows. We watched with amusement as their drone snagged a tree and ended up in the water. The next day, we came across them again, this time acting out one of those "Wow, look at that!" moments that are the meat and drink of the genre. Our brave, bare-chested hero was on a sandbar, down-and-dirty, nose-to-nose with the crocs as the camera whirled from the nearby boat. I was heartily amused at his folly, but our guide was justifiably horrified that this kind of intrusion, and those kinds of risks, were being perpetrated. A serious incident could spoil it for the rest of us. True, Yacare Caiman won't eat you (they were juveniles in any case), but they do have big teeth, and I agree that

Juveniles, nose-to-nose

this kind of thing is not to be encouraged. Nature should not be treated first and foremost as our plaything.

On the river, we also came across a family of Giant Otters, another wildlife attraction of the Pantanal. Like the Jaguar, they just got on with their business, which seemed principally to consist of having a good time. They swam playfully in a cluster as we followed them downriver, before they mounted the bank and gathered in a heap to settle down for the evening, cavorting and squabbling as they looked for the best spots. We were spellbound. Like the Jaguar, they were fearless, allowing us to watch from close by. They were graceful, handsome, with fearful teeth and, above all, they were relaxed, sociable and … well, just happy.

In places like the Pantanal, where spectacular wildlife presents itself for our viewing, we are always on a knife-edge between imposing or intruding and doing no harm. Our encounter with the Otters felt like mere spectatorship, so little attention did they pay to us

A bundle of Giant Otters

Hyacinth Macaws

and so unaffected by our presence was their behaviour. Probably, the same was true of the Jaguar. Even bandana-man and his TV crew were doing little more to intrude than we were, and they were probably putting more into the local economy. True, when it came to their antics with the Caiman, they were courting trouble, being foolish and showing no respect, pandering to unthinking, domineering views of nature. But then I recall our participation in the spectacle of finding the Jaguar and the episode of throwing fish into the river to attract a swooping hawk, so that those of us with cameras could try to get 'that perfect shot'. Sometimes, birders can also treat nature as if it were a plaything. A voice in my head keeps insisting that perhaps the difference between bandana-man and birder was more one of degree than of kind. But then, in the Anthropocene, in all our encounters with nature we deal routinely with degrees of harm.

Of course, I visited the Pantanal above all to see the birds. The chance to find Hyacinth Macaws was one of the many attractions, and we were not disappointed. I also saw a host of other new species. But the trip sticks in my mind not so much for the birds I added to my list, as for my memory of the Pantanal's magic as a wild place – its abundance of wildlife of all kinds and its sweeping, flat landscape of wetlands and woodlands.

I came away with a sense (rightly or wrongly) that here was a rare place where we could get a glimpse of what much of the world must have once been like, home to an astonishing abundance of wildlife, relatively secure in habitats that humans had yet completely to transform with their agriculture, their industry and their commerce. We could not, of course, see how human inhabitants interacted with this environment before the European invasion. Many of their communities are long gone, decimated by contact with Europeans. Nor could we experience whatever megafauna – perhaps giant armadillos, sabre-toothed cats and giant ground sloths – may have roamed these floodplains before encroaching humans helped drive them to extinction thousands of years ago. But the Pantanal nevertheless feels like a vast natural refuge, almost a pre-human throwback.

But this landscape is, of course, being shaped by humans to the detriment of wildlife. Appearances can be deceiving. We were seeing the best bits. Ranchers settled the Pantanal over two centuries ago. It is 95% privately owned and home to some 8 million cattle (still fewer cows than the crocs, then!). Where there are grazing cattle in such numbers, ecosystems are transformed. And climate change is also beginning to have an impact. A prolonged dry season in 2019/2020 resulted in unprecedented levels of damaging fires across huge parts of the dried-out landscape.[27] Again, in 2020/2021 even more widespread fires spread across 30% of the Pantanal biome. Slash-and-burn agriculture and the deliberate burning of pastureland by ranchers set the fires going. They spread via the smouldering of dried-out peat just under the surface, in conditions caused by the dry season drought conditions that have come with climate change. The region saw its lowest level of rainfall for half a century in 2020.[28]

So, while vast and seemingly still able to support a rich and diverse ecosystem, the Pantanal is nevertheless fragile and vulnerable, not only to climate change but also to the impact of schemes for modern development and exploitation. Even the raised road that we travelled on is a threat to the natural flow of water across the land (hence, the number of bridges). Schemes have been around for many years to moderate the river flows and control the seasonal floods with ever more ditches and dykes so as to increase the area suitable for grazing and other agricultural uses. There is also a plan to build a new Transpantanal Highway connecting all the way north to south. So far, remoteness and inaccessibility due to the seasonal flooding remains a barrier to more intensive development. But for how long?

The great majority of birders and other ecotourists try their best not to leave a heavy footprint when they visit such a place. Of course, the dusty highway is there for them as much as it is for the stock drivers. But we tell ourselves our presence brings economic benefit and offers incentives for conservation. We provide an economic alternative to more intensive forms of development that might degrade the ecosystem and diminish the Pantanal's attraction to ecotourists. This will probably not, in the long run, be enough.

27 Ana Ionova, 'Brazil's Pantanal region experiences unprecedented fires during rainy season', *Mongabay*, 10 March 2020; Catrina Horn *et al.*, 'The world's largest tropical wetland has become an inferno', *New York Times*, 13 October 2020.

28 Ana Ionova, 'Devastating fires engulf Brazilian Pantanal wetland – again', *Mongabay*, 23 December 2020.

CHAPTER 8

Birding at a Crime Scene

In December 2016, we visited Cambodia on a ten-day birding trip organized by the Sam Veasna Centre in Siem Reap. Two of us, with a driver and a guide, motored across Cambodia, visited a variety of habitats and targeted some rare and very special birds. We also visited temples and other remains of a past civilization. From the 9th to the 15th centuries, Cambodians held sway over most of what later came to be known as Indochina. Angkor (modern Siem Reap) was for much of the period the centre of the Khmer empire. Angkor Wat and countless other temples across the country are a lasting and visible legacy of this civilization. Decline set in, Thai armies invaded, and Angkor was abandoned in 1531. To the west, Vietnam grew in power. In the second half of the 19th century, Cambodia was colonized by France.

In more recent times, periods of civil war commencing in the 1950s post-colonial era culminated in the 1975 Khmer Rouge insurgency. The resulting Pol Pot regime (1975–1979) and its genocide of their own people have left a dark legacy. Things stabilized in the years after Vietnam invaded and overthrew the Pol Pot regime in 1979. A new regime was established, and international mediation helped bring normality. International Tribunals convicted senior members of the Pol Pot Regime of war crimes. Today, Cambodia's Government – the same as was installed after the Vietnamese invasion – maintains close economic and political ties with Vietnam and, increasingly, with China. Internal political opposition is suppressed.

Cambodians have a unique and complex sense of place and history. Tales of victimhood and loss set against distant, past glories act as starting points for contemporary hopes of renewal. The yearning of many Cambodians for a recovery of their lost past also colours their relations with the natural world. A telling symbol of this is Cambodia's 'national mammal', the Kouprey, a species of majestic wild cattle endemic to Cambodia that figures prominently in Angkorian temple carvings. It was last seen alive in the 1980s. Sam Veasna, a naturalist and pioneer conservationist after whom the centre organizing our trip was named, died from malaria while vainly searching for Kouprey in Northern Cambodia in 1999. Some still hope Kouprey may turn up in some remote pocket of forest. Most believe it is extinct. It is at one and the same time a symbol of pride and shame, of hope and despondency.

Kouprey on a roundabout, Senmonorom, Mondulkiri Province, Cambodia

The Sam Veasna Centre, set up in his memory by friends, is a conservation-focused NGO based in Siem Reap. It offers ecotourism, including birding tours to a variety of Cambodian destinations, and it partners with international NGOs to support local conservation initiatives. In 2016, the centre won the Gold Medal at the World Responsible Tourism Awards for 'Best Contribution to Wildlife Conservation'. Centre workers help set up and maintain local lodges and train villagers to cater for visitors; they fund schemes to incentivize local farmers to combat wildlife hunting and to protect habitats; and they run educational campaigns in schools and train local wildlife guides.

Earnings from visiting birders contribute to a variety of local conservation and educational projects at a number of critical sites in Cambodia. Iconic bird species they help to protect and conserve at these sites include Bengal Florican (Critically Endangered), White-winged Duck (Endangered), Giant Ibis (Critically Endangered), White-shouldered Ibis (Critically Endangered) White-rumped, Red-headed and Slender-billed Vultures (all Critically Endangered) and Greater Adjutant (Endangered).

Many of these species inhabit the little that is now left of a once widespread lowland habitat across Southeast Asia, the Central Indochina Dry Forests.[29] Cambodia contains some of the largest remnants, on the Northern Plains and in the east of the country.[30] This type of forest contains mainly deciduous dipterocarp trees, forming an open forest woodland with canopy coverage ranging from 40–80%. The understory is grassland. The French colonialists aptly named it '*forêt claire*'. The landscape is wet for 4–5 months of the year and dry the rest of the time. In the wet season, the grasslands flood and in the dry season the tall grasses wither and turn brown. The water drains away, but water holes remain to sustain the wildlife. Evidence from the Angkor period indicates that the Khmer cultivated large parts of this landscape; they built numerous temples and irrigation works, the remains of which are to be found throughout the region.

29 World Wildlife Fund for Nature (WWF), *The Global 200: Tropical and Subtropical Dry Broadleaf Forests, Southeastern Asia*, https://www.worldwildlife.org/ecoregions/im0202

30 Christian Wohlfhart *et al.*, (2014), 'Mapping threatened deciduous dry dipterocarp forest in southeast Asia for conservation management', *Tropical Conservation Science*, vol. 7, no. 4, pp.597–613.

Temple ruins in the forest, Prey Veng

Associated with this landscape was a megafauna that was, by some accounts, as rich and spectacular as any that the savanna landscape of Africa has to offer. Aside from the Kouprey, other large mammals that roamed in huge herds in the wooded grasslands included Asian Elephant, Gaur and Water Buffalo. The Eld Deer was numerous. Predators included Asian Tiger, Leopard and herds of wild dogs. The large mammals helped create and maintain the hollows and wallows that sustained wildlife in the dry season, including bird populations such as the ibis and adjutants.

Another mammal also present in these grasslands was the Banteng. Banteng are domesticated across the region and are widely known as Bali Cattle. Wild Banteng in their original habitats, across the whole of Southeast Asia, now number less than 10,000. In a strange twist of fate, the largest single concentration of wild Banteng today is a feral colony of about 10,000 animals in the Garig Gunak Barlu National Park in Arnhem Land, northern Australia. About 20 were brought to Arnhem Land by the British in 1849 as part of an ill-fated attempt to settle the Coburg Peninsula at Port Essington. The Banteng were released when the colony failed, and they thrived. They are valued by the aboriginal owners for their meat and as a now-familiar part of the landscape. They also provide a source of income for locally managed sport hunting expeditions.

We spent several days visiting Cambodia's Northern Plains with our guide from the Sam Veasna Centre. We saw none of the mammals, because they are virtually all gone. We were fortunate to find a single Bengal Florican, a few remaining ibis and vultures and a roosting pair of White-winged Ducks (the Greater Adjutants were elsewhere, in search of wetter landscapes). The dry forest, while beautiful and majestic as a landscape, is now a tragically impoverished ecosystem. Most of this destruction happened within living memory.

These remote, sparsely populated regions were sites of fierce post-colonial civil war and conflict for nearly 50 years. Successive militias and insurgents roamed the open forests, living off the land and disrupting the traditional ways of life of villagers, who had for many generations farmed, hunted and taken resin from the trees. The marauding armies participated in and encouraged commercial hunting and opened up links to the international wildlife trade.[31] Guns replaced the snares traditionally employed. The widespread famine induced by the catastrophic policies and actions of the Pol Pot regime was probably the last straw for the remaining wildlife. It may be no exaggeration to say that the fauna was ultimately eaten to extinction, or close to, by the starving human population. Birds fared slightly better than mammals, although the Giant Ibis was also thought extinct until it was rediscovered in the 1980s.

In the Northern Plains, the village of Tmatboey, where a Sam Veasna lodge is run by the villagers, is the site for Giant and White-shouldered Ibis. On our first evening, we watched about 20 of the latter as they flew in to roost in bare trees, for which the farmer was being paid not to chop down. Elsewhere, at Boeng Toal a 'vulture restaurant' has been set up by the centre and local villagers to sustain the remnant populations of vultures, close to a nearby camping ground, which is set deep in the forest. Dead cows are placed in front of a hide to attract the vultures into view. Local hosts set up our camp and cooked dinner. At Prey Veng village, next to a well-preserved, huge Angkorian-era baray (an artificial stone reservoir) another lodge has been built for birders and is managed by the local villagers, who are trained as hosts by the centre. Not far from here, White-winged Duck fly in and roost in a stand of tall trees that soar above the rest of the forest canopy. In the wet season, adjutants feed in the baray.

We ventured to these remote places in a four-wheel drive vehicle down furrowed, off-road tracks winding amidst the trees through the vast grasslands, and we stayed overnight at each. Restoration and recovery of the mammalian wildlife on these Northern Plains is almost a lost cause. Asian Elephants survive only in a few pockets and are still poached for the wildlife trade. Eld Deer, Gaur and Banteng are very rarely encountered. But there is more hope for the birds. Meagre and still fragile populations of the endangered species seem to have stabilized with the help of conservationists. Local villagers are willing helpers,

Prey Veng, hosts and guests

31 Colby Loucks et al., 'Wildlife decline in Cambodia, 1953–2003: exploring the legacy of armed conflict', *Conservation Letters*, vol. 2, 2009, pp.82–92.

once persuaded and given support; visiting birders and other ecotourists bring a steady stream of income – a dollar goes a long way in rural Cambodia.

Cambodia has other wildlife treasures. The Mekong River divides the country in half as it runs north to south. We visited Kratie, on the banks of the Mekong, and birded from a boat at Kampie Pools, looking for endemic Mekong Wagtails, flitting from one tiny island to another in the midst of the slow-moving river. And we also watched as Irrawaddy Dolphins, in one of their last Mekong refuges, surfaced and dived around our boat. The dolphins are fast heading for extinction as upriver dam building, far beyond the borders of Cambodia, alters the flow of the river.

Now, savouring these memories with mixed feelings, we were driving east down Highway 76 to our next stop, in Mondulkiri Province. Our destination was the Keo Seima Wildlife Sanctuary, an area of nearly 3,000 km^2 containing lowland, mixed evergreen and deciduous forest, extending north and west from the border with Vietnam. The biggest town in the province, Senmonorom, holds a population of 7,500 people. The region is home to the Bunong people, who live in scattered villages, variously growing rice for subsistence and a few cash crops, while also exploiting forest resources such as resin. Recently, settlement by people from elsewhere in Cambodia, looking for land and a livelihood, has resulted in growing demands on the region's resources. Mondulkiri is booming thanks to growing cross-border trade with Vietnam.

We saw some of this trade with our own eyes. As we headed east, it was late afternoon. The road was busy with mainly local traffic, but also larger trucks, some of them carrying logs and mostly heading with us towards the Vietnamese border, where timber merchants ask no questions. The ultimate destination for much of the timber is China. Almost imperceptibly, the road began filling up with more and more vehicles, also heading east. Most were motorbikes, which trickled in one by one from side trails and joined the line of traffic.

All these busy bikers carried cut logs, some of them ludicrously large, strapped crosswise to the rear of the bike. Like high-wire walkers with their balancing poles, the riders somehow managed to stay upright as they motored down the road with their loads.[32] Looking around us, nearly every vehicle carried its share of freshly cut wood. Back seats of ageing Japanese sedans were stacked up to the roof; beaten up vans, back doors open, were stuffed with logs, sticking out far behind, scraping the bitumen and threatening to lift the front wheels off the road. The forest was being shipped out, piece by piece, by an army of paid carters and petty thieves, their loot heading for the timber yards and furniture factories across the border.

This is not the place to apportion blame, nor to go to remedies. In the Keo Seima forests, close to highways and even further afield, the impact on wildlife of this accelerating deforestation is potentially devastating. More than 60 flora and fauna species found in Keo Seima are listed as Threatened or worse on the IUCN Red List. Aside from some of the mammals already mentioned, the sanctuary contains the world's largest known populations of Black-shanked Douc Langur and a large population of Southern Yellow-cheeked Crested Gibbon. The Asian Tiger (the Indo-Chinese subspecies) is now considered extinct in the region.

We birded close to the highway in logged, heavily degraded habitats where we found sparse populations of barbets, pigeons, bulbuls, leafbirds, woodpeckers and other species that cope with forest edge and disturbed habitats. We had to venture much further, down

32 Dramatic photographs and a running commentary on logging can be found in a thread under 'newsworthy/ logging' on the blog *Cambodia Expats Online*.

Grey-eyed Bulbul, Seima Wildlife Sanctuary

muddy roads to more remote villages and tiny protected forest patches to find (after some difficulty) forest birds such as the Germain's Peacock Pheasant and Bar-bellied Pitta. The particular patch we visited was patrolled as a reserve, funded through foreign and local NGOs (including the Sam Veasna Centre) to provide a refuge for birds, gibbons and other forest creatures. A 'Gibbon Camp' has been set up to accommodate visiting ecotourists.

Cambodia has an elaborate, detailed set of legal provisions regulating the logging of old growth forests. It also has all the right-sounding named ministries and agencies with their armies of rangers to enforce these laws. This official paraphernalia was as much evident out on the road as was the thriving thievery. We drove behind trucks that carried certified logs, each of them meticulously individually numbered as verification of their legality. Maybe it wasn't all just for show – or maybe it was.

Out birding the next day, as we pulled up by the road to enter the forest, a smart four-wheel drive with two green-uniformed rangers in the front seats pulled up and looked us over. Later, as we walked down the trail, another forest cop drove by on his motorbike. Around the corner was a pile of cut logs, and all along the trail was evidence of the business, carried out in plain sight under their watch. Our hotel car park nearby was full of polished sedans and four-wheel drives and the hotel itself was buzzing with smartly dressed men attending a work retreat. They were police chiefs.

Policing can be a thankless and dangerous job and the Keo Seima forest rangers face a near-impossible task. Forest exploitation in Cambodia, as in many comparable countries, is conducted by a combination of corporate and local, big-time and small-time, ill-meaning and well-meaning, actors and interests. The dilemmas and pressures that the rangers and police face come from all quarters. A good deal of serious economic and political muscle

Keo Seima Protected Forest

is behind the captains of the logging industry, in a country not noted for the rule of law. Military units hold some of the logging concessions and participate in illegal logging.[33] And villagers complain when over-zealous patrols, seeking to curb logging, apprehend them for legitimately cutting trees for their own use, such as building homes.[34]

Some villagers have participated in organized, illegal logging when faced with outside disruption to their traditional ways of life and the opportunity for new sources of income. Also, some are employed as rangers to protect the forest and the wildlife. Their work is supported by partnerships between government ministries, international aid agencies and NGOs (and, more peripherally, by income earned in local communities from ecotourists such as birders). In Keo Seima, some of the funds come from the REDD scheme (REDD stands for 'reducing emissions from deforestation and degradation'), under which governments, with the participation of local communities and others, agree to take action to reduce deforestation. International funding comes via the UN and is drawn from contributions from rich nation governments that participate in international carbon reduction schemes.

One of the international NGOs that is active in Cambodia and in the Keo Seima Wildlife Sanctuary is the Wildlife Conservation Society (WCS), founded in 1895 and based in New York at the Bronx Zoo. It regularly partners with the Sam Veasna Centre and it also helps coordinate the REDD scheme for Keo Seima. On their website, on 1 January 2018, an article recorded the achievements of 'community patrol teams' in the Wildlife Sanctuary in tracking down illegal logging camps, confiscating equipment and vehicles, and apprehending loggers.

33 'PM calls on soldiers to end role in illegal logging', *The Phnom Penh Post*, 25 January 2019.

34 Catherine Walker, *Testing the Validity of a Theory of Change Approach in Keo Seima Wildlife Sanctuary, Cambodia*, MSc Dissertation, Imperial College, London, September 2016, p.24.

These patrol teams are drawn from villagers and led by local law enforcement officials, with support from WCS. A month later, on 2 February 2018, the same website carried 'A Statement from WCS on the Killing of Three Conservation Heroes in Keo Seima Wildlife Sanctuary'. One of them was a Ministry of Environment ranger, the second a military police officer and the third a team member of a project run by WCS in Cambodia:

> 'Soknai, 37, Wathana, 34, and Khna, 24, were killed when returning from the O'huoc border area after locating an illegal logging camp and confiscating chainsaws and motorbikes used for transporting wood.'

Teurn Soknai was brought up in a local village. He had been a moving force in setting up the Gibbon Camp and in protecting the reserve that we had visited to see the Peacock Pheasant and the Pitta. Later, arrests were made. A defence by one of the accused alleged that the cause of the shooting was a dispute over unpaid bribes.

We knew nothing of events such as this during our visit and we felt no sense of danger. The police chiefs in the hotel and the smart rangers were a reassuring presence and our driver and guide were savvy, responsible and careful guardians of their foreign visitors. For some years now, Cambodia has proved to be a safe destination for tourists of all kinds. Ecotourism is a growing part of the industry and much is done by the authorities to make it safe and comfortable. Criminal activities such as those leading to violence against the enforcement patrols have not targeted foreigners.

The so-called 'Wildlife Sanctuary' where all this took place used to be officially called 'Seima Protected Forest'. Whether by design or not, the obvious irony of this descriptor has been substituted with one that appears more hopeful. Of course, it is still a misnomer. There can be no such sanctuary, in a literal sense, if wildlife shares the forest with modern humans, especially new settlers or profit-seeking public officials and businesspeople. While a mutually beneficial level of co-existence and harmony between the local indigenous population and the remaining wildlife seems once to have prevailed, and is still feasible under ideal circumstances, in recent times this has become a distant, vain hope. Outside forces and compelling incentives have, to this point, been too powerful.

Against this bleak prognosis and in the shadow of criminal violence, it is humbling that there are Cambodians who continue to work to protect their forests and wildlife. They view their work to attract visiting birders as an important part of their efforts, but they do much, much more, including risking their lives. Our guide from the Sam Veasna Centre embodied the commitment shared among a growing band of Cambodian nature lovers and conservationists. Their hope and energy serve as a counterpoint to the despondency that I was feeling that day, as we watched the forest disappearing down the road, piece by piece, into the distance.

CHAPTER 9

The Spiny Thickets of Madagascar

Madagascar is famous for its unique wildlife. Whole families of plants, mammals and birds are endemic to the island, including an extraordinary array of weird desert plants and the country's iconic lemurs. Birders visiting Madagascar for a few weeks have a very good chance of snaring nearly all of its 100-plus endemic bird species. This is thanks in large part to a network of national parks and private reserves that preserve small areas of natural habitat, where the birds shelter in place, in a country where the landscape more generally has been radically transformed by humans. There is plenty of opportunity for the visitor to experience the wildlife that evolved over millennia on the island, even if this is only available in a remnant form.

Birding in Madagascar involves long bus trips between isolated pockets of different natural habitats, through a wider landscape that shows ample evidence of centuries of destructive forms of 'slash-and-burn' agriculture. Some of Madagascar's remaining forests are also under threat. They contain many species of precious woods, such as rosewood and ebony, that are in high demand. Lax regulation results in a thriving illegal export business in such commodities.[35] High levels of poverty and population growth put intense pressures on the land, and governments have generally lacked either the capacity or the will to halt the destruction.

Travelling through such a country brings into stark relief the contrast between the privileged experience of the touring birder and the daily lives of the general population. Good birds do not by any means all inhabit lush forests, pleasant woodlands or green hillsides. Birders also visit arid deserts and other habitats where human settlement, if found at all, is marginal and where infrastructure is rudimentary. Here, not only are the means of making a human living from the environs precarious, they also often challenge a birder's reason for being there, by helping destroy the natural habitats they have come to visit.

35 Malakiva Vitawahare, 'Conservationists call for lasting ban on trade in Malagasy precious timber', *Mongabay*, 3 May 2019.

Such a combination of human hardship and the desperate measures taken to eke out a living, with the potential to destroy a unique wildlife habitat, is acutely evident in the southwest corner of Madagascar, an area of dry country and near desert often referred to as the 'spiny desert'. In this landscape of sub-arid thorn scrub, one half of the genera and 95% of the species of flora are endemic to the region. There are eight regionally endemic birds. For a birder seeking to see as many of the country's birds as possible, it is a must-visit destination.

The region lies in a rain shadow, with a rainfall of 350 mm per year and a 9-month dry season. Drought can last several growing seasons, and with it comes the risk of famine. We visited in the midst of an El Niño drought in 2016, with food shortages and famine beckoning.[36] We drove south and then west from Fianarantsoa, along a modern road through an increasingly dry and dusty landscape, heading to the west coast for the main town in the region, Toliara, a trading and administrative centre. Our destination was a private reserve further along the coast near Ifaty, where there was comfortable accommodation and the prospect of good birding.

Along the way as we headed south, we passed through a string of sizeable settlements and areas of relative agricultural plenty, but the further south and west we went, the drier and more sparsely settled the land became. We stopped at intervals for roadside birding, on occasion venturing down a dusty track in search of a local endemic. The effects of the drought were plain to see. Once or twice the human impact was driven home by a direct encounter: a small child standing transfixed in the dust among the huts of his village as we walked by, and two smiling boys with water containers strapped to their bikes, miles from home, who stopped to watch us as we birded from the main road. Each brief encounter spoke volumes of the precariousness and hardships of daily life.

In this landscape, at least so far as one could see from the road, larger trees have more or less disappeared, leaving a seemingly endless expanse of desiccated, scrubby deciduous thickets, interspersed with evergreens and succulents, all waiting for the next rains,

36 'Madagascar: 1.5 m face hunger because of drought, UN says', *BBC News*, 27 October 2016.

which may be many, many months away. This vegetation is well-adapted to long, dry spells. Endemic birds such as the Red-shouldered Vanga can be found, albeit few and far between (this is not a landscape of abundance). A scattered rural population ekes out a living with a few livestock, chickens and small plots growing root vegetables and such. Many of the residents are formerly landless settlers from elsewhere in the country occupying vacant, marginal lands. But as the lack of rain makes even small-scale agricultural pursuits unfeasible, they turn to other means of survival. Most prominently, they exploit the landscape for wood, which they use to produce charcoal.

Charcoal production is widespread across a large part of Madagascar (not to mention the rest of Africa) and charcoal has rapidly become the cooking fuel of choice, not only for those living close to the source, but also for many city dwellers. Villagers set off into the scrub and collect pieces of wood by hacking away at the bushes and cutting down the remaining trees. They cart the wood out on bicycles, or they dig a pit on the spot, fill it with wood and set it alight. They cover the hole with dirt and let the wood smoulder, starved of oxygen, to produce the black charcoal.

Meanwhile, in the towns and villages stretching east and north along the highway, a network of middle-men and women, traders, bullock cart drivers, truck owners and distributors do their business. Driving through these villages, we couldn't help but notice that typically in front of each house on the roadside stood a neatly bundled plastic bag of charcoal, or several, waiting to be picked up. Somewhere down the road, trucks are waiting at a collection point for the bicycles and bullock carts to deliver the sacks, and to aggregate them into shipments to the market towns and the cities. And so, the destruction goes on.

Charcoal stoves at a local eatery

Loading sacks of charcoal

Deforestation due to expanding settlement and agriculture has already depleted Madagascar of most of its forests. The dominant landscape in the central parts of the island these days is rolling grassland, dotted with a species of palm that is resistant to fire, and not much else. The recent uncontrolled growth of charcoal production is another nail in the coffin of the remaining forest and natural scrubland. Living in the dry, marginal agricultural lands of the south-west, when faced with the vagaries of crop failure, the short-term certainty of a regular cash income from charcoal is a godsend. But in the longer term, the accessible supplies of wood disappear. Villages that were once surrounded by scrub and by trees are now surrounded by near desert. So, the tracks snake further into the landscape and new settlements spring up down the road, where the scrub is still exploitable. The boys with the water cans lived in one such settlement, where there was no water supply.[37]

As a result, the spiny forest and thickets are being degraded and are diminishing. Compared with more resource-rich and inhabitable parts of Madagascar, where human settlement and agriculture have already destroyed much of the forest, it is generally supposed that the unwelcoming spiny desert is more secure. Satellite imagery still shows big expanses with limited human disturbance. But the trend is only one way, and the pace of destruction is relentless. Only about 3% of the remaining habitat in the spiny desert area is in reserves, and most of it is not well-managed.

But as we drove past the dusty villages along the road, we knew that our destination held the promise of presenting us with most of our target birds. We were heading for a 60-hectare private reserve not far up the coast from Toliara. The villagers were not destroying this remnant of the forest, which was fenced and protected. Nearby Hotel Solidaire is associated with a voluntary organization, L'ONG Bel Avenir, which focuses on social development and assists in conservation efforts. The profits from our stay went to the NGO. Most of the target regional specialties (Thamnornis, Chabert Vanga, Crested Coua, Archbold's Newtonia and others) were accessible

Chabert Vanga

37 Norimitsu Onishi, 'Africa's charcoal economy is cooking. the trees are paying', *New York Times*, 26 June 2016.

Ifaty Nature Reserve

in this park; with the help of the local guides, we had no trouble ticking them off in a couple of hours.

The birding was easy, the birds were spectacular and confiding, and the accommodation was comfortable. We stayed two nights and we were soon off back up the same road (there is only one good road in and out) to our next forest patch further north. We passed that dusty village once again and observed the degraded landscape through new eyes. Ifaty has slightly higher annual rainfall than further inland, but the main difference is the degree of protection afforded by the reserve owners. Like so many birding experiences in such places, we had benefited from the efforts of local landowners supported by a foreign NGO with an eye to eco-tourism, who had safeguarded for us our precious ticks. We could indulge in a pang of guilt and a feeling of compassion for the conditions in which many of the local people elsewhere extracted their meagre livings. The ecological damage they were wreaking on a unique habitat was regrettable, but our own precious protected patch had been quite enough for our purpose.

We had achieved what we came for, thanks to our brief privileged exposure to a fenced-off fragment of the spiny forest. We had paid our bills, which supported the reserve and the conservation of that tiny remnant of habitat. The fate of the remainder and the threats it faced were beyond our control. The drought and the imminent starvation were part of an alien world that we were leaving behind and (aside from savouring our birding successes) could try to put to the back of our minds. Tragically, such regrets and clumsy excuses are part and parcel of the experience of a foreign birding tourist in the world's poorest countries, where the poor are desperate, citizens and governments alike are constantly on the lookout for new economic opportunities, and habitat destruction goes largely unchecked.

CHAPTER 10

David Attenborough Moments

Birding can be frustrating. Even though we are paying full attention, moving slowly and quietly with bins at the ready, very often our sight of a bird is a fleeting, unsatisfactory one. Potluck plays a big part when we are walking a trail or standing and scanning the hedgerows and telegraph wires. Of course, fieldcraft is also important, the knowledge that leads us to the most favourable habitat or picks out a birdsong that we can identify. But even when we come across a bird (or it comes across us), what happens next is up for grabs. Some are curious, others are preoccupied and indifferent, but very often they flee, in which case we get a brief glimpse and an unsatisfactory flight view – sometimes not good enough for confident identification.

Sometimes, we can play or whistle a call and get a target bird to fly in to check us out. Repeated playback often stimulates the bird to stick around for a bit, albeit often in an agitated state that prevents lining it up for a good look (although, by this point, for the birder the target's responsiveness to the call has partly done the ID job for us, so a good look is less urgently needed, if all you want is a tick). A fieldscope can enable us to see birds that are unaware of us at a distance, perhaps quietly preening, as if close-up. But this, too, can be frustrating if the bird is far away, in particular those blurry images of an indeterminate wader a mile across the mudflats.

Although that side of birding is all part and parcel of the challenge, what we all crave now and again is a David Attenborough moment. I think most birders have seen episodes of David Attenborough wildlife films and would instantly recognize what this is: one of those precious instances in a birding life that is forever imprinted, a moment when a special bird is seen, perhaps unaware or oblivious of the viewer's presence, in clear view, prolonged and (preferably) close-up. We catch our breath; we feel a sense of awe and excitement. Afterwards, we stand around and talk about it, sharing the wonder and the thrill. This is not the same as the birder's thrill of a lifer; it is a moment of joy at a close encounter with wildlife.

David Attenborough moments can occur for even the most hardened list-obsessed birders. Arjan Dwarshuis, a Dutch birder who holds the world record for the number of birds seen or heard in a calendar year, recorded an interview that was published on Birdlife International's website in which he described the trials and tribulations of his adventure.[38] He was asked: what was the best bird of the year? He nominated the White-necked Rockfowl, a rare, spectacular ground-dwelling bird he saw in Ghana. On describing the encounter, and the reasons he chose this bird, he concluded by calling it 'my David Attenborough moment'. While I read much of the rest of the interview with suspended judgement, expecting to have my prejudices about Big Year listers confirmed (more interested in the list than the bird (see Chapter 13); rushing from one tick to another without pausing to enjoy the birding experience; and worse) this depiction of the moment just about saved his bacon. Rather, as the TV viewer on their lounge gasps at the magic and wonder of an Attenborough close-up of an unfolding sequence of events in the normally unseen daily life of a wild creature, this Big Year lister was captivated by the moment, in his case on the spot rather than in the lounge room. Clearly, Arjan is more than just a manic lister (and I apologize for thinking otherwise).

While what we think of as David Attenborough moments are not the norm, they are more and more part of the standard menu on organized birding trips. But most such moments don't happen by chance, just by walking a trail or sitting quietly. Our close-up views of rare or spectacular birds are more often than not staged for us. One common form of such staging is to set up hides or blinds (with seating provided), placed so as to give a view of a particular species – perhaps at a lek or a display ground.

Another ruse is handfeeding of elusive forest-dwelling species, attracted on a regular basis by a local expert out of the undergrowth to a feeding station, at a particular time of the day, often after a familiar human call to announce the moment. Achieving this requires much skill and patience by the practitioner. In the Americas, requiring little or no skill and therefore more ubiquitous, is the line of hummingbird feeders in the garden, with a viewing station close by so we can take in the sight of the visiting hummingbirds that are attracted to the sugar water. On these occasions, nature does not just give itself up, we must interject ourselves into it with varying degrees of intrusion and with the use of artifice. Many of our most memorable moments observing nature do not come naturally.

I have watched David Attenborough's BBC TV series *The Life of Birds* again and again, as I have several others in his wildlife series. The ten episodes were first shown in 1998 and, without being consciously aware of the connection, I am sure in retrospect that the pleasure I gained from watching them played a part in my decision to take up birding seriously a few years later. Wildlife movies and TV series such as these are the source of many peoples' closest experiences of nature in the modern world. On the one hand, this has sparked heightened appreciation of the natural world and perhaps a greater concern for conservation. On the other hand, while they spur some of us out into the field, for most others wildlife and wilderness adventure movies have become a cosy substitute for experiencing nature directly. They lull us into a false sense of security that nature is still alive and well 'out there' in some remote, wild place, waiting to be visited by David and his intrepid camera crews, who will bring us the images. And birders, living and reliving their David Attenborough moments, are not immune to such complacency.

I occasionally rewatch memorable Attenborough scenes on YouTube, such as the time he was bowled over by a testosterone-fuelled Capercaillie in Scotland, or a scene in a gloomy Borneo bat cave where he climbs a mountain of guano that is alive with scuttling

38 Birdlife International, *News*, 24 April 2018.

cockroaches. I have relived some of those moments on my own travels. When I was in the same bat cave, I didn't get down and close with the cockroaches as he had done (although I got quite close enough for my comfort), but my memory of his vivid descriptions and the choking sounds as the ammonia from the bat guano entered his lungs were brought to life by my own experiences. Later, just outside the cave we watched Bat Hawks performing impossible acrobatics as they singled out prey in the streaming clouds of tens of thousands of bats as they emerged at dusk. The same thing had happened in the film.

This feature of such moments – the mediated and the immediate blending into one – is a direct product of the artifices of modern media, coupled with the extent of our exposure to it. In the past 20 years, this effect has been accentuated by all the new ways of recording wildlife and accessing media in the digital age. Looking back at that moment outside the bat cave, I am not quite sure whether I am remembering the real thing or the film, the real world or a virtual one. This blending of the immediate and the mediated, both at the time and in our memories, reflects a deeper feature of many Attenborough moments: the growing importance in our birding lives of artifice and technology aimed at enhancing the experience.

This last point struck home powerfully when I was birding in New Guinea. Black and white films from the 1950s depict Attenborough's expeditions into the New Guinea Highlands to capture moving images for the first time of some birds-of-paradise mating displays. He and his film crews have revisited on several occasions. During my trip, at one site the guide pointed to the spot where David sat to provide commentary on a Twelve-wired Bird-of-Paradise performing his tricks on a stump – indeed, the very same performance that I later watched from a nearby vantage point. The guide also pointed out a spot where David had filmed a display, but which had later been deserted as a display ground because of the repeated visits by film crews and the disturbance this caused.

Wilson's Bird-of-Paradise

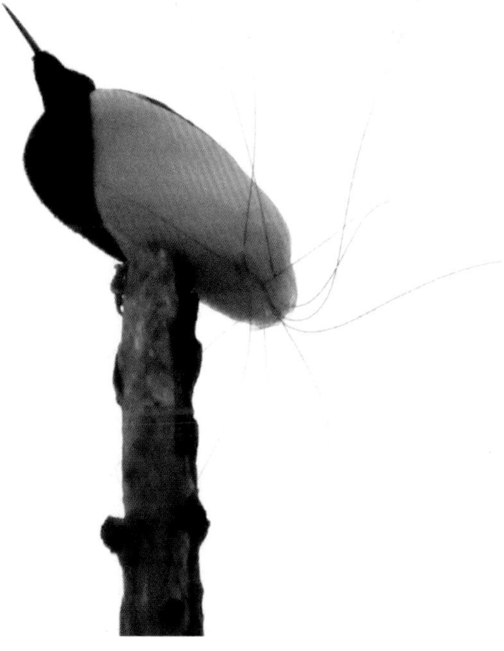

Twelve-wired Bird-of-Paradise

Some of the most memorable of Attenborough's bird-of-paradise episodes are those of the Wilson's Bird-of-Paradise, a startlingly plumaged bird with a ridiculously bright blue, bald pate at one end and two curly wire tail feathers at the other (in between, the colours and patterns have to be seen to be believed). This species is found on two islands – Batanta and Waigeo – off the north-western tip of New Guinea. David filmed his on Batanta, while we visited Waigeo. But the scene was identical. The depiction in the TV episode includes shots of David peeping through a window cut into the canvas screen and the palm leaves that front the hide. The film cuts to the bird, seen through the same window, clearing away the leaves that David had just strewn on its display ground to provoke it into action.

On our visit to Waigeo, our guide also threw a few leaves around for encouragement and then retreated. I looked through exactly the same kind of window cut into the hide; the bird also followed the ritual of obsessively tidying the ground by tossing leaves around; and subsequently his efforts were rewarded by a visit from a female, before whom he did his dance. 'Wow! this is just like watching David Attenborough,' was my first thought. I took my own amateur videos and later posted them on YouTube.

Indeed, not only was I experiencing the bird close-up, but I was also in my mind's eye watching a re-run of the Attenborough episode. The similarities between my experience of watching the bird display in the wild and watching the TV show were striking. My standpoint was the same – watching through a hole in the hide like the one through which the TV camera lens was poked and through which a cutaway also showed David peering out. The show was staged for us in both the live event and the film: the birds entered from off-stage into our line of sight and performed for us. Indeed, the setting was already a stage, chosen by the bird as a place to do its dance, not just on the occasion of our visit but also on other days. With this knowledge, the hide had been set up at a good vantage point, local guides patrolled the area, and the birds were more or less habituated. Much of the time, I was watching through my own camera lens. I re-enacted the filming. My birding companions and I drew in our breath and whispered involuntary exclamations, like a living-room audience. We were both remembering and creating virtual experiences while we were simultaneously living 'the real thing'.

This scenario was repeated several times on my trip to New Guinea, when we visited other display grounds and sat spellbound while these extraordinary birds displayed in front of us. The male Magnificent Bird-of-Paradise was another spectacular performer, seen through the window in the hide placed in front of his display ground. Of course, experiencing this directly, however much it might be mediated through memories of the same or similar scenes on the TV, is a bit different to the TV viewing itself. Our private viewing in the hide was privileged, but the manner in which we saw these birds was a simulacrum of the staging that was also necessary for filming and broadcasting to a mass audience. Birders have to go to a lot more trouble than sitting down in front of their TV in order to add birds-of-paradise to their life list (as distinct from their 'seen on TV' list). Often the sites are in remote places. And of course (so we tell ourselves), we see them 'in the wild'.

But we are kidding ourselves. When we see a close-up of bird behaviour on TV, such as displaying or singing, we know that a lot of preparation has gone into filming the sequence. Sometimes, the person behind the camera has had to sit in a hide for weeks or months to get the right shots. We acknowledge the artifice and admire it. The nature film clearly takes

Magnificent Bird-of-Paradise

us several removes away from nature itself but succeeds by artfully offering us the illusion of being there. We acknowledge the illusion. Similarly, the lengths that birders have to go to in many cases to get our close-ups also create an illusion of being in the natural setting, but one we are not so ready to acknowledge. Hides have been built and birds have been habituated to human activity in the vicinity. Despite being so close, we are clearly removed, seeing something staged for our benefit, through a window in a blind (and often, through a hidden lens – our bins or our camera viewfinder). Fortunately for us, the birds seem to carry on as if everything were normal. But of course, things aren't normal. We are happily experiencing artificially constructed and mediated fragments of nature.

The creation of such illusions about 'being in the wild' and 'entering into the world of nature' to enjoy its wonders is happening for birders all the time, on a number of levels. Later in this book, I will describe many encounters with wild birds which have been effectively 'corralled' into safe spaces such as reserves, and there habituated to the presence of birders and others. Some of these birds may have been hand-reared and released, others relocated to this safe location.

These cases include Kiwis on Tiritiri Matangi Island in New Zealand; Norfolk Island Parakeets in their protected enclave; Crested Ibis being looked after in the pine trees around a village in China; and Orange-bellied Parrots in Tasmania, monitored and fed at their one remaining nesting site. I will also describe visits to feeding stations where we sat and watched tamed birds, many of them normally very cryptic and elusive, hop boldly into view in front of us. Again, the David Attenborough moments I experienced in these cases were made possible by human intervention and artifice. The encounters were all uncomfortably like visits to the zoo.

But there are some magical close-up encounters that require none of this kind of intervention and staging, when we just 'come across' such a scene. Some of the most compelling of these situations are those that occur in places where whole populations of birds have survived through isolation from human dangers and have no fear. Humans never settled there. In these rare and special cases, no artifice of any kind is necessary. There, birds seem to be tame by nature. To them, we are just another harmless creature in the background.

These places are often uninhabited, remote islands. On some islands, this eventually had catastrophic consequences when modern humans did arrive, most famously in the case of the extinction of the Dodo on the island of Mauritius. First seen by Dutch sailors in 1598, it was last seen in 1662. Hungry sailors and invasive species did for it within a human lifetime. On a few other such islands, fortune and circumstance has meant the indigenous creatures, for the most part, have survived.

The Galapagos Islands is a rare example of such a place. Here, our views of the birds are both prolonged and close-up. If not exactly in the scene as part of their lives, we are at least no more than part of their scenery. This is what makes the Galapagos such a unique experience, a magical wonderland of nature where we are seemingly invisible to the creatures around us. It is as if the Anthropocene had passed this place by. In recent years, it has arrived in no uncertain terms as ecotourism has boomed. But at least, we don't eat the wildlife.

The Galapagos Islands were, for obvious reasons, a favourite filming location for David Attenborough and his crew. So, too, are remote rocky outcrops where albatross, petrels and penguins breed and seem unfazed by the approach of visiting humans. Elsewhere, only very rarely are we fortunate enough to experience close-ups and intimate moments without artifice and without hiding. Perhaps this was Arjan's experience of the Rockfowl (or perhaps he was in a hide at a protected site where the birds are habituated). That is why a fleeting, accidental moment in a forest when we encounter a special bird close-up, even if it passes in a flash almost before we can take it in, is so special.

Just part of the scenery: Nazca Booby posing with birder, Genovesa

Nature films can capture many such moments in a manner that birders would not normally experience. Skilled camera operators sit and wait in hides, sometimes for days, at a site where they can reasonably expect the birds to appear. Often, they have to

Geomalia, Anaso Trail, Sulawesi

move to several possible sites before they strike lucky. Such must have been the case, for example, with some notable recordings of the behaviour of manakins at their leks – for example, the Lance-tailed Manakin with its amazing dance-floor act, when several males put on a collective show for the benefit of the dominant member of their troupe. But most birders cannot be so patient, unless they stop birding and just devote their time to observing. Only the most avid listers, targeting a single rare and elusive species to take their list past 9,000, are likely to devote this kind of time and effort until the quest succeeds. For the rest of us, time is precious, and we move on; there are so many other new birds to see.

Most of my close-up and intimate encounters with iconic species that were achieved without the help of artifice were brief, and part of a wider, hopeful search in a particular habitat. One such occurred in the Lore Lindu National Park in the mountains of Sulawesi, when we were walking the Anaso Trail. One of the target birds for all of us was the Geomalia (*Zoothera heinrichi*), an enigmatic, thrush-like bird endemic to the highlands of Sulawesi (it is named after the same Gerd Heinrich who figured in Chapter 3).

The Geomalia use to be placed in its own monotypic family, but has been reassigned by taxonomists to *Zoothera*. It is classed as 'Near Threatened', but this classification may be a bit rose-tinted, given the pace of deforestation and human disturbance within its restricted range. We came across it on the trail, just by quietly walking along. It hopped off in front of us, jumped onto a log only a few metres away and stood there for a few seconds looking at us, before disappearing. It was a highlight for all of us.

We often refer to birding as being 'in the field', an expression common amongst all observers of nature. The natural scientist does 'fieldwork', distinguished by its strict protocols and rigid regimen to ensure validity and reliability of observations. Nature is retrofitted as their laboratory. We birders also construct artificial observational standpoints out in the field, better to see and record the subject. Playback of calls as we walk along the trail is perhaps the least intrusive of such devices. In this chapter, I have described other more elaborate and often more intrusive ones. In so doing, we are always in some sense retrofitting the natural setting as an artificial, human-made stage so as to make that observation more congenial to our particular limitations and desires.

Just so, we create our David Attenborough moments of magic and wonder, filing them away in our birding memories. Some of us add our images to the digital cloud alongside his digital archive, accessible with a couple of clicks on everyone's electronic devices (firewalls permitting). Some of our personal memories become almost indistinguishable from memories of the clips – mine and everyone else's – because of the same staging.

But not so my Geomalia moment and others like it, which stand alone as memories of direct, unmediated, personal encounters with the natural world. And yet, it is not just me that has that Geomalia as an image in my files. I have seen others just like it on the web, from the same location, along the same trail (accessible on the Cornell Lab of Ornithology website). This is where lots of birders visiting Sulawesi go to look for Geomalia. When I visited, the setting seemed relatively untouched, other than by walkers of the trail (including local woodcutters, judging by the presence of the log on which the bird posed). But it's quite possible that one day some enterprising local with an eye to profiting from avian tourism will build a hide and start putting out worms on that cut log, just to make sure a Geomalia is on the stage the next time birders walk up the trail with their big lenses.

CHAPTER 11

World Birders, Patchwatchers and Nature

Perhaps I mix with the wrong crowd, but I have observed that, for a good number of the fellow birders I travel with, appreciating birds and nature for what they are is secondary to enjoyment of the activities entailed in searching out, finding and recording new birds. We are listers as well as bird lovers – we aim to add as many species of birds to our life lists as we can. We enjoy travel and we look forward to the camaraderie of like-minded folk on our long-distance birding trips. We like to talk about the top birds we have seen and where we have ventured to find them. Our favourite bird is the latest tick. Conversation on the bus on a birding trip is much less likely to be about the birds themselves than to consist of war stories of past travels and of birding triumphs and disappointments. We are world birders, who have turned our placid pastime into a globe-trotting pursuit of as many new birds as the passage of time and the size of our bank balances will allow to us.

Being a world birder and being a nature lover are not mutually exclusive. No doubt, many of us got into it because we just liked being out and about, looking at birds, in the local park. We still do. However, how and where we end up is in many ways far from being the place where a nature lover with a simple passion for birds might expect to arrive. To understand where this place is, it is useful to contrast the world birder with the 'patchwatcher'.[39]

These two 'ideal types' stand at either end of a continuum. Individual birders will, at different times, occupy positions at any point along it. There are many ways to slice and dice the birding world and draw fine distinctions between birders of different kinds, but no individual seems to fit neatly into any one box. There are many ways of enjoying birds, and the world of birding accommodates many different inclinations and tastes. The dichotomy I present here is just one among others that we might highlight.

Patchwatchers stay at home and bird in their neighbourhood – their 'local patch'. They choose a particular piece of local habitat where birds are to be seen – a city park or a nature

---

39 Dominic Couzens, *A Patch Made in Heaven: A Year of Birdwatching in One Place*, London: Robert Hale, 2012.

reserve, for example. The quality of the habitat is important and valued for itself as well as for the birds that it attracts. They regularly (perhaps even daily) walk well-trodden paths and look for familiar birds, their nests and their fledglings. They probably also keep a keen eye on signs of other creatures, and on the state of the woodlands and the waterways.

For most of the time, patchwatchers are happy with the familiar. They like to be on their patch most of the year so they can follow the natural rhythms of the seasonal comings and goings. They are not driven by the need to constantly add new sightings to their life list, although they are excited when a new bird turns up. They become local experts, eyes and ears trained to recognize every form of wildlife they regularly come across. If migrating birds visit their patch, they eagerly await the annual migrations. They probably keep a life list of birds they see on their patch and a 'year list' to compare one year with the next. They may be interested, in so doing, to track changes in populations of local birds over time and to record new arrivals on the local scene, particularly new breeding birds. Amateur naturalists began to do this in the 19th century, recording the state of the natural world in their locality through the passing seasons. Patchwatchers are their direct descendants. They are quite likely to dabble in ornithology and they will be among the stalwarts of the local birding club.

World birders visit other birders' patches, and many more remote places that are nobody's patch, with the sole purpose of finding birds that are new to them. World birders value the new and the foreign for themselves. Their ambition is to see as many birds as possible. The list that really matters to them is the life list of all the birds they have ever seen, and above all they want it to grow and grow. Their bookshelves will be stocked with dozens of field guides covering every country and region on Earth. To help them find new birds, world birders enlist the help not only of patchwatchers in the places they visit, but also of professional birding guides. Birding tour companies take them to the places where they can find the endemics and rarities they desire.

Birders who prize seeing everything there is to see must act more urgently. At each place they visit, they probably have only one shot – world birders rarely go to the same hotspot more than once, unless a trip schedules repeat visits from a nearby lodge, or they missed a 'must-see' bird on the first visit. World birders don't just stay put and watch passing birds, they hunt down their targets, adopting numerous stratagems and shortcuts to make sure they 'clean up'. Moments of contemplation or quiet appreciation of the natural world are few and far between in the pursuit to see as many target species as possible.

In this pursuit, they are likely to impose their human presence and priorities on their subjects in a way a patchwatcher probably doesn't. Lodge owners provide hides overlooking feeding stations, where local birds are more or less habituated to a human presence. Walking the trails, birders often play recordings of bird calls and songs to attract them into view. The best strategy is to wait to hear the call of a target bird, record it and then play it back. With any luck, it will come in to take a look and, hopefully, show itself. The bird hears its own dialect and is curious about the intruder. A second-best stratagem in suitable habitats is to 'toot' the sound of a local species of owl, either with a playback recording or by voice, as this will attract many small birds who fly in to mob the perceived danger in order to drive it off. When deploying these aides, birders don't so much look for birds, as get the birds to come to them.

In other words, world birders are much more proactive and intrusive. These birding tricks of the trade can pose potential risks for the well-being of birds, for our benefit. Some nature lovers argue that calling in birds with a recording can be harmful and disruptive, for example by raising levels of stress in breeding birds defending a territory.[40] And some forms of habituation (in particular putting out food to attract birds so we can see them close-up) can make birds more vulnerable to their predators, including non-birding humans.[41] Birders are, of course, aware of the risks. Professional guides, lodge managers and bird touring companies have reputations to guard, so they have an incentive to behave responsibly. But their biggest incentive is to deliver the birds. Sometimes, things go too far. Local guides, eager to earn their keep, sometimes hound and herd docile, ground-dwelling birds into a birding group's presence; or birdsong recordings are played repeatedly and loudly in pursuit of a better view, even after the bird has come in to take a look and most have seen it. Many birders have been to well-known birding hotspots where the birds no longer show because it is believed they have been 'taped out', that is, become wary and unresponsive to the repeated playback of their call by successive groups of birders; or perhaps they have deserted the location for another, quieter spot.

Patchwatchers cherish the natural world on their patch. World birders approach nature differently. They view the habitats and ecosystems they visit rather as if they were stage sets for the drama and excitement of adding birds to their lists, as much as being natural spaces that offer enjoyment just for the way they are. The intrusiveness they are happy to accept as part of their birding experience is a sign of this mindset. It reflects a downvaluing of nature as the primary object of enjoyment.

Another sign of this mindset is that, rather than avoiding degraded habitats and artificial settings that attract birds, world birders gladly accept some of these places as top birding sites. If they wanted only to experience the natural world 'at its best', they would not visit many of the birding spots that they do. In one sense, this is unremarkable and to be expected. Many birds readily adapt to transformed or degraded habitats because natural processes have always created such places. 'Forest edge' birds, for example, like disrupted, marginal ecosystems. Humans have created such habitats in growing abundance – for example, the trees planted for shade along roads and around buildings, or along the watercourses that irrigate or drain fields of crops, in landscapes that were once lowland forest ecosystems. These places are now what most of us experience as being 'in the wild'. Many species have adapted to thrive in these places.

So, a walk along a dusty track being used by farmers on motorbikes and tractors, with barking dogs and farm animals all around, may be a very productive birding excursion, however irksome to the senses. A good deal of time on a trip is spent 'roadside birding', where birds are visible from the road at the forest edge and in the nearby

Roadside birding in Indonesia

40 David Sibley, 'The proper use of playback in birding', *Sibley Guides*, 11 April 2011 (online resource).

41 Benjamin Geffrey, Diogo S.M. Samia, Eduardo Bessa and Daniel T. Blumstein, 'How nature-based tourism might increase prey vulnerability to predators', *Trends in Ecology & Evolution*, vol. 30, no. 12, 2015, pp.755–765.

treetops. On such excursions, every passing bus, truck and motorbike invariably sounds its horn and slows down for a friendly thumbs-up to the foreigners-behaving-strangely, before roaring off in a cloud of dust and fumes. Hardly a pleasant day in the forest but still, 'good birding'.

World birders regularly encounter, as a matter of course, the impacts of human-caused habitat transformation in ways that may be disturbing to a nature lover. It is a common experience to head out for a patch of habitat which the guide knows from a previous visit is likely to harbour a lot of good birds, only to find that both the habitat and most of the birds are gone, replaced by smouldering tree stumps, piles of logs, banana groves or a palm oil plantation. We shake our heads and drive on to the next hotspot. We mostly take all this for granted. Spirits may be lifted when we spend a day in largely undisturbed forest, but such days are increasingly the exception, not just because such habitats are disappearing, but also because, just as often, we choose to bird elsewhere. The primary objective of world birders is to add to a growing list of species on their life list. Engaging with nature as might an ecotourist pure and simple is secondary, or perhaps incidental.

It goes without saying that dedicated world birders have to enjoy travel. World birders as globetrotting tourists are as much wrapped up in the process as in the purpose. It is easy to get hooked, not only by the excitement of the new and the unknown, but also by the daily routines. The mundane rituals of a birding trip are seductive, once they have become familiar: setting up the mosquito net at night; washing the shirt in the shower; brewing from the precious stash of ground coffee in the micro dripper (when a kettle is provided); swallowing a late night snifter from the flask in the quiet of one's room; wondering at the dinner table what local delicacies and mysterious concoctions are going to emerge from the kitchen; and suffering any unfortunate consequences in silent patience. The discomforts provide only momentary irritations – and, in any case, there is always the prospect of some idyllic forest lodge waiting for us down the road, run by a bird-loving gourmet chef with a well-stocked bar.

Most tours include ordeals of 4 am starts and tedious travel along bumpy, dusty or muddy roads between one forest patch or watering hole and another by often primitive, nearly always uncomfortable (and sometimes scary) forms of transport. The horror stories of the missed or cancelled flights; the altered itineraries due to impassable rivers because of unseasonal rains; and the hotel bookings that were cancelled before arrival, are perversely all part of the fun – the battle scars world birders wear with pride.

Birding tourism is a fast-growing industry. Some intrepid 'do-it-yourself' birders construct their own overseas itineraries, relying on previous online trip reports or contacts with local birders to find their way around. But most rely on organized birding tours put on by specialist birding tour companies. These companies are growing in number and in the scale of their activities. One of the largest in 2018 boasted that it offered 'over 300 tours to over 100 destinations on 7 continents'. They compete by advertising their success in seeing more birds on a tour than their competitors – especially endemics and rarities. They stimulate interest in new destinations, seeking out and promoting exciting new itineraries. World birders like to go to out-of-the-way places that are off the well-trodden paths of most tourists. They scan the offerings and pore over the published trip reports and trip lists, carefully selecting the companies and tours that maximize their chances of seeing new species, many of them in remote locations.

Highly skilled and knowledgeable birding guides lead the tours. They are the rock stars of the industry, their reputations and track records picked over in conversations at the back of the bus during those seemingly endless journeys to the next birding site. Indeed, their skill and knowledge are astonishing, and their dedication to and enthusiasm for their profession exemplary. Many just started out as birders; some are trained ornithologists. Increasingly, in bird-rich destinations in the tropics, the birding tour companies are local, rather than international. Most used to be run by expatriate western birders, but more and more they are run by local birding guides, who often have strong links with grassroots conservation networks.

The support infrastructure for all these tour operators is impressive. Lodges and hotels at or near key birding hotspots are set up to cater for the birding visitors. Specialist agents organize the logistics and negotiate with the authorities to acquire permits (including, in some places, police escorts). National Park rangers, village heads and many other local officials are co-opted and offered inducements to smooth the way. Local guides are trained up, drawn from the surrounding villages. Money and other resources filter down into the local economy, providing jobs for drivers, porters and hotel staff.

The growing scale of this industry has its downsides. For the most part, all actors in the birding tour industry are aware of the potential harm they can do by bringing growing numbers of visitors into sensitive habitats. Often, the visit is to a fragile remnant of a fast-disappearing natural ecosystem. It is in everyone's interest to try to conserve it and to keep the birds safe for future visitors. But whether it is by improving access and setting up infrastructure, by the mere passage of human traffic and the disturbance this brings, or by some of the potentially harmful effects of the more intrusive birding activities mentioned earlier, avian tourism can be a threat to fragile wildlife habitats and to the birds themselves.

But in the bigger picture of human impacts on nature, the potential harms of these intrusions are a tiny detail in the overall scheme of things. The more disturbing issue to me is the state of mind that this kind of birding both reflects and promotes. It mimics and participates in the wider economic and social forces that lead to continuing environmental degradation and habitat destruction. World birders are privileged, acquisitive niche consumers who are hooked on the pleasures of their conspicuous consumption of birding activities.

In an important sense, birding is inextricably part of the industrial and post-industrial rat-race, in which we are driven to strive for more stuff and more status symbols for their own sake. In our case, it is the status of the impressively long list and the inclusion on it of much sought-after rarities, preferably in places that are remote and almost inaccessible. Perhaps we are only different in degree from all those in the Anthropocene who are driven in other ways to partake of increasingly unsustainable forms of production and consumption that extract value from (that is, exploit) the world's fast-depleting natural resources. Our view of nature is just as instrumental as theirs.

But wait a minute, before my self-flagellation goes too far, there is much more to the story. This is not a binary, all-or-nothing matter. Most ecotourism, including avian tourism, is one of the few economic forces currently countering some of the worst effects of biodiversity loss, including threats of extinction. This is best seen in small things on the ground, rather than in the larger economic forces that seal the fate of whole biospheres and ecosystems through, for example, massive deforestation and agricultural expansion on an industrial scale. In this context, the interests of birders and the global birding industry can provide one reason for local landowners, government agencies and tourism operators to offer up some resistance and to act to defend and look after some remaining fragments of habitat and the increasingly rare species that require them for survival.

In poorer countries in particular, where every dollar counts, the economic calculus needs some 'plus signs' on the side of conservation in order for governments and many local communities to pay attention. The preceding chapters have all pointed out how my trips to all corners of the globe have been facilitated by local conservation efforts, often undertaken with a view to attract birders. Every international birding trip I have taken has provided examples of the way birders and the birding industry support and sustain local enterprises and government agencies that strive to protect and enhance local habitats in the face of surrounding destruction:

- Village communities in New Guinea curtailing their hunting practices and placing their local knowledge and skills at the disposal of tour operators, setting up facilities to view birds (such as hides adjacent to established display grounds) and helping birders to access them by offering accommodation, maintaining trails and organizing camping trips;
- A dive resort owner in Indonesia supporting the preservation of surrounding forest (through purchasing it), enabling them to tap a new market for birders as paying customers;
- Conservation-minded national foundations, NGOs and landowners in Brazil, Colombia and Ecuador embarking on international fundraising drives to purchase hectares of forest and establish lodges, while providing birding services to help fund their ongoing activities. For example, in Colombia, the Pro Aves Foundation through private purchases preserves 60,000 hectares of prime habitat across the country and runs over two dozen lodges on these reserves, catering specifically for birders;
- National Park rangers and managers, in places where government budgets are hopelessly stretched, who depend on formal and informal fees paid by foreign birders and other visitors to sustain their work; and
- Local environmental enthusiasts and activists who enlist support from national and international NGOs, establish local lodges and train local community members to help protect birds and provide guides for birding tours.

International birding tourism would be impossible without such local activism, enterprise and support. Some of these local efforts are supported and encouraged by an international network of NGOs that provide funding and expertise, as well as egging governments on to do the right thing. Birders are often members of or donors to these organizations. The result of all this is a small glimmer of hope in the battle to conserve natural habitats and to fend off extinctions.

There is, however, an elephant in the room: our contribution as carbon-emitting globetrotters to the climate change crisis. I address this in the final chapter of this book.

That aside, it is one thing to suggest that some world birders seem to be less mindful of nature than most patchwatchers, another to suggest that they may, as a result of their birding quests, do more harm. In defence of the world birder against the virtue claims of the patchwatcher, on balance the impacts of birding tourism are not unambiguously negative. If we wonder whether our determined efforts to see rare, endangered birds in remnant Sumatran rainforests are in one way or another disturbing their habitat or perhaps even harming the birds themselves, we should remember that the birds' continued presence quite likely means that the local hunters and trappers have been warned off (or have become birding guides) and the loggers kept at bay by those protecting the habitat for our benefit. Worse intrusions will happen if we stay away. We could all decide to become innocent contemplative patchwatchers, stay home and forget about our world list but, given what is going on around us, that would not necessarily mean a net gain for wildlife.

CHAPTER 12

Modern Birding as a Point of View

A Northern Hawk Owl turned up in Metro Vancouver, a rare visitor from the frozen wintry north, and we set out to see it. Its location had been shared discreetly on birders' networks. Snow was on the ground, and the site was a 20-minute walk from the end of the road where we parked. A scan across the fields with the bins revealed a tell-tale sign of the location of its daytime perch: a cluster of tripods and birders, close to a copse of bare trees. We crunched through the snow to the spot, set up the fieldscope and feasted on the view of the bird on its tree stump, the image filling the field of vision as we screwed down the zoom.

Owls in all their close-up detail are among the most charismatic of birds and this one was no exception. Nonchalantly preening, it occasionally turned its head and graced us with a scornful glare of its yellow eyes. The camera replaced the scope on the tripod, and images were duly captured. Passing dog walkers asked what the fuss was about. The owl was visible with the naked eye, but we offered them a look through the scope. The reaction was what always happens in this situation: 'Wow!', 'Just look at that', 'Isn't it gorgeous!'. I always wonder, when I give non-birders this kind of glimpse of what thrills me every time, why they don't instantly become lifetime birders themselves. Maybe the dog walkers loved their dogs even more. Everyone to their own.

Meanwhile, the 20 or so birders who had come to record the event that day stood around chatting, their long lenses ready, waiting for a better pose. There was an air of satisfied togetherness, a common understanding that this was the kind of moment that helped get us up in the morning. For me, this bird was a lifer; for other birders present, it would at least have been a first for their Metro Vancouver list. The bird flew off, maybe irritated by all the attention, and perched on a nearby telegraph pole, eyeing the fields for possible prey. Most of us hung around, waiting for it to come back, or choose an even closer perch.

Northern Hawk Owl, metro Vancouver

This is the kind of thing birders do – give up a morning or a day in their life, drive out to the outskirts of town, tramp through the snow lugging a tonne of gear, look at a rare bird through an eyeglass, and then stand around sharing the moment by talking about it, or about other such episodes they want to compare this one to. So how would we explain what we were doing to the proverbial visiting Martian? How do we account for it to ourselves? More generally, what are the origins of this oddly compelling pastime?

Birdwatching as we know it today is largely a 20th century invention. There is a simple and rather obvious reason for this: the advent in the late 19th and early 20th centuries of wearable, high-quality field glasses or binoculars, the result of a series of technological advances. You can't be a birder without binoculars (although, these days a few birders just carry around a high-quality digital camera with a long lens to spot the birds). Today, good quality binoculars are affordable, and the best are of astonishingly high quality. Nearly every keen birder invests in a good pair of bins and treasures them. Lose them on a trip, and (if no one has a spare pair) a birder may as well get on the first plane home. I pack a backup pair each time I go away.

But there is a lot more to the story of the origins of birding as a pastime than this one technological advance. The term 'birdwatching' is first found in the written record in the 1890s. It took some decades before it came to be widely accepted and used in its modern sense to describe a recreational pastime. In the interim, it was used mostly to refer to a method for the scientific study of birds with the new technology, as distinct from inspecting stuffed dead birds and their skins. In the UK at least, the term was also used to describe the voluntary and paid 'birdwatchers' who, under the auspices of the recently formed RSPB, hid in bushes and looked out for infringements of the new bird protection laws. The RSPB had a Bird Watchers Committee to coordinate these efforts.

Before birdwatching as a recreation, however, there were other activities undertaken by people who were just as enthusiastic about and even as obsessed with birds as is the modern birder. Often, this was part of a wider interest in nature. Throughout the 19th century, observing nature in one form or another had been a common pastime among the leisured classes. For some of the more enthusiastic, this may have taken them outdoors to gather wildflowers for pressing and sketching, or to collect seashells. Connecting with nature in this and other ways became fashionable among the growing urban middle class. Bird pictures and ornaments featuring stuffed birds were popular in well-off households. Bird feathers were an important part of many wearable fashion items. The wealthy subscribed to lavishly produced books of lithographs illustrating newly discovered natural delights, including birds, from across the globe.

Birds were also favourite literary subjects, especially for the romantic poets, who clearly paid close attention to them in the outdoors. To take one example, John Clare's poem *The Yellowhammer's Nest* begins with a cowboy flushing the bird from its nest by the stream and ends with a lament on the fate of nestlings eaten by a snake. In between, one passage describes the nest and its eggs in careful detail:

... – 'tis rudely planned
Of bleached stubbles and the withered fare
That last year's harvest left upon the land,
Lined thinly with the horse's sable hair.
Five eggs, pen-scribbled o'er with ink their shells
Resembling writing scrawls which fancy reads...

There is much more in the rest of this poem that reflects not only a poet's but also a naturalist's eye on the world. Clare clearly spent some time and effort observing, listening to and enjoying the Yellowhammer and its way of life. He was a close observer of birds and their behaviour, as well as a poet.

Alfred, Lord Tennyson's arresting short poem *The Eagle: A Fragment*, penned in 1851, suggests that he also closely observed his subject in the wild:

He clasps the crag with crooked hands;
Close to the sun in lonely lands,
Ring'd with the azure world, he stands.
The wrinkled sea beneath him crawls;
He watches from his mountain walls,
And like a thunderbolt he falls.

Tennyson's eagle is in another world, a world of wonder and myth, observed from a distance rather than described in close-up, intimate detail. The poet is content to sketch just a few evocative images, such as that vivid description of the eagle's claws. The rest is landscape, mood and menace, befitting a bird of prey, a symbol of power.

The poets watched, listened and took away vivid images that fed their imagination. Nature inspired wonder and reflection. But it is not Clare's or Tennyson's poetic vision, inspired by their absorption in nature, but the naturalist in Clare, the observer and accurate recorder of nature's minute details, that I more readily recognize as a precursor of the modern birdwatcher.

Amateur naturalists in the 19th century were closer to hard-nosed fact-gatherers and scientists than to dreamy poets. The increasingly dominant mood of the age was practical, detailed, empirical. Keeping a record was essential. If primarily interested in birds, the more serious among them increasingly identified as ornithologists, specialists in the scientific study of birds. However, ornithological study in the 19th century was in large part conducted on dead birds, not outdoors but in museums and libraries which held collections of bird skins and eggs. That study entailed minute description of plumage, careful measurements of the whole and of the anatomical parts and direct comparison so as to establish similarities and differences among species. Feathers and skins, along with eggs, could be preserved in library or museum drawers. Wealthy individual collectors, scientific institutions and ornithologists accumulated huge collections of bird skins from all corners of the globe. Taxidermy brought these exotic discoveries to the public's attention via dramatically mounted and displayed collections in museums or at exhibitions.

Ornithologists as well as taxidermists relied for their specimens on field collectors. Many of these collectors were in occupations that entailed travel and left plenty of time on their hands, such as officers in the military.[42] They went looking for birds. They needed to have highly developed field skills to be successful (although a popular technique appropriate in some settings was to blast off a shotgun into the crown of a tree and hope something fell out).

Other field collectors, like Alfred Russell Wallace, were also explorers and natural scientists. Wallace funded his expeditions by collecting insects and shooting birds, selling the bird skins to wealthy aristocratic collectors through his London agent. Charles Darwin employed a shooter, Syms Covington, who accompanied him on his expeditions.[43] Pioneering ornithologists John James Audubon in the USA and John Gould in the UK shot birds (or got others to do the shooting for them), practiced taxidermy and produced impressive, illustrated books depicting stuffed birds' crafted poses – works of art but also records for science. Both were businesspeople, turning their passion into a living.

Those shooters and collectors are recognizable characters from my observation of some modern birders, particularly the ones who strive first and foremost to add to their list. The same can also be said of another group of 19th century nature enthusiasts who engaged in the pastime of 'birdsnesting', namely seeking out birds' nests and collecting and preserving eggs. This was an accessible, inexpensive outdoor activity in the 19th and early 20th centuries both for recreation and for the sake of science.

42 Scott Weidensaul, *Of a Feather. A Brief History of American Birding*, Orlando, FL: Harcourt, 2007, pp.110–120.

43 For an imaginative reconstruction of Covington's life, full of historical detail, see Roger MacDonald, *Mr Darwin's Shooter*, Penguin Books.

'Birdsnesting' has an entry in the *Encyclopedia Britannica* (1911). It was sometimes expressed as 'birds' nesting', more commonly as 'bird-nesting' and most often simply as 'egg-collecting'. Colloquially, egg-collecting was also known as 'egging' and the collectors as 'eggers' (the same linguistic route to a catchy shorthand has produced the term 'birders'). Egg-collecting combined three things that gave it wide appeal: satisfying the scientific curiosity, outdoor adventure, and indoor collecting and trading. It was popular among young people, for whom the attraction was possibly having a good reason to scramble into thickets and to climb trees. Early photographs of egg-collectors at work show the same daredevilry among the adults as well. The fieldcraft and cataloguing were informed by the emergence of a separate branch of natural history – 'oology'.[44]

A steady stream of books was widely available about nests and eggs and on the fieldcraft and techniques of collecting. That excerpt from Clare's poem about the Yellowhammer could almost have been an entry in one of those books. Some of the publications were strictly scientific or ornithological, others were directed at those with a more general interest.[45] Catalogues and periodicals catered for collectors who bought and sold eggs and kept them in specially built wooden cabinets.

Egg-collecting was a paying occupation for some, as was trapping or shooting birds. Eggs had commercial value – albatross eggs (for example) for albumin; rare eggs for selling to collectors; and eggs of all sorts for the table. The commercial value of dead birds included being specimens for ornithologists and taxidermists; feathers for the fashion industry or for stuffing eiderdowns and pillows; and food – birds of all kind trapped or shot in the wild (as in 'Four and Twenty Blackbirds') were a much more common item on the table in the 19th century than they are today.

But commercial shooting of birds – or 'market hunting' as it came to be called at the time – turned out to be not so much a precursor of birdwatching as a salutary example in contrast to which modern birdwatchers came to form their identity. Birdwatching came into being at exactly the same time as a cultural and political backlash emerged against the excesses of shooting and collecting. Towards the end of the 19th century, a growing consciousness of the value of nature as something to be treasured created a climate of growing hostility to shooters. It reached the public consciousness that they could drive even familiar birds to extinction – the Great Auk and the Passenger Pigeon, for example.[46]

Particular opprobrium fell on killing of birds such as egrets in huge numbers to provide feathers for women's hats. Successful campaigns against using feathers in this way, led by well-to-do women, were a major influence on changing popular perceptions of nature on both sides of the Atlantic. In the UK, the RSPB had its origins in groups at the forefront of this campaign. In the USA, the Audubon Society's first beginnings were in 1886, and they too campaigned against the use of feathers for millinery decoration.

Through such efforts, the idea of nature conservation began to take hold in peoples' minds. It emerged just as human society was beginning to develop and put to use technologies capable of the mass destruction and slaughter of wild places and creatures, respectively. Legislation of the early 20th century to protect birds was aimed primarily at reining in the excesses of shooters but also covered egg-collecting. With exceptions, such

44 Carroll L. Henderson, *Oology and Ralph's Talking Eggs*, Austin, TX: University of Texas Press, 2007.

45 Ernest Ingersoll, *Nests and Eggs of North American Birds*, (1880–1881); and Richard Kearton, *Birds' Nests, Eggs and Egg Collecting* (1890).

46 Errol Fuller, *The Passenger Pigeon*, Princeton, NJ: Princeton University Press, 2015, pp.14–19.

as for scientific pursuits, birdsnesting was outlawed by the 1920s. 'Egging' as a hobby continued to be popular in the UK and Australia into the mid-20th century but tightening of laws and heavy fines have mostly brought it to an end.[47]

In the minds of most nature lovers as the 20th century was ushered in, there was a big difference between market hunting and shooting for sport. The Audubon Society and the RSPB both developed close relations with sporting hunters, such as duck shooters. Some of the same people who set up the Audubon Society were also active in these circles, not so much to discourage hunting as to help conserve bird populations for future generations of recreational shooters. Their growing concern for limiting the slaughter, especially of migratory birds, was behind the creation around the turn of the century of nature reserves and parks, the establishment of regulated hunting spaces and seasons and the licensing of game shooting.

This American model of nature conservation is very closely related to the cultural significance of shooting and hunting as a way of experiencing nature. Hunting with firearms and venturing into the wild were, and continue to be, inextricably bound together for many Americans across all social classes. This is unlike the situation in the British Isles, with no frontier and fewer wild places. Sporting hunters were mostly from the upper class, shooting on exclusive, well-tended private estates, while working people who did much the same thing were poachers and were sent to prison (or, until mid-19th century, to Australia), unless they were legally shooting crows or eagles as agricultural pests, or working for the landed gentry as gamekeepers.

The anti-shooting movement around the onset of the 20th century sought more to regulate and license than to abolish. And some of the excesses of shooting and collecting for the sake of ornithology did not escape the opprobrium of the reformers. By now, ornithology was an established, institutionalized profession in scientific establishments and universities. Ironically some ornithologists, with an insatiable thirst for specimens for their skin collection, were upping their game just as the public sentiment was turning. Distinguished American ornithologist Eliot Coues, writing in 1903, advised any budding ornithologist to aim for collecting "…*(a)ll you can get* – with some reasonable limitation', namely 'fifty or a hundred of any but the most abundant…' (as if there were no limit on the latter).[48] Coues at the same time scoffed at the 'Audobonians' for their sentimentality, calling them 'the opera glass fiends'.[49]

But not all ornithologists looked so unkindly on the amateur enthusiasts. Many clubs and societies active in the late 19th century to cater for bird lovers were initiated by ornithologists. A landmark event in the development of modern recreational birdwatching was a 'Christmas Bird Count' in North America in 1900, organized by Frank Chapman, who had edited the popular magazine *Bird-Lore* and was then working as an ornithologist at the Smithsonian in New York.[50] This event was launched as a counter to the traditional Christmas Bird Shoot. The aim of the Bird Count was for a team to record the most species seen and identified (but not shot) within specified geographical limits. This first Bird Count

47 Ian J. Mason and Gilbert H. Pfitzner, *Passions in Ornithology: A Century of Australian Egg Collectors*, Fyshwick, Canberra: CanPrint, 2020.

48 Elliott Coues, *Key to North American Birds*, vol. 1 Boston, MA: Dana Estes & Co., 1903, pp.12–15, quoted in Weidensaul, op. cit. p.142.

49 Weidensaul, op. cit. p.143.

50 *Ibid.*, pp.148–149.

was undertaken by 27 enthusiasts equipped with binoculars, in 25 locales. It has been held each year ever since, these days immensely popular among birdwatchers as a combination of social event, annual ritual and sporting contest.

With the advent of high-quality field glasses, ornithology swiftly took off in new directions. The focus changed from studying specimens in pursuit of taxonomical knowledge to behavioural studies of birds in the field. Ornithology evolved through new methods of field observation and data collection, such as ringing or banding, for which techniques developed in leaps and bounds in the first two decades of the 20th century. But study of skin collections first formed in the 19th century still goes on today in order to resolve taxonomic questions. And confirmation of discovery of new species continues normally to require 'type specimens' to be shot or trapped, preserved, catalogued and made available for study. But with modern DNA sampling and other techniques, a newly discovered bird species these days may in some cases be confirmed without a full type specimen.[51]

British ornithologist Edmund Selous published a book titled *Birdwatching* in 1901. It was a scientific text, a record of his field observations reflecting his strong belief that field glasses, rather than guns, should be the primary tool of the ornithologist. That birdwatching with the help of binoculars was also growing in popularity among the general public is evident from a paper the biologist Julian Huxley wrote in 1916 in the ornithological journal *The Auk,* in which he lamented the fact that the growing band of recreational birdwatchers wasn't being encouraged to contribute their observations to scientific studies.[52] Huxley emphasized the importance of good field binoculars and the need for the observer to have 'a knowledge of what to search for…'. The perspective of a birdwatcher should be guided first and foremost by cool, informed, objective observation, enabling accurate record-keeping. Huxley had, perhaps unknowingly, anticipated something of the essence of the modern birder.

But not everyone heading for the woods or the wetlands was driven either by the collector's urge or by scientific curiosity. *In situ* observation of nature, including birds, as an expression of a love and enthusiasm for natural things, was increasingly popular. The romantic movement, beginning over a hundred years earlier, had already established walking in the countryside as a recreation for the better-off. Until then, if you walked in the country, as distinct from in manicured parks and gardens, it was normally a sign you were poor. Later, romantic poets such as Wordsworth became associated with a love for rural landscapes and a desire for their preservation. Being 'in nature' for its own sake took on increasingly mystical and transcendental tones as people read Ralph Waldo Emerson's essays and poetry and Henry Thoreau's classic *Walden*, published in 1854 (albeit the book was not a popular success in its day).

Of more direct impact in promoting the idea of the benefits of connecting with nature was the 'nature study movement', which gained strength in the 1890s and flourished in the early 20th century.[53] Nature study became a core part of school curricula in the USA, the UK, Australia and elsewhere. In this guise, the movement was firmly rooted in a scientific view of the modern world, and its leading advocates included prominent science educators. Getting young people out into the field to observe nature, away from the stuffy classroom, was not only good for health but also a pedagogical device for instilling the rigours of

51 'To kill or not to kill? Scientists debate specimen collection', *Mongabay,* 11 November 2015.

52 Julian Huxley, 'Bird-watching and biological science Part 1', *The Auk*, vol. 33, no. 2, 1916, pp.142–161.

53 Kevin C. Armitage, *The Nature Study Movement*, Lawrence, KS: University Press of Kansas, 2009.

London Transport Poster (1918) promoting travel to the outskirts of London

scientific inquiry. It also served the end of educating young people in the value of conserving nature.

At the same time, some in the nature study movement emphasized the spiritual benefits, advancing notions about connecting with nature as a remedy for the evil influences of city life and the material straitjackets of industrial modernity. A growing band of weekend nature lovers tramped the countryside. Getting out into the country and walking or 'rambling' grew in popularity as a weekend recreation among middle-class city dwellers. Meanwhile, the countryside and the newly established nature reserves became increasingly accessible with modern means of transport. Visiting places of natural beauty on weekends and on vacation opened up the natural world, including birds, to a whole new set of people as the new century progressed.

This burgeoning interest in being out and about in nature was accompanied by a growing nature literature, often written by scientists but for wider public consumption. The books were directed at people wanting to experience nature in the outdoors, not just on the page. They had titles like *Popular History of Animals, The Field Naturalist's Handbook* and *Familiar Wild Flowers*. This last was published in 1878, by Professor Edward Hulme, F.L.S, F.D.A, and contained '40 exquisite coloured plates'. The publication on birds in this series by W. Swaysland was in four volumes and contained high-quality coloured prints by a prominent natural history artist, Archibald Thorburn.[54] The book catalogued a selection of British birds that a recreational observer of nature might see, with extensive text on their appearance, behaviour and habits.

A four-volume work of reference on birds could not be considered a 'field guide' suitable to be carried while out and about. It is widely agreed that the first such was published in the USA in 1889 by naturalist, bird lover and environmental campaigner Florence Merriam Bailey.[55] One of her aims was to inform and encourage an interest in birds in support of greater conservation. Young people were in her mind as readers. The book presented and described birds using not only scientific but also colloquial, sentimental language, in particular by representing birds anthropomorphically: some were good citizens and worthy characters (such as 'Mr Robin'), others had less commendable habits and mores. Narrative

54 W. Swaysland, *Familiar Wild Birds*, London: Cassell, 1901.

55 Florence Merriam Bailey, *Birds Through an Opera-Glass*, New York, NY: Chautaqua Press, 1889. See also Schaffner, op. cit. (cited in the Introduction to this book).

descriptions contained comments on which species deserved greatest protection and which might be shot at for sport with fewer qualms. In similar vein, campaigner and nature writer Mabel Osgood Wright's 1895 book *Birdcraft* included anecdotal and educational material as well as illustrations with descriptive text to aid identification.[56]

Almost simultaneously with Bailey's book, Richard Kearton's 1890 volume on egg-collecting was published in Britain.[57] His book better resembled a modern birding field guide than did Merriam's, albeit only with respect to eggs. It was slim enough to be taken into the field and had colour prints and monochrome photographs, with terse, matter-of-fact descriptions of where to find and how to identify the nests and the eggs of the most common British birds. It was a rudimentary field guide for the committed egger. It went to eight printings, including a revised edition in 1896, before a new, more generously illustrated volume appeared in 1907 co-authored with his brother, Cherry (who was an early pioneer of nature films). This edition contained entries for many more species.

Drier, descriptive material became more prominent in handbooks as recreational outdoor nature study, aided by carrying binoculars, became more popular. In the USA, Chester Reed's series of *Bird Guides*, first published in 1906, had a sharper focus on identification and were clearly designed for the field. They were pocket-sized volumes with an illustration and accompanying text on each page. They flew off the shelves, selling 300,000 copies in five years.[58] Clearly, there was a demand for this kind of handy volume from a fast-growing band of nature lovers who were observing birds in the fresh air and wanting to know exactly what they were looking at.

But it was not until the 1930s that what we might recognize today as a fully-fledged modern birding field guide was published, by artist and birder Roger Tory Peterson.[59] In Peterson's book, identification of birds seen through the binoculars was clearly the name of the game. This was a book for the specialist birdwatcher with mainly one thing in mind: identifying birds in the field. Peterson adopted a form of presentation that emphasized the detailed explication of the 'field marks' distinguishing one species from another. Anything else we might perceive or feel when looking at birds, or project onto them, had become superfluous. The book was like an illustrated catalogue, detailed in its descriptive and illustrative entries for each species and single-mindedly focused on being able to tell one from another through the binoculars.

Peterson's *Field Guide* symbolizes what birdwatching had become – and still is: an activity concerned primarily with finding and identifying species of birds in the field based on scientifically based standards and criteria. The author's description of his own induction into birdwatching tells in microcosm the path that was taken to produce this result.[60] Arriving in New York in 1925, he joined the Bronx County Bird Club and met their members' mentor, Ludlow Griscom (1890–1959). Griscom had studied ornithology at Cornell University and he lived and worked in New York until 1927. His specialization was using field marks to identify birds (his thesis was on field identification of ducks).

An apocryphal story is that Griscom won a bet with another ornithologist who doubted that he could identify a distant tree-top warbler reliably with his binoculars. They shot the

56 Mabel Osgood Wright, *Birdcraft: A Field Book of 200 Song, Game and Water Birds*, New York, NY: Macmillan, 1895.

57 Kearton, op. cit.

58 Weidensaul, op. cit. p.199.

59 Roger Tory Peterson, *A Field Guide to the Birds*, Boston, MA: Houghton Mifflin, 1934.

60 Roger Tory Peterson, 'In Memoriam: Ludlow Griscom', *The Auk*, vol. 82, no. 4, 1965, pp.599–605.

bird in question and his identification of a Cape May Warbler was proved correct. Griscom was not just an ornithologist, he was a birder who enjoyed 'Big Days' and other forms of competitive birding, and he loved his life list. The Bronx birdwatchers roamed Central Park testing each other's identification skills using 'the Griscom method', and Peterson was hooked. His book, some ten years later, was a product of this experience and it laid the path for all subsequent field guides.

Since Peterson, the publishing industry has produced many hundreds, even thousands of such books. If you want to understand birders and birding, the modern field guide has all the clues. Field guides cover a region or a nation and aim to be comprehensive. Meticulous, detailed illustrations, drawn by specialist artists, show every bird that might be encountered. They depict the key field marks that distinguish each species to the eye. Juvenile, male and female plumage, plus seasonal differences may be described and illustrated. Birds most likely to be seen in flight (such as hawks) are depicted both perching and also in silhouette on the wing, from below; ducks are shown as if on the water, as well as flying and standing; and so on. Additional details are supplemental to these identifying marks and poses and have the same purpose. Detailed measurements are provided. Brave attempts are made to represent calls and songs on the page; range maps are included to show where one can expect to see the bird at different times of the year; and the text indicates whether the bird is a year-long resident, passage migrant, winter or summer visitor and so on.

The modern field guide is not so much a general description or analysis of the natural setting or daily lives of birds, as a species-by-species account of their distinguishing features. In the illustrations and text, scientific rigour and complete accuracy are essential. The illustrations are less depictions of the natural word than of the museum specimen. Any detailed information about general natural history provided, like everything else in the volume, aims to aid in identification. A short introduction will describe the habitats found in the region covered – climate, typical flora and fauna, geological features and topography. The paragraph on each species gives a more detailed account of habitat and feeding habits, as these are key pointers to finding and identifying each species. But our binocular vision in the final analysis homes in on the field marks of a particular bird that identify it as a species to the eye (and, to a lesser degree, to the ear).

The field guide, in sum, is a concrete representation of the way a birder views nature. You don't so much look at or listen to birds as part of the wider context of the natural world, nor at their human or social contexts, but as individual bundles of features that sort one species from another. The text is dry and cool, packed with detail; it does not wax lyrical about the beauty or the charm of a bird or offer any other kind of superfluous commentary. The imperative – the challenge – is to identify what you may see and to label it.

Looking at that Northern Hawk Owl in Vancouver, I was doing two things: first, as a bird lover, enjoying the spectacle and beauty of an owl perched on a snow-capped stump in broad daylight, perhaps wondering what message it might have for us behind that baleful stare; and second, as a birder, field guide in hand, noting its size, plumage and behaviour in order to confirm that it was indeed a Northern Hawk Owl. The dog walkers were bowled over by the first way of seeing but oblivious to the second. The poet in me was moved by the owl's beauty and mystery, but the birder in me was excited by the rarity of this species in this place and, especially, the fact that it was a lifer.

To the dog walker, this was just another owl, in the same way as, to Tennyson, his eagle was just another eagle (I suspect the species was a White-tailed Sea Eagle, but it was none the worse observed or appreciated by not naming it as such). Indeed, all eagles share the same essential features and evoke similar reactions and emotions from most people, but not the birder. A birder has to know the species. Similarly, if a birder hears a nightingale they are permitted to go into raptures, like John Keats in his poem *Ode to a Nightingale*, but not before they have carefully discerned from the tones and cadences that it is, indeed, the song of a Common Nightingale and not of some other songbird (including its close relative, the Thrush Nightingale). As a birder, I may appear to be looking at and listening to birds in nature, but I am actually looking for species that are in the field guide.

Field guides make no sense without binoculars and other optical instruments such as high-powered field scopes with a single zoom lens, mounted on a tripod, some able to magnify close to 100 times. A more recent technological development, following the same trajectory, has been the digital camera. Whether it is through the medium of the binoculars, the field scope or the camera zoom lens, the view we have on nature is specifically a birder's eye view: narrowing the field of vision, blotting everything else out, focusing on the bird and reducing it to a set of field marks as represented in the field guide, better to identify it as a species.

Bird song is a key identifying characteristic of a species, just as much as plumage and other visual clues, and field guides have battled bravely with trying to represent songs on the written page as successfully as the illustrations represent appearance. Poets have tried as well, as in Gerard Manley Hopkins's opening lines to his poem 'The Woodlark':

> Teevo cheevo cheevio chee:
> O where, what can that be?
> Weedio-weedio: there again!

Big lenses on the Kazakhstan Steppes

Fully equipped for a day in the field

Sorry Gerard, not good enough! Modern birding field guides are not concerned with poetic effect but with the attempt at precise accuracy: 'lee, lee-lee-leeleelee**leelülu … ee**-lü **ee**-lü **ee**-lü **ee**lü-**ee**lu-**ee**lue**e**lu … tluee tluee vi vi vi **tellellellell …**', etc.[61] A few field guides have tried sonograms, visual graph-like representations of the audio signal of a song or call – unsurprisingly, they haven't caught on with your average birder. Again, fortunately, technology has come to the rescue. We can now download a real-life soundtrack from xeno-canto, an open-source database, and play it on our smart phones out in the field.[62]

Birders rely on 'having a good ear' to remember and recognize songs and calls. Not only do accessible sound recordings make this knowledge easier to acquire, but they also make it easier to 'call in' a bird, enabling the birder to see it and also helping to confirm its identification. Recording bird song is not something that is a normal part of a day's birding for the average birder, although most professional bird guides do it as part of their trade. Sound recording equipment can be quite a burden.

Other forms of modern technology, particularly digital technology, have reinforced and accentuated the birder's way of relating to the natural world. One very recent development is online reporting and recording of bird sightings by individual birders on a central online database, eBird, which provides a way of telling other birders what you have seen. This has dramatically enhanced the birder's ability to track down target species in any given locality. If I plan to visit a new place, I go to eBird through the app on my smart phone or laptop and in a few minutes, I am able to save a record of previous sightings to my digital device. If I want to find a particular species to add to my list, I can look for the locations of recent sightings, then visit and try my luck.

Citizen science has also gained a new tool in eBird, helping to realize Julian Huxley's wish that birders' observations could be incorporated into scientific inquiry. Bird records submitted by birders have become an important database for scientific analysis. The advent of eBird has provided a new, widely adopted method for doing this and, in turn, transformed birding for many birders, who now go 'eBirding', which is to say, they follow strictly the protocols and guidelines entailed in entering a suite of details on the eBird app about each sighting. These protocols mimic the work of field ornithologists by refining the birder's existing field habits and recording practices. The details entered may include notes on identification, the precise GPS location, number of individuals sighted, the presumed sex and age (juvenile or adult) and some aspects of behaviour, in particular breeding behaviour. A digital photo may be uploaded to help confirm the accuracy of the ID.

The purpose of all this is scientific: eBird is now used both as a historical record of key features of bird populations and also as a tool for constructing precise, scientifically

61 Lars Svensson et al., *Birds of Europe*, Second Edition, Harper Collins, London, 2009, p.250 (entry for the Woodlark).

62 https://www.xeno-canto.org/

designed bird surveys. For the latter, birders are recruited as volunteer citizen scientists. Breeding bird surveys, and the construction of Breeding Bird Atlases based on them, have been undertaken by ornithologists for many years, but the advent of eBird has helped widen the participation of birders in such activities. Some North American state-based Breeding Bird Atlases are now conducted through eBird portals, using the eBird database facilities, with birders encouraged to volunteer. Today, ornithology is wielding even more influence over birding as a pastime than ever.

The modern preference for the term 'birder' rather than 'birdwatcher' aligns with the underlying point of view I have been describing. There is no general consensus on the terminology, but one often quoted distinction was made by the American Birding Association (ABA), shortly after it was set up. In their journal, *Birding*, vol. 1, no. 2 (1969) they set out their definitions:

> *Birder*. The acceptable term used to describe the person who seriously pursues the hobby of birding. May be professional or amateur.
>
> *Birding*. A hobby in which individuals enjoy the challenge of bird study, listing, or other general activities involving bird life.
>
> *Bird-watcher*. A rather ambiguous term used to describe the person who watches birds for any reason at all, and should not be used to refer to the serious birder.

The authors may have been part tongue-in-cheek, but they hit the mark, nonetheless. That birding is described as a 'challenge' and 'serious' is telling. The 'challenge' has a number of dimensions: first to find the birds you are seeking out, for which knowledge of habitat, range and general fieldcraft skills are necessary; second, to 'get on to' the bird with your bins or fieldscope so as to have a chance of identifying it; and third, to know enough confidently of the relevant field marks or song patterns to name what you have encountered as a species or subspecies.[63] Perhaps the best reason for using the term 'birder' rather than 'birdwatcher' is not mentioned directly, but it ties in with the rest: the skills required for ID aren't all being deployed by 'watching'. An important skill for a birder is to be able to recognize bird songs and calls – birders must listen as well as look if they are to be proficient. Indeed, this is a formidable challenge and one of the most prized skills of a 'top birder'.

Mention of the 'challenge of listing' is particularly significant in the way the ABA typified the hobby of birding. On the one hand, lists are kept as a simple record of observations, as would be the case in any kind of scientific 'bird study'. But at the same time, the description of listing as a 'challenge' suggests something else altogether: a competitive spirit – to have the longest list or lists. It's almost as if birding is a sport. Indeed, as discussed in the next chapter, listing is a central, defining feature of birding.

In sum, as distinct from idle pleasure, birding demands dedication, knowledge and skill, not to mention energy and fortitude (no sitting quietly under a plum tree for these folk, like John Keats writing his *Ode*). Looking back at the precursors of birding, we can see in all of this echoes of the birdsnester (the collecting urge of the cataloguer and lister); the naturalist-cum-explorer striking out into new places and making discoveries; the shooter

63 Jonathan Rosen, 'The difference between birdwatching and birding', *The New Yorker*, 17 October 2011.

or hunter (the thrill of the hunt and the language of 'targets' and 'bird counts'); and the early ornithologist (the objectivity and precision of identification of species by their form and appearance). The weekend rambler-cum-amateur naturalist and the romantic poet revelling in the beauties of nature are only dimly in view. Nature conservation, which was a powerful influence on the early development of birdwatching, has also somewhat receded in importance compared with other motives and priorities, although there are recent signs that this priority is being recovered.

My point is not that individual birders do not marvel with wonder at the beauty of what they see, nor that they are not enthralled by the magic of coming across a rare bird in the forest or by the beauty of the forest itself, nor that birders do not care about conservation. But what sets birding apart from simply looking at and enjoying birds, or caring about birds and nature more generally, is a specific point of view, resting on a set of enabling technologies. What shapes the modern birder's perspective is not wonder or mystery, charm or delight, but rigorous classification, objective certainty and quantification; not enchantment, but its forensic, bean-counting opposite; not just the pursuit of leisure or recreation, but also hard, rigorous work; not contemplation and appreciation of nature for itself, but active pursuit and objectification of it, in the form of searching out and accurately identifying species to add to the list.

CHAPTER 13

Listing and Listers

Every birder I know keeps organized lists of their sightings. Most of them know exactly the total number of species on their life list. When on a trip, their aim is to make new entries. Listing seems to be just a regular part of birding, but hardcore listers have a bad press. Some of them are the twitchers who trample on people's lettuces, desperate to see a rarity that has unexpectedly turned up; or they are the birders who only lift their binoculars when a lifer is in view and drop them immediately it is identified and added to the list, keen to rush on to the next one. The list, not the bird, seems to be the priority.

While nearly all birders do keep a list – many, more than one – this negative view of listing is not always deserved. Whether it's observing trains, planes, butterflies or birds, and whatever the reason, the wish to record the observations seems obvious and natural. After a few hours watching birds and trying to identify them, making a list in a little black book or on a smartphone app wraps it all up very nicely. It is a record of one's observations, an aid to memory like a diary and a launching pad for future outings and observations. All this sounds very innocent – just good common sense.

So, what's entailed in a birder's list? The first step in listing is accurate identification – there is no point keeping a list if all the entries are in the form of 'small, brown bird' or (somewhat more useful) 'a kind of thrush' (or '*Turdus sp.*', listing shorthand for 'unknown species of the genus *Turdus*'). Normally, the unit of record is the species, although some birders also record subspecies. Each birding excursion results in a 'trip list', whether it is on one day or over many. This list is a record of birds seen (and, for some, heard) on particular days in particular places. A record of the date and location are usually part of the list. Some such lists, for sake of completeness, will record the number of each species encountered – one Wedge-tailed Eagle, 12 Australian Magpies, etc.

I only keep a list of birds I have seen, not the ones I have only heard. I suppose I had always thought of birding as 'birdwatching', so I just adopted this norm as a matter of course. It's a matter of personal preference, but for some purposes it does make sense to list the ones heard as well as seen. If we were doing birding surveys of a scientific kind, identification by a distinctive song or call is as valid an observation as an ID by visual clues, so the lists drawn up in this case will include both. For birders, the skill of recognizing bird calls and songs is an important part of their fieldcraft but still, for most of them, the main ambition is actually to set one's eyes on the singer.

As more trip lists are accumulated, they can be consolidated in at least two ways: first, a list of species found in a defined location, from multiple trips; and second, a list of the birds found within particular time periods, either in particular locations or in all locations. A list of species encountered everywhere, at any time, is one's life list. The latter will only record each species on the first occasion it was observed, regardless of location. The easiest way to compile such a list is to enter one's observations by ticking off birds on a checklist of all species one might encounter (hence the expression 'a tick' for a species seen for the first time). If one is a world birder, that checklist is the complete avian taxonomic list.

From somewhat straightforward beginnings, things can very easily get out of hand. Many birders create separate lists for places commonly visited or, beyond this, a set of lists combining such sightings by district or region (a county list, for example). Patchwatchers most likely keep a patch list. The next step may be to keep a year list. Each New Year's Day, it all begins again. Patchwatchers might do this to track changes in their local bird populations over time. Birders willing and able to travel may also set their eyes on a country list. On a birding trip, once I have said I'm from Australia, I'm often asked: 'what is your Australia list?' The most ambitious birders will have their eyes fixed on a world list, perhaps along with separate country lists. Some birders may now be looking to top the total in their previous year's local/county/state list, just to give them something to aim for each year and – quite commonly – in order to top everyone else's list, as if it were a competitive sport.

At some point, one must begin to wonder what some of these listers are enamoured with, the birds or the lists? Perhaps the ultimate in listing mania is the 'Big Year', the non-stop birding odyssey to see as many species in a calendar year as one can. At the time of writing, the record for a world Big Year is held by a Dutch birder; his list for 2016 (both seen and heard) was 6,833 species. Big Year birding certainly captures the popular imagination, as the success of the 2011 movie of the same name illustrates. But there are even crazier lists and listers. I have heard tell of the birder who keeps a list of birds seen on TV live broadcasts (gulls on the cricket pitch, crows flying by during the wartime correspondent's live reports from the battlefield). And there is an online group of Google birders who trawl the world of Street View looking for birds, sharing fuzzy images from the background and trying to identify what has been accidentally captured in the shot so as to compile a Street View list.[64]

Extreme listing of this kind expresses in exaggerated form a number of aspects of birding, in particular the enjoyment of the challenge of identification and, for many, a competitive urge. Competition for seeing the most birds in a year within the ABA 'checklist area' is particularly keen. The ABA has a special page on its website setting out the rules and the conditions, its so-called 'Recording Rules'. It is a badge of honour to be the ABA top lister, that is, the one who has seen the greatest number of species within the ABA area in a calendar year. Exactly how this boundary should be drawn is not so straightforward as it sounds, and much serious attention has been applied to it:

64 Ryan F. Mandelbaum, 'These birders flock to Google Street View to spot birds around the world', *Gizmodo*, 10 December 2018.

The **ABA Area** is defined in the organization's bylaws and in the *ABA Checklist*. It includes the 49 continental United States, Hawai'i, Canada, the French islands of St. Pierre and Miquelon, and adjacent waters to a distance of 200 miles from land or half the distance to a neighbouring country, whichever is less. Bermuda and Greenland are not included.

Among a select few 'mega-listers', there is a keen race to be the top world lister among all birders – the current leader has a species list that is creeping up towards 10,000. I sometimes secretly envy these birders for having seen all those birds, but at the same time I do think some of them are a bit crazy. Although, I once travelled with the then top lister and he was perfectly nice.

Undoubtedly, for many of these top listers it is the thrill of the chase, or the irresistible attraction of the impossible challenge that urges them on. Like climbing Mount Everest, responding to such a personal challenge is not strictly speaking a 'race'. But the competitive urge and the function of the list as a kind of score separating winners from losers are clearly evident in the phenomenon of the 'bird race'. With origins in the first Christmas Day Bird Count in 1906, this phenomenon has been an important part of birding ever since, often described as 'Big Day birding'. A reading of the ABA 'Big Day Count rules' makes it clear that there can be a serious competitive intent in Big Day listing – many of the rules clearly seek to forestall opportunistic behaviour (and just plain cheating) aiming to pad the list unfairly.

Each year in Hong Kong there has traditionally been a bird race on a designated day run by the Hong Kong Birdwatching Society, when teams of birders compete to see the largest number of species in the Territory. Much strategizing goes into the chase and competition can get quite keen. For several years, a visiting team from Singapore would fly in and sweep the board, leading to dark mutterings from the locals about the reliability of their sightings. Hong Kong and Singapore have always been keen rivals, about all sorts of things.

India adopted Hong Kong's bird race model in 2005, with teams competing all across India. The competition got so keen and unseemly that after a few years the organizers decided no longer to award prizes for the winner and runners-up, but to call every team a 'winner' and to emphasize the role the Big Day can play in recruiting new birders to a 'fun' activity. Indeed, bird races have always embodied educational and recreational purposes as well as competitive ones. But nearly all fun games have winners and competition is a key motivator – indeed, this is why the race, not the birds, is thought to be the thing that will attract more young people to birding.

The Big Year leader and the top lister are both men – no surprise, from my observation of the demographics and the behaviour of the many birding companions I have encountered. Regardless of whether my own observational sample is skewed, it does seem to be the case that competitive listing is 'heavily male biased'.[65] Men tend to be the top listers and the keenest and most aggressive twitchers. Of course, gender is not determining and many social, personality and cultural factors are also at play. A number of famous birding listers have been women. There are always exceptions, while statistical analysis too easily descends into gross stereotyping. And things change. In the study quoted above, there were some data to suggest that the male bias was much less in evidence among younger birders.

65 Caren B. Cooper & Jennifer A. Smith, 'Gender patterns in bird-related recreation in the USA and UK', *Ecology and Society*, vol. 15, no. 4, 2010.

Most birders, male and female, young or old, manage to stop somewhere on the way down the slippery slope towards listing for its own sake in its various forms. For them, the list is simply a means to an end, which is identifying and then recording birds. But there is something about the list as an intrinsic part of the birder's pastime that is irresistible in itself. This an example of what the American Sociologist Robert Merton called 'goal displacement' in which something that is a means to an end becomes the end in itself.[66] He applied this idea to what he called the 'pathology of bureaucracy', that is, the tendency for public employees to become so enamoured with 'red tape' that they forget what they are really there for. In the same way, we might talk of the 'pathology of listing'. The list becomes the main point of it all. This may be particularly so when the list is also a score.

But listing is not always pathological, nor is it necessarily competitive. Keeping lists can be a valuable and enjoyable aspect of birding that enhances the experience of looking for and looking at birds, for all types of birder. The value of the life list is immediately apparent for the birder who wants to keep an aide-memoire of trips and sightings. It is a record of a lifetime's birding activity. Maybe there are other records as well, such as a collection of notebooks containing field notes (like a diary), or a filing cabinet full of the trip lists that were provided by bird tour companies, with ticks added to record the sightings. But the life list is the ultimate repository of all those birding memories and the point of first access to them.

Second, the life list is also valuable for organizing future birding activity. The existence of a life list of ticks immediately creates another list – of birds one would like to tick in the future. It is the gaps in the list that motivate many birders to go birding. One's life list, cross-checked against established lists of species' geographic ranges at different times of the year, indicates what trips one might take in order to see as many new birds as possible. For just about anywhere you might want to visit to do some birding – a National Park, a nature reserve, a local park, or even an area as non-specific (in birding terms) as a city or county – some person or organization has published a checklist of birds that have been seen at that location. The Internet has made publicizing or accessing such checklists a click or two away, so you can see very quickly whether you might see some new birds if you visit.

Technology has played a big role in the facilitation of listing and giving it added value. In the age of the Internet, one can log into websites that exist for the purpose of recording lists of observations that can be retrieved by other birders, as well as by the original lister – eBird is one such, providing a global database that can be accessed by all. In other words, birders' trip lists become a shared public resource of checklists, not just vanity projects. This has been one of the most important developments in birding since the advent of high-quality affordable binoculars. Listing now is not just the work of a bunch of obsessive listers, but a public service activity shared by a community. In the digital age, birders, like everyone else, are networked. Listing on eBird also announces and records local rarities (see Chapter 15). And eBird and 'eBirding' has turned many more birders into citizen scientists than was previously the case.

So far, so good, but there is another dimension to listing that embodies a set of temptations for the unwary birder teetering on the slippery slope to obsession. I refer to the mechanics of listing, or the technology. I know one birder who has seen thousands of birds and is still using loose-leaf binders, rulers, erasers, sticky inserts, different coloured inks and such like to maintain the list he first started 50 years or more ago. To him, it's a matter of

66 Robert K. Merton, 'Bureaucratic structure and personality', in Merton, *Social Theory and Social Structure*, Glencoe, IL: Free Press, 1957, pp.195–206.

pride that he can keep it going. Most of us, however, are not quite such confirmed luddites.

My own first list, set up in the age of the PC, was a word-file table, with columns for each component of the list. A new sighting allowed entry of a new bird in the right place in the taxonomic order simply by adding a row to the table. Number codes in the columns were used for countries, date of the encounter and bird families to allow them to be sorted. I managed to keep this going for quite a few years, and it was perversely a lot of fun, but as my life list grew in length and the table covered more and more pages, I finally lost patience. Taxonomic changes completely threw it out; it was unbelievably clunky; and I began to insert sub-codes and categories to allow for finer sorting just because I could, to the point where it really was in danger of becoming an obsession.

A spreadsheet was the obvious answer, but I have an aversion to spreadsheet software. Fortunately, technology came to my rescue. Digital bird recording software was just taking off and I found a programme that was to my taste.[67] On my computer I now have a database, *Scythebill*, that contains my list and, thanks to the software's features, the capacity to turn the life list into numerous sublists, should I wish to do so. I keep the data in the digital cloud so I can access it from any computer that has the software installed.

This database can show me how many birds I have seen in total and I can also view reports for any country and, in some cases, smaller subdivisions such as states and counties, all with a few clicks of the mouse. I can also see year lists and trip lists if I wish. Entering new sightings is easy. I can choose to enter every sighting or just the new ones, or maybe only new ones for that country or region. To my taste or needs, the amount of detail I enter about the location can either be very general or very fine-grained. In addition, once my entries are complete, I can generate reports country by country that show me how many lifers I might see if I visit. Perhaps the coolest thing is that periodic updates are available to download that include changes to the taxonomic order (either IOC or Clements, according to my preference) as they are released. A few minor adjustments to my life list to account for splits and lumps and everything is fine.

To do this, however, I must try to record subspecies as well as species. When a myzomela I have seen both in Sumba and in northern Australia is later split into two species, the location data in the entry I made for both sightings would automatically signal that I may have seen two, not one species. It's up to me whether I record a new tick. If I do, all of a sudden, when I reopen the software with updates and adjustments completed, it shows me that I have a new lifer, an armchair tick! The fact that these two birds are pretty much identical is another matter altogether (see Chapter 17).

So far as I can tell, I am not yet such a slave to this listing software that it has taken over my life, although I do find myself spending a lot of time playing with it. Since I took up bird photography in a modest way, one other feature has me captivated, for I can embed my own digital images of each species in the database so that they can be called up when I review my sightings. There is also a place to enter notes referring to each entry, such as time of day, weather, habitat, anything noteworthy about the bird's behaviour and so on. All this adds a new dimension to the value of my list as an aide-memoire. In my experience, listing software does not act as an invitation to succumb to the listing obsession, even though it may seem to have this capacity (if you are already hooked, it is certainly a better version of the drug).

67 Gerco Hoogeweg, 'Birding listing software review', *Surfbirds.com*, 3 March 2017.

Red-headed Myzomela, northern Australia

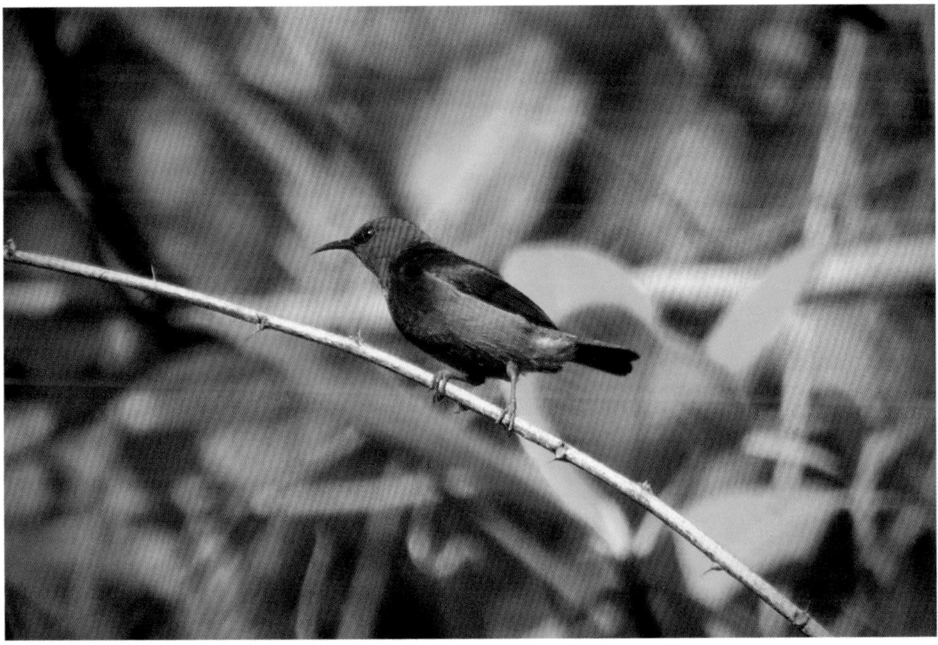

Sumba Myzomela, Lesser Sundas

There is just one thing about listing that does properly elevate it to the status of an end in itself. On a birding trip, at the end of the day, the evening ritual of 'doing the list' is an intrinsic part of the experience. If I birded alone, I relive the day for myself as I enter the list on my database. If I was with others, the group can go through the checklist together and tick off the day's sightings. We relive the disappointments and the highlights of the day and go over arguments about dubious or uncertain IDs. Individuals who dipped on a bird receive more commiserations. The lucky one who saw the rarity or the lifer when everyone else dipped tries not to gloat too much. The one who first spotted a bird and pointed it out to everyone else gets patted on the back all over again. Arguments about whether a bird on the trip checklist deserves full species status (like the aforementioned Sumba Myzomela) may be fiercely engaged. These arguments usually peter out harmoniously as everyone begins to fall asleep over their list due to the 4 am start.

Later, having taken the trip list home at the end of the trip, there is the new pleasure of entering the sightings from the handmade trip list to my life list on the computer, sometimes discovering in the process that I have a lifer that I mistakenly thought was a bird seen on a previous trip. Exploration of online sources and field guides might enable confirmation or identification of the subspecies, if it were not already known. Then I go through all the photos I took on the trip and add the best ones to the database as well. Again, 'doing the list' is like reliving the trip. It is also often educational as I follow up on questions about similar species, range, habitat and so on. And what I have at the end of the day is a rich, permanent record of a life of birding that can be revisited at my leisure.

So yes, I really like my list, I look after it assiduously and I have always wanted it to grow because I have wanted to see as many new birds as possible. The list does, in one important sense, have a life of its own, generating armchair ticks as taxonomic changes get registered on the database. But this is a quirk of taxonomic decision making, beyond my control and independent of my attachment to the list. I have never been interested in competitive listing in any form, but I suppose I would still have to describe myself as a 'lister'. However, my only meticulously kept list is my life list. I don't keep strict country or locality lists, but I did for a while for my amusement keep an office-window list and a rooftop list in Hong Kong. But I don't particularly care if my attachment to the list and to listing as I have just described it means you want to put me in the category of manic or pathological lister. I know one when I see one and really, truly, that's not me.

CHAPTER 14

Authentic Birding

For a variety of reasons, the vast majority of birders are pretty scrupulous about which birds they include on their life list. I have seen Budgerigars in cages in all sorts of places, but I only added the species to my list when I saw a wild one in its native Australia. But what do we count as a 'wild' bird? And why is this so important? After all, a budgie is a budgie is a budgie, so surely it should go on my list wherever and however I see it. But this isn't how birding works. It's just not done to go birding in an aviary at the zoo, or at a bird market in Hong Kong. There are both unwritten and codified rules and standards that govern what we can count on our lists.

As we saw in the previous chapter, for many birders, the list is an intrinsic, indispensable part of birding, and getting it right is a top priority. The norms and rules about this are of two main types: first, what constitutes a reliable identification; and second, what, aside from

Wild Budgerigars, Mount Isa, Queensland

this, is a listable bird. The first set of rules are generally unwritten, as it all really depends on the integrity of the individual birder (although some kind of confirmation or vetting is sometimes required, such as in most bird races). Most birders take the view that if it's just your list we are talking about, it's up to you what standards you adopt in claiming a tick. But birders are alive to their reputation among their peers, so they mostly adhere to some standards about reliable identification. Honest mistakes are part of the learning process; continually making unlikely claims about rare sightings that no one can verify is a rapid, downhill slide to ostracism.

The second set of rules are more precisely elaborated and clearly written down somewhere, and these are the ones that I shall deal with here. Birding is an institutionalized activity involving lots of participating organizations, many millions of birders and a large number of businesses small and big, turning over billions of dollars a year. Not surprisingly, there is a fair bit of red tape involved. International ornithological bodies lay down and modify the taxonomic list that frames our identification of species and our quest for new ones. Birding societies such as the ABA set rules for birding events and competitions, such as bird races. Birders are expected or sometimes required to follow such rules if they submit their sightings to local rare bird notice boards, or to databases such as eBird, in order that more or less scientific records can be kept and to enable compilation of reliable lists for the benefit of other birders. Avian tourism businesses publish trip reports, meticulously listing all the birds seen at the places visited; their credibility is important to them, so they by and large adopt and reinforce the rules.

So, back to that question: what, according to these rules, is a tickable bird? As one authority puts it, the bird should be 'alive, wild and unrestrained when encountered'.[68] This may seem pretty straightforward (like those budgies), but not so: plenty of room is left for uncertainty. What counts as restrained? One of the low points in my birding adventures was when a tour guide in Argentina drove us down a back road to see a rhea. It was quietly browsing in a large, fenced paddock on a farm. Should I count it as a sighting? Was it really unrestrained? Rheas don't fly, so how high can a rhea jump? To take another case, I have seen a Besra (a species of small hawk) emerge from a bush after a dramatic plunge from a nearby tree, with a Swinhoe's White-eye in its claws. The White-eye certainly was not unrestrained, although I presume this rule doesn't apply to prey. But that aside, was the victim still alive?

An apocryphal story doing the birders' rounds is of a group of birders looking for a rare flufftail in a paddock (or perhaps it was some other small, ground-dwelling bird that is reluctant to fly – the story varies on this point). They decided to spread out and beat the paddock in a line. A few minutes in, an anguished cry announced that someone had accidentally stepped on the bird, which was hiding in a tussock. 'Is it still alive?' was the response from the birder at the end of the line as he sprinted over for a look, not so much in sympathy for the plight of the creature, but to determine whether or not he could count it as a tick – that is, so long as he got there in time.

The exact meaning of 'wild' in the ABA's rule book raises some knotty issues. To count as such, a bird's occurrence must not be '...because it, or its recent ancestors, has ever been transported or otherwise assisted by man (*sic*)...'. For a start, we can rule out domesticated birds, which may be captive-bred and also habituated to a life with humans, not to mention

68 American Birding Association (ABA) *Recording Rules and Interpretations* (version 2014(b)) (available on the ABA website).

restrained. But so-called 'exotic' species living free (birds clearly from another part of the world, presumably transported by humans) may be counted if they are part of an established population. We generally refer to these as introduced species. Some countries, like New Zealand, have a lot of established, introduced species – settlers brought them over from the British Isles in the 19th century as part of the acclimatization movement to make themselves feel more at home (there were Acclimatization Societies to organize this properly). In other cases, exotic birds are most likely escapees from cages, or 'feral'.

To cover these cases, the ABA has a formal definition of 'established', basically meaning a population that is breeding and self-sustaining and has been *in situ* for at least 15 years. This is clearly the case in New Zealand for European Goldfinches, for example. Under the ABA criteria, the Budgerigar used to be on its checklist for Florida, but in 2015 it was decided that the population (presumably, descendants of escapees) had failed to sustain itself and was extirpated. If a birder saw a Budgerigar in Tampa after 2015, it shouldn't be on their list. Some birders make it a point of principle not to count introduced or feral species, but only to tick them if seen in their original range. This is going a bit far.

Most bodies of rules have a way of ending up being a bit daft, as more exceptions and unforeseen circumstances are woven into their fabric. These rules are no different. There are reliable records of birds arriving in foreign lands after hitching a ride on a ship. Somewhat puzzlingly, the ABA does not count this as 'transported or assisted by man': 'A wild bird following or riding a ship at sea, without being captured, is considered travelling unassisted by man.' Really?

Here's another one: if you are releasing a captured wild bird (for example, after mist-netting and ringing) you can't count it as a wild bird just because it flees unrestrained. You have to see it resume its 'normal behaviour' first (although why fleeing from humans or escaping from a cage isn't 'normal behaviour' is a mystery).

Another borderline case is of birds that have been captive-bred and trained by humans to act appropriately in the wild after release. Captive-bred Whooping Cranes in the USA have been trained on their migration route by a pilot in a light aeroplane. After release and successful integration, they can be counted as 'wild'. Indeed, there is an ABA rule about this: 'an individual of one of these species may be counted only if the population it belonged to had successfully hatched young in the wild prior to the encounter'.

There is more. Some forms of human intervention and assistance, however significant or intrusive, do not negate the wildness of a bird for the purpose of recording it as a valid sighting. Specifically, '...(a)n otherwise wild bird that voluntarily uses ... a feeder, nest box ... or other unnatural device, without being captured, is still considered wild.' The key thing is whether the bird is 'voluntarily' making use of the nest box or feeder, that is, the helping hand of humans is not *forcing* a bird to appear in the birder's line of sight (this is the logic we have already seen applied to the avian stowaway). So, 'otherwise wild' birds that have become habituated to handfeeding or have become induced to approaching humans and human habitation for other reasons, are fine. For the purposes of adding to the list, a tame bird can be deemed wild. Habituation is not the same as restraint.

Most birders, keen on adding to their lists, obviously approve of this rule – many birds on some birding trips are sighted because someone has taken the trouble to habituate them. There are some doubters, not so much because they dispute the logic of the rules but because they have a principled objection: they frown on such human interventions for the harm they can do. As discussed already in Chapter 11, there is evidence that habituation can change the character or personality of a wild population, leading its members to be bolder and less wary of predators (not just humans) and hence more at risk of dangers of all kinds. National Parks for such reasons often display 'Don't Feed the Animals' signs – mostly, of course, to no avail.

If done carefully – such as providing the right food and taking measures to protect the feeding birds from predators – handfeeding in protected locations of the kind that caters for visiting birders can help sustain local populations of vulnerable and threatened species. So far, we don't have conclusive evidence that this causes more harm than good. Birds are adaptive and intelligent creatures. When humans appear, this often creates opportunities as well as threats. The birds learn and take advantage. If someone appears day after day with a handful of worms and doesn't appear threatening, then why not hop over and take some? Especially if there are young mouths to feed.

On the face of it, an otherwise wild bird that has been tamed is not being observed 'in the wild'. Indeed, the rules about which birds we can count say nothing directly about this. Yet I have a nagging sense that 'in the wild' is where we should be looking for birds for an authentic birding experience. But what does it mean? A definition that might help is one contained in the USA 1964 Wilderness Act:

> A wilderness, in contrast with those areas where man *(sic)* and his own works dominate the landscape, is hereby recognized as an area where the Earth and its community of life are untrammeled by man, where man himself is a visitor who does not remain.

But 'wilderness' won't do as a standard of authenticity, as by this criterion, I don't think I have ever birded in the wild – everywhere is more or less trammelled. Another possible meaning applicable to the specifics of birding might define it as the kind of habitat a species naturally evolved to populate. We call such places 'primeval swamps' and 'unspoilt forests'. We can see all around us the results for wildlife of outright destruction of such habitats – the pre-existing birds disappear. But what we also see is ecosystems and landscapes that have been radically modified, but which we still think of as in some sense 'natural' (such as practically the whole of the British Isles outside the towns and cities). There seems to be plenty of birds there as well (although this is becoming less so in recent years) and they clearly are, in some sense, in the wild.

Humans, as they expanded in number and range, shared ancient habitats of other creatures and everywhere was changed by their presence. Swifts, swallows, House Sparrows and many others adapted to take advantage of human settlements and artefacts millennia ago, and these adaptations are now inextricable from all the other conditions of their wild existence. They, not we, decided what 'in the wild' means. Australian Aborigines for 60,000 years used fire to manage the landscape in many parts of Australia, transforming habitats. Birds and other creatures adapted – some thrived; some, no doubt, declined; others, more specialized in their needs, ended up in enclaves of pre-existing habitat if they were not to be extinguished.

Modern European agriculture has reshaped these Australian landscapes once again, and more drastically. Many species of birds have just got on with it, or perhaps even benefited as a result. But (to name just two) the Mallee Emuwren and Black-eared Miner in

Mallee Emuwren

western Victoria and eastern South Australia are now on the very brink of extinction due to destruction or radical modification of the Mallee landscape by modern humans.

But the story is complex. Terms like 'wild' and 'nature' are contested, not fixed or settled.[69] Contrarian environmental historian Eric Rolls traced the history of the Pilliga forests in New South Wales, showing that the disturbance and transformations wrought by European settlers actually promoted the growth of denser native scrub and forest, increasing the abundance of many species:

> ...for Eric – a farmer – 'wild' nature was feral, mongrel, hybrid nature, nature stirred up, nature enlivened by human presence and intervention.[70]

Although, it might be hard to explain this to the Mallee Emuwren in its vanishing habitat.

There may be an appropriate language to accurately describe these ecological and landscape changes, but 'the wild' is not part of it: this term mostly serves to capture a diverse and often contradictory set of values or sentiments about the natural world that we can express in all sorts of ways and with all sorts of wild and not-so-wild places in mind. From a perspective of inhabiting urban, suburban and industrial landscapes (including those shaped by modern agriculture), these sentiments are more often than not attached to places that are imagined rather than real. But reality is complicated. Australia's Aborigines harmoniously inhabited what we newer Australians call 'the outback', as 'country' to which they attach myths and other cultural meanings. It was all they knew, they helped shape it through the use of fire, and they thrived, along with a teeming native wildlife. To the first settlers of Australia, what they saw was either good grazing or alien, hostile wilderness-cum-wasteland. To inhabit it

69 Joachim Radkau, *Nature and Power; A Global History of the Environment*, Cambridge: University of Cambridge Press, 2002.

70 Tom Griffiths, 'The Writing of *a Million Wild Acres*', in Eric Rolls, *A Million Wild Acres*, Sydney: Hale and Iremonger, 2011, p. xix.

in their way, they changed it again. Wilderness, the wild, wasteland, country, grazing land, the outback and so on are names for some of the same non-urban places, but invested with different economic, historical, cultural and psychological meanings.

Genuinely undisturbed wilderness landscapes are so few and far between and increasingly so remote that it's all a bit academic. For birders, looking at birds in significantly human-influenced habitats is the norm. One of the reasons we find birdwatching so appealing is that many birds thrive among us in plain sight, despite our best efforts to alter their habitats. Perhaps the most popular place for people to watch birds is in their backyard. Many an outing, bins around the neck, is likely to be to a municipally cultivated and tended park or to a nature reserve that is not far from human settlement. Many such reserves allow or encourage human activities other than just 'being in nature', such as hiking, camping, trail-riding or shooting.

However, most birders probably like the idea of birding in wild places (in the minds of most of them, probably, this means as close to wilderness as they can comfortably get) and would claim to be nature lovers who place intrinsic value on such an experience. We wish to go to a National Park, or on longer birding trips to places like Antarctica or remote New Guinea, in the hope of seeing new birds and also to experience some of the remaining wildlife habitats that are least trammelled by humans – these are the *really* wild places. However much this may be an illusory quest, we are genuinely looking for an authentic experience of birds in their natural habitat as well as for the chance to see authentically wild birds.

But to put it bluntly, in whatever way me might define and idealize it, experiencing nature and being in the wild are incidental to the birder's main aim, which is to see a wild bird and count it. A birding hotspot where one can see wild birds does not always have to be a place of natural beauty, a wild place, or even in the countryside. Sometimes, it does have to be a very specialized habitat, such as one that contains a sufficient number of very tall, ancient trees with suitable nesting holes, which can only be found in relatively undisturbed forest. But the best place to find other sought-after birds may be a sewage farm, a rubbish tip, a drainage pond on an industrial estate or a hotel patio with a line of hummingbird feeders. In other words, birding is about seeing wild birds (so deemed) more than it is about birding in the wild.

If you are a birder, the main selling point in going somewhere for the birding is how many species you can expect to see, especially if they are new birds for the life list. 'The wild' is simply where the wild birds are. In this respect, the travelling birder is unlike other ecotourists, for whom authenticity of experience is the whole point (albeit within reasonable bounds of convenience and comfort). An ecotourist would not welcome a 4 am start to visit a sewage farm, for example.

Perhaps there is, however, one circumstance in which all keen birders do thirst after birding 'in the wild': when you have seen all there is to see in the accessible habitats, all that's left is to head for the more remote, uncomfortable, inaccessible places – the wilderness, even – where the remaining ticks are to be found. But is this because of a love of nature and wild places? Probably not. It's simply an imperative if you want to go on seeing new species.

Ecuador is a prime birding destination for keen birders. For a visiting birder wanting to see as many wild birds as possible, the best itinerary might be one that is designed to visit a series of lodges situated on a variety of protected forest reserves and, in the process, be taken from one feeder to another, or from one hide to another, where more or less habituated wild birds are on tap. Ecuador, where the birding industry is well-developed, is just the place where such an itinerary is feasible. You don't have to hack your way through virgin forest looking and listening for birds in the hope of coming across them, although you would probably spend some days doing something like this, albeit mostly on well-marked, frequently trodden trails. Many of the destinations will be a public reserve or a private property where you are directed down one short trail after another to a hide or to a line of benches, giving a view of a protected lek or a well-stocked feeding station. A stop at the local café with its hummingbird feeders in the garden is also certain to be on the itinerary. Back at the lodge, the bananas are put out at set times to suit both the birds and the birders.

Increasingly, the accessible habitats that hold the key species of a region are shrinking and, in those fragments that remain, birding tourism may be an important source of income. The local custodians have learnt to offer what many birders want: wild birds that are readily accessible so that they can be viewed well and easily photographed. In Ecuador and Colombia, there are well-known birding sites where property owners and birding guides have learnt the knack of 'calling in' individual members of key target species, such as antpittas, to be fed by hand. These species are normally elusive and very difficult to see in the depths of the forest and the success in taming them in this manner is astonishing.

A pioneer was Angel Paz, a farmer who welcomes birders to Refugio Paz de las Aves, near Mindo in Ecuador. To complete the experience, Angel has also set up a hide to observe

Feeding time for the Blue-naped Chlorophonia, Santa Marta, Colombia

Andean Cock-of-the-rock at the lek, Refugio Paz de las Aves, Ecuador

Albeiro and Chestnut-naped Antpitta

lekking Andean Cock-of-the-rock. The visitor's package also includes a snack of baked delicacies and coffee from the farm kitchen, overlooking the hummingbird feeders. In Colombia, the Rio Blanco Reserve near Manizales is where the local guide, Albeiro, who learnt the technique from Angel, calls in up to five species of antbird and antpitta to his feeding stations – 'venga! venga! venga!'.

For birders, the experience of having birds presented for viewing, rather than having to go out and look for them, is an increasingly common one. Reserves that harbour protected rare birds are now among the primary destinations of world birders. They are sometimes artificially restored natural habitats. There has been an exponential growth in recent decades in interventions that aim to save species and populations of endangered birds from extinction, including capture and release into new, safer habitats on reserves, coupled with captive breeding to boost declining populations. For birders, these interventions assist them to find and see birds that might otherwise not be accessible. All sorts of new questions about authenticity are posed, most of which can be brushed aside according to the rules about what constitutes a wild bird, as long as the habitat in which one sees the birds (however artificially produced or protected) is one where they are free to fly around and do their thing.

Some of the most notable and extreme cases of this are to be found in New Zealand. Not only did the acclimatization movement in the 19th century bring songbirds and rabbits, but it also brought stoats and foxes. Rats mostly arrived more surreptitiously in the bilges of boats – some of them, along with dogs and pigs, in the boats of earlier Pacific Islander visitors and settlers. New Zealand's wildlife (what was left of it after the land was cleared for European-style agriculture) was completely unprepared for these predators. Mammals with their sharp teeth were entirely new on the scene (the only land mammals in New Zealand before human settlement were bats) and so most indigenous birds and reptiles had evolved no defences. By the mid-20th century, only small fragments of the original populations of birds were surviving. To preserve them and try to restore their numbers, drastic measures have been taken.

A number of offshore islands have been cleared of sheep, rats, stoats, possums, goats and whatever else was not indigenous, including weeds. Native plants have been reintroduced where they had disappeared, and birds and other native creatures relocated from mainland locations where they were hanging on (but still under threat). For the most-threatened species, captive breeding schemes have been the main source of the reintroductions. Strict *cordons sanitaires* are imposed to prevent re-invasion. To visit Kapiti Island, for example, I had to book in advance on one of the boats that are authorised to transport a limited number of daily visitors and, before I was allowed to board, I had to empty my backpack to show I wasn't harbouring a pet ferret, or worse. On the mainland, a growing number of areas have been elaborately fenced and eradication of invasive species has been undertaken within the fenced areas, followed by reintroductions.

More recently, these piecemeal efforts, albeit highly successful, have been supplemented by more ambitious goals to undertake the complete eradication in New Zealand of the principal invasive species that continue to threaten the indigenous wildlife. How this is to be done is an ongoing, sometimes fractious debate, perhaps with no satisfactory resolution. A prominent local businessman in 2013 launched a public campaign through the Morgan Foundation to eradicate all cats, including pets, unsurprisingly without much traction on the stage of public opinion. The idea is almost certainly a dead fluffy kitten too far.

Birding on dry land in New Zealand is now undertaken for the most part by visiting these sanctuaries. Some of them offer other tourist attractions, such as the one near Rotorua where a forest canopy walk has been constructed and the total eco-experience can include hair-raising zip-line rides through the trees. Normally, a birder is guaranteed a sighting of the main targets at these places. Outside the fenced areas, some indigenous species of birds have adapted and survived, despite the challenge of predators, by taking advantage of humans' helping hands. In these cases, it may be the habituation of the birds to human inducements that allows the birder to get their tick.

Elsewhere in this book (Chapter 16), I describe at greater length my experience of seeing the near-extinct Orange-bellied Parrot on its breeding grounds in Tasmania. The tiny surviving population in the wild is being sustained partly as a result of releases each year of captive-bred birds, and partly through protection of the one remaining breeding site. The birds seemed habituated and we saw some of them at feeders. Nothing in the rules says we can't count them as wild birds, but they did seem a bit too much like budgies in an aviary for comfort. Nevertheless, they are on my list. So, too, are the translocated New Zealand endemics I have seen on Kapiti Island and in other sanctuaries (despite the fact that, in some cases, these islands were not originally part of their natural range).

A 'helping human hand' is taken advantage of and deployed at every turn by birders. Even when birds are not habituated, or protected in enclaves in some way, thereby making them easier to find, we use artifice to make finding them easier. The most commonly deployed is 'playback', which we have already discussed in Chapter 11. When, as a novice birder, I first encountered this in the company of an expert guide in Thailand, I was amazed to see how much easier it was to see birds in this way than just by wandering around, listening and looking. My guide was a veritable Pied Piper. But my sense of delight and satisfaction was followed almost immediately by the nagging question: 'But isn't this cheating?'. I got over that pretty quickly, as I came to realize just how much I gained as a birder from using playback – I saw many, many more birds than I would have done otherwise.

But I do prefer at least the illusion of authenticity. In Ecuador in 2016, we visited a chocolate farm near Mindo, where the owner, who is a bird enthusiast, had located a Rufous-crowned Antpitta the year before in an area of well-preserved forest on his property. He regularly visited its territory to study the habitat and survey the birds, and so the bird, normally very shy and elusive, was now somewhat habituated to a human presence. We had to walk up a steep forest trail for an hour or two to meet up with the owner. We clambered down a slope and soon encountered the Antpitta, which was following an ant swarm. It came close, seemingly unafraid (no playback needed) – and of course, so did the ants. We had to get down low to see it through the undergrowth, and few of us escaped being bitten as a result.

Rufous-crowned Antpitta, Mashpi Chocolate Farm, Ecuador

The photo I took – the bird, mostly obscured, peering at us warily through the dense undergrowth – says a lot. Although I had much better views on that trip of several other spectacular species of antpitta thanks to handfeeding, this one was my bird of the trip, because I experienced the forest close-up while encountering the bird in its element. The authenticity of that experience, to my mind, was composed of a number of things: sweating up the forest trail in undisturbed forest; seeing the bird behaving naturally in the undergrowth; and being in the middle of the ant swarm. The last is an astonishing thing in itself. The forest floor was alive with insects. The ants' invertebrate prey was rushing to escape, and birds were picking off the fleeing insects in a feeding frenzy. Being in the middle of all that is to inhabit a different world compared with sitting on a bench at a feeding station.

For me, being in what I think of as a wild place does matter. Forget the fine distinctions, it all comes down to taste and preference. As long as I am fit enough, I will enjoy the experience of birding in old growth forest, on remote mountain slopes and in lowland swamps, whether or not I see the target birds, in spite of the fact that discomfort is almost certainly an essential part of this experience (see Chapter 3). As a species, we left the wild behind or tamed it in pursuit of our security and our comfort. Mostly, when we get really close to nature, it is uncomfortable. It is also unpredictable, including with respect to what birds we will encounter. This, to me, is one of its attractions.

But also, for these very reasons, I'll spend some of my time in other, less-than-wild places where I can still see wild birds – indeed, where I probably have a better chance, especially if I am looking for something in particular for my list. I mean, I am a birder as well as a nature lover. I value both nature and my list (and I also appreciate some home comforts now and again).

And although I express a preference about 'being in the wild', I don't harbour too many illusions about it. My experience of pristine forest is often as much manufactured for me as is the experience of seeing hand-fed antpittas. The Rufous-crowned Antpitta was there for me to see only because the landowner had looked after the forest, had encouraged the bird to stay and, perhaps, had got it accustomed to human presence. He could tell us where to find the bird and he had cut the trails through the forest to allow us to get there. And we were in that forest in the first place because he had advertised the site through birders' networks. During our visit, we sampled the chocolate from his factory, and we all bought some to take home. That bird, as well as being a wild bird in its natural habitat, was a commercial asset, as long as it could be induced to stay around.

As birders, we are part of a complex web of activity that entails human intervention in, including profiting from, the lives of wild creatures. Sometimes our birding takes us to places that look and feel like undisturbed, unspoilt ecosystems. Sometimes this is just an illusion, even upfront a fake, an imitation, a reconstruction. In an age of extinctions, artificially preserved wild places are also artificially stocked with rapidly vanishing wildlife. When we get to these places, feeding stations often offer great views and good photographic opportunities. Constructing authenticity in whatever sense we choose, individually or according to rules adopted by the birding community, is itself part of the many ways we navigate our interactions with nature-in-decline in the modern world.

CHAPTER 15

Rarities

When I first read the phrase 'common where found' in a birding field guide, I fell about laughing. Common already means you can easily find it, surely, so what does 'where found' add? Is the bird common or rare? But leaving aside its mild absurdity, the phrase is interesting (and also turns out to make a lot of sense) because it hints at the complexities and subtleties of rarity, both as a state of being in nature and also as a human construct.

Rare birds make up many of the mega targets of a birder, but just what bestows this rarity value? It tells us something about the things that make birders the creatures they are to unravel why they cherish and chase rarities. Rarity is not the only object of desire, of course. Asked to name 'birds of the trip', a group of birders after three weeks of travel and hundreds of sightings will draw up a list comprising (in varying combinations) the rarest; the most beautiful and spectacular (awesome, graceful, colourful, bizarre); the cutest; the best close-up view; and one that took a member of the group past 7,000 on their life list (quite probably it was a 'common where found' LBJ).

But rarity is my focus here. Let's begin with the semantics. A common expression we use to convey rarity is 'few and far between'. As a starting definition it can't be bettered. If you are watching the passing traffic, cars striped like a zebra are going to be very few and far between (both in time and space) – that is, rare. In the population of cars, they occur at a very low density. Low density is an observed phenomenon in nature as well – many species of plants, animals and other organisms have evolved in this way. If we do a survey of living things in a few square kilometres of any tropical forest, a list of species will emerge that will comprise a group that are abundant and a much larger group of species that are less common, including some that are very scarce. This is a consequence of many different evolutionary circumstances and pressures, a fact of nature.[71]

Actually, we don't know all the reasons for rarity, and multiple interacting factors are at play. For example, carnivorous apex predators will be among the rarities in our survey. Apex predators are limited in population by the size and density of the populations of their prey. Some predators also self-regulate their breeding behaviour to manage their population size

71 Eric Dinerstein, *The Kingdom of Rarities*, Washington DC: Island Press, 2013.

in order to maximize prey availability to their offspring. Many predators set up territories and fiercely defend them against competing members of the same species, or sometimes members of other species with similar prey demands. This also regulates population size and density. Predator territories can be quite large; hence individuals (or maybe family groups of individuals) are few and far between. Similar types of dynamics, with a whole lot of different mechanisms at play, can show how interactions between all species and their food sources (which are often specialized) might produce self-reinforcing cycles of either abundance or rarity.

Eagles are apex predators, but not all eagles are considered equally rare. There are more Golden Eagles (around 250,000 worldwide) than Gurney's Eagles, for example, because the former occupies a range that covers several continents, whereas the latter is restricted to New Guinea and neighbouring islands. On eBird, there are over 170,000 reports of sightings of Golden Eagle and only 307 of Gurney's Eagle (doubtless, fewer birders in New Guinea help account for this). Many archipelagos and isolated islands, such as Madagascar and Sulawesi as well as New Guinea, have their own endemic species of raptors which are very few in total number because of range restriction, as well as being far between within this range. The Madagascan Fish Eagle, for example, is normally described as very rare (also around 300 sightings on eBird).

These island species of birds of prey, which are less numerous than ones that range across continents, tell us something more general about rarity, namely that isolation is a major factor. Geography is critical to understanding rarity. Isolation is a major driver of speciation and can occur on islands, on mountain tops, in valleys and so on. Isolation is not a matter only of distance but also of the nature of the barriers that prevent populations from mingling together as they evolve. Wide rivers such as the Amazon can isolate one species from another, if the birds are loth to fly across water. Birds are ancient species, so volcanic activity, land erosion, continental drift, climate change, rising and falling sea levels and so on have all played their part in speciation, making and unmaking barriers and islands, shifting populations apart and sometimes bringing them back together.

Isolated populations of birds that evolve into distinct species may, simply for reasons of geography, be small in size, whether or not the individuals occur far between in their habitat. They may, indeed, be 'common where found'. On tiny Norfolk Island, stuck out in the middle of the South

Madagascan Fish Eagle

Pacific (Chapter 18), two of the endemic island species are the unimaginatively named Norfolk Island Parakeet and Norfolk Island Gerygone. The first is one of the rarest birds on the island (maybe even less than a hundred); the second is one of the commonest, with a population of as many as 10,000. This Gerygone is certainly 'common where found'. But Norfolk Island is only 35 km^2 and the Gerygone is found nowhere else. We might want to call that 'rare' but, if so, it is simply in the sense that the single, relatively small population is very isolated, not that the individual birds seem to be either few or far between, nor hard to find once on the island.

Islands of isolated habitat occur on land as well. The Stresemann's Bush-Crow comprises a population estimated at around 9,000 breeding pairs and is restricted in range to an area of about 6,000 km^2 in the Borana region of Southern Ethiopia, surrounding the town of Yabello. There is no immediately apparent difference between its habitat and in the many thousands of square kilometres surrounding, where the bird is absent. But this patch of savanna has a cooler, drier and more seasonal climate due to topography. Hatchlings of the Bush-Crow are adapted to this climate but cannot survive in the adjacent areas' higher temperatures.[72]

Having reached Borana, you need to go to a bit more trouble to find the Bush-Crow than in the case of the Norfolk Gerygone, but they turn up often enough if you drive through the landscape. The human residents of the region doubtless think they are pretty common. In fact, the bird is recently getting less so. In addition to pressures on the savanna bushland ecology from a growing human population, the species' survival is vulnerable to climate change. Birders may be well advised to put this bird on their bucket list, it may well be about to get a lot rarer.

All species that are small in number and found in one spot are especially vulnerable to extinction. Small, isolated populations may have very low genetic diversity, which can be a vulnerability in itself, although this is perhaps less important than the threats arising

Stresemann's Bush-Crow, Yabello, Ethiopia

72 Paul F. Donald *et al.*, 'The restricted range of the Ethiopian Bush-Crow *Zavattariornis stresemanni* is a consequence of high reliance on modified habitats within narrow climatic limits', *Journal of Ornithology*, vol. 153, 2012, pp.1031–1044.

from external factors, such as an extreme weather event, invasive species (including a new pathogen) and climate change. One event could summon the death knoll. A recent case is the Cozumel Thrasher, which has not been seen for a number of years, although it was once quite common on the island of Cozumel, off the coast of Yucatan in eastern Mexico. Hurricanes in 1988 and 1995 devastated its preferred habitat, and sightings after those dates were very few. The last (unconfirmed) sighting was in 2006. Ornithological authorities have not yet declared the species extinct – it might just turn up one day, although hope is almost gone. Other factors must also have been at play, such as the impact of invasive species, as hurricanes have always been common on Cozumel. But either way, it was the isolation and small size of this single population of the species that was its critical vulnerability.

Nothing is rarer than the last surviving member of a species. In this age of extinctions, 'rare' with respect to wild creatures is now pretty much synonymous in most peoples' minds with 'going extinct'. If you do a web browser search for 'rare birds', what pops up is not a list of birds that are rare as a result of evolution over many millennia, but of birds that are declining in numbers (and facing extinction) due to relatively recent human activity – hunting, habitat destruction, invasive species and so on. A recent publication titled *The World's Rarest Birds* is a lavishly illustrated volume of those species that are closest to extinction worldwide, with scant, if any, mention of reasons for rarity other than the impact of humans.[73]

Although species with small, isolated populations are especially vulnerable to the impacts of humans, some extinct species were neither few nor far between before they were driven to extinction, as the notorious case of the Passenger Pigeon illustrates.[74] Millions used to live in North America across a wide range. They were hunted to extinction at the end of the 19th century because they were viewed as a pest – they would descend on orchards like locusts and demolish them – and because they provided good sport. In a few years, this species went from very abundant to rare to extinct. A number of bird species with rapidly declining populations today were also once very numerous.

The benchmark for rarity in this sense is the IUCN Red List and its categorization of species into: 'Of Least Concern'; 'Near Threatened'; Vulnerable'; 'Endangered'; 'Critically Endangered' and 'Extinct'.[75] Just to pick one example, the Sumatran Ground-Cuckoo (listed as Critically Endangered) was probably always rare compared with some other species in its shrinking lowland forests. Ground-cuckoos tend to be relatively low-density species, but the Sumatran species is now much rarer because of human destruction of nearly all of its forest habitat. Growing hunting pressure also plays a big part. It is estimated that at most there are only 250 left in the wild, in isolated forest pockets. Even once-common species in the same forests, such as the Sumatran Leafbird, are facing threats of extinction (on the Red List it is classed as Vulnerable). In this case, trapping for the cage bird trade is a key factor – in Sumatra today you are perhaps just as likely to see this and other species in a cage on someone's front porch, or in the bird market, as in the forest.[76]

Rarity as a result of a vanishing population is perhaps the gold standard of rarity value for a birder. After all, if I don't get to see it soon, I never will. And if it's so rare that it

73 Erik Hirschfeld *et al.*, *The World's Rarest Birds*, Princeton, NJ: Princeton University Press, 2013.

74 Erroll Fuller, *The Passenger Pigeon*, Princeton, NJ: Princeton University Press, 2014.

75 International Union for the Conservation of Nature, *Red List of Threatened Species* (online resource).

76 Muhammad Iqbal et al., 'Now you see them, now you don't: how representative are field surveys when most birds are caged? A case study from the lower montane forests of southern Sumatra, Indonesia', *Birding Asia*, vol. 33, June 2020, pp.19–24.

hasn't been seen for decades, the chance of rediscovering it is a birder's nirvana. Birders and ornithologists can be driven into a frenzy in their efforts to track down such 'Lazarus species', as the case of the Night Parrot in Australia amply demonstrates.[77] Once seen quite frequently in the 19th century by European settlers in the outback, the Night Parrot disappeared from view as these settlers transformed the landscape with their roaming livestock. The Night Parrot is elusive, mostly feeding at night and it is easily misidentified from fleeting glimpses in the gloom. The search for firm evidence of its whereabouts became the holy grail for generations of bushmen, bird lovers and scientists, spawning many tall tales, false alarms, jealous disputes and broken reputations. The cast of characters involved in the quest was, to say the least, colourful. The antics of some of them and the dramas of the quest regularly made the news. Its rediscovery quite recently in remote Queensland caused a minor media sensation (and yet another spectacularly damaged reputation).[78]

Our understanding of just how rare a bird is, or whether it is extinct, depends on someone seeing it and counting it. This hints at another feature of the phenomenon of rarity, of particular relevance to birders: as I hinted in the case of the Gurney's Eagle, rarity is in an important sense always relative to an observer and in part a function of the number of observers and observations. The more ornithologists and birders who are recording in particular locations, the less rare the birds in those places may seem to be, because there will be more records. In addition, the more elusive or cryptic a bird, the fewer times it will be observed so, again, the rarer it will seem.

Indeed, from a birder's perspective, rare birds are the ones they are the least likely to see, unless they go to an awful lot of trouble. I have already mentioned the Sumatran Ground-Cuckoo, now very rare indeed because most of its habitat has been destroyed. It is also very elusive, creeping through the undergrowth of gloomy lowland forests, so it is hard to see even if it is encountered, as I learnt to my chagrin: we dipped on the bird when birding in Sumatra, as it circled around us close by, calling, without showing itself. Indeed, the likelihood of encountering a bird, rather than the actual size of its population or its distribution is, for birders, the key consideration. And once we define 'rare' in these terms, a whole new universe of rare birds arises – and others that might seem to be objectively rare become less so.

While staying in Vancouver in 2018, I was a bit taken aback at the interest aroused by the appearance of a Great-tailed Grackle on a piece of waste ground in the city. The local birders' online bulletin boards were crackling with excitement as people posted their 'rare bird alerts'. As I soon discovered, this was the first recording of the species for Vancouver. Now, there is no way the Great-tailed Grackle is a rare bird in the greater scheme of things, but it is clearly very rare in Vancouver. Great-tailed Grackles are common in all sorts of habitats from Peru north to California. Most birders in those parts of the world probably consider them trash birds. They are not for the most part migratory, except in the far north of their range. They are considered a vagrant in Canada.

In this case, it was not the bird that was rare, but its encounter with Vancouver birders on their home patch. The Grackle was a 'local rarity'. Birders classify individual members of a common species which are vagrants as rare because they don't normally occur on their local patch. In fact, vagrancy and the appearance of 'accidentals' is a regular feature in nature, not only due to longer-term range expansion but more often because migratory birds now and again get blown off-course or take a wrong turn.

77 Another example is the New Zealand Petrel – see Chapter 6.

78 Penny Olsen, *Night Parrot*, Clayton South, Victoria: CSIRO Publishing, 2018.

Local vagrancy events are always headline news items for the birding community. The ABA podcast's first item of business is always the 'rare bird segment', when notable records of birds-in-unexpected-places are read out – a 'first recording for North Carolina…' and so on. This may be another case where it seems as if the list is more important than the bird (see Chapter 13). They don't announce sightings of rare birds like the Whooping Crane, which is one of the rarest birds on the continent (250 remaining in the wild, at most), unless it is also in the wrong place.

Likewise, the Hong Kong Bird Watching Society Bulletin has a section recording the monthly rare bird sightings in the Territory. A committee of the wise solemnly and meticulously tries to validate each sighting. They are a cautious, even suspicious, lot – many claims are rejected; but then, some of them are reinstated once a confirmed sighting of the same species is made at a later date. The biggest headline is for the 'new to Hong Kong' bird, more noteworthy for some than the annual appearance at Mai Po marshes of a handful of critically endangered, globally rare, Spoon-billed Sandpipers on migration. And, of course, the 'newness' is a record of a new observation, not necessarily a first occurrence.

I once saw a Varied Thrush in New York's Central Park; indeed, I took most of a day out of my sightseeing itinerary to find it. Its appearance had made headlines in the *New York Times*, no less. The Varied Thrush is a common bird in the north-west of North America and in winter it migrates down the west coast, some individuals as far as north-west Mexico, but mostly over relatively short distances and into lower altitudes. Occasionally, birds turn up in the USA east of the Rockies (in Central Park, for example). The Varied Thrush has even been found in the UK, the first recording being in Cornwall in 1982.[79] In that same winter an unusually high number of North American visiting rarities (including the American Robin, one of North America's most common birds) caused great excitement by popping up in the British Isles, due most likely to the weather conditions.

A (not at all rare) Varied Thrush, Vancouver

79 S.C. Madge *et al.*, 'Varied Thrush: New to the Western Palearctic,' *British Birds*, vol. 83, 1990, pp.187–195.

The appearance of good numbers of migrating vagrants or accidentals happens every year in the UK, which is well-placed to pick up a whole host of off-course migrating birds, both from east and west. The sheer variety of surprising visitors has produced a whole branch of modern birding, commonly labelled 'twitching'. Twitchers will drop everything to fly or motor to the far corners of the British Isles to see a rare vagrant. Many of these birds make landfall on the fringes of the UK – Scilly Isles, Shetland, Cornwall – and twitchers will make a mad cross-country dash to get a glimpse before the bird in question disappears off the map. Most drop out of sight as quickly as they appeared because they don't survive for long, being exhausted and facing an alien environment. There's something macabre about wanting to witness an impending demise before it's too late, but the twitcher's purpose in all of this (aside from adding excitement to their lives) is to get these local rarities on their list of birds seen in the UK.

Twitchers tend to have a bad press in the popular image and are frowned upon by some other birders.[80] It's never much appealed to me, I have to say, but it's all pretty harmless in the bigger picture. Visiting the UK from Hong Kong and out with a local birder in Norfolk, the main target was to find a Pallas's Leaf Warbler that was known to have arrived, way off-course on migration, at a local birding hotspot. To me, it was something of a ho-hum moment, because they are a common migrating bird in Hong Kong. Without wishing to lump all birders who get excited by a local rarity, such as this stray warbler or the Grackle in Vancouver, into the category of mad twitcher, the same underlying factor is at play in causing the excitement: not rarity itself, but rarity value measured by the number of prior local sightings in that locality and, in consequence, the fact that it was a new bird for the local birders' lists.

At the same time, I agree that ornithologically speaking, the arrival of these local rarities is interesting and noteworthy, so there may be good reason to get excited. In the case of the leaf warbler, if the incidence of annual sightings of this species grows significantly each year, it may suggest that a subpopulation has found a new way to thrive, by taking the 'wrong turn' on migration and yet still managing to get through the wintering season and to find the way back to their breeding site. More generally, trends in such sightings can also be important data in showing the effects of climate change in a particular species' range, including perhaps the Grackle. However, I venture to suggest that most twitchers are not primarily driven by ornithological curiosity.

There is another category of rarities for birders that can be defined by how frequently *they* visit the places where a species can be seen. Accessibility and remoteness are at play here. Not only birders, but also ornithologists suffer from the torment of not being able to access a place where little-known and never-seen birds exist. We might label them as 'rare' just for this reason, even if when we got there, we were to find them abundant. The Foja Mountains in New Guinea are uninhabited and practically inaccessible. Visits by western explorers and scientists have been very few. Members of recent expeditions have discovered a new species of honeyeater and been the first to see the rarely encountered Berlepsch's Six-wired Bird-of-Paradise doing its courtship dance. Neither were particularly hard to find around the expedition campsite, particularly as many of them showed no fear of humans.[81]

Around 30 bird species are endemic to the Andaman and Nicobar Islands, which are Indian territories not far off the coast of Indonesian Sumatra. One can visit the main

80 Melissa Manyntz, 'What is a Twitcher?', *The Spruce*, July 2019.

81 Dinerstein, op. cit. pp.30–32.

Andaman island but others in the archipelago are off-limits for all but a very few who get Indian government permission (being a birder on its own doesn't qualify, for some reason). The endemics on those islands are tantalisingly out of reach, among the ultimate rarities on a world birder's wanted list.

The accessibility factor highlights most clearly the birder's 'list value' definition of rarity. Birds in remote places are especially desirable as additions to the list because these are the ones that are going to comprise the gaps and leftovers after just about everything else has been seen. It's very easy to see the Norfolk Gerygone if you go to Norfolk Island, but most birders might leave Norfolk Island until pretty late in their birding career, or maybe never get there at all (life is too short): there are plenty of other places to visit that will produce more new birds before heading for distant, remote Norfolk Island. But at some point, the really dedicated lister has to go there.

Remoteness from birders' normal haunts is best illustrated in the case of seabirds. Some, such as petrels and prions, roam widely in the oceans most of the year and nest on a few remote, rocky islands (sometimes in their tens or hundreds of thousands). Some species are relatively few in number and distinguished as species by the very fact that they only breed on a particular oceanic rocky outcrop. Others are far more numerous. Either way, we have to go a very long way (on a boat, to boot) into the middle of nowhere to be sure to find them. We rarely make such journeys, hence the rarity of our sightings.

In sum, 'local rarity', 'rarity value' and 'common where found' make most sense as observers' constructs of rarity. They describe the rarity or otherwise of encounters rather than the objective rarity of the bird itself. Rarity is not simply a fixed, quantitative concept. What is rare for you may not be rare for me. But surely, 'going extinct' is as hard and fast, as objectively rare, as you can get – there is something absolute and finite about rarity in this sense. Yet the concept of rarity as the chance of an encounter with birders, rather than as an objective measure, gives pause for more thought in this case as well.

Somewhat ironically, more and more of the world's rarest species by the IUCN criteria are actually increasingly easy for birders to find (and common where found) precisely because they are rare. This is because their rarity gives rise to conservation efforts: captive breeding and reintroduction to the wild, supplementation of diet at known breeding sites and protection from human hunting and natural predation. Our visits to protected areas where they are being looked after are often encouraged as a source of support for the conservation efforts. The birder knows where to go to see the remaining populations and the local keepers know exactly where to take us, even if there are only a few hundred individual birds to be found.

Birders more and more visit places where birds that are on the brink of extinction are being looked after in the hope of saving them. They go extinction birding. They know where to go and, when they get there, the birds are often easy to find. An example is the Asian Crested Ibis, a bird that is routinely seen by birders on some Chincse birding tours despite the fact that the population in the wild is only around 500. Active protection coupled with captive breeding and reintroduction are keeping this population going. In fact, it is now increasing as a result of these efforts. Once widespread across North East Asia, the Asian Crested Ibis became almost extinct in the wild, apart from a surviving population in a small area in Shaanxi Province of China in the Qinling Mountains, which was rediscovered in 1981. The species feeds in paddy fields and nests in pine forests. When we visited, we

Asian Crested Ibis, Shaanxi, China

encountered a large group perched in their roost trees, obviously unfussed by our presence. All were ringed and apparently well looked after; so were we (well looked after, that is) in the accommodation provided in the nearby village.

Not all extinction birding is as easy as this, although more and more of it is getting easier. The Asian Crested Ibis once upon a time seems not to have been all that rare, but a close relation, the Giant Ibis, was probably never abundant within its range in Indochina. It is now near to extinction (estimated total population in 2012 was about 350 birds) due to habitat loss and hunting, and it is found only in Cambodia and southern Laos. Nature protection and conservation in these countries is not nearly so well resourced or managed as in China. Population numbers are still thought to be in decline.

Through the good offices of the Sam Veasna Centre in Siem Reap (see Chapter 8), birders can visit a lodge where local people monitor the birds in that vicinity and protect them against hunting. But still, finding the Giant Ibis is not as easy as the Asian Crested Ibis. It took us, with the help of a village guide, one dusk excursion and two early morning treks to find a pair on their roosting tree at dawn, before they flew over the plains in search of distant swamps and hollows. This bird is rare in every sense – uncommon where found, critically endangered with a population in the hundreds, and pretty hard to find. But still, because it is rare and for this reason is being looked after (to the extent feasible), the determined birder can generally get to see it.

Rarity in all things is something that humans have always coveted and prized. All birders are caught up in the thrill of seeing a rare bird, whether it is a first-record grackle on a piece of waste ground in the local patch or a critically endangered ibis on the wooded grassland plains of Northern Cambodia, magically appearing in the dawn light. Most of the images in this chapter are trophies from my own rare bird encounters – fruits of my pursuit of birds that are variously by nature few and far between; once common where found, but now vanishing; hard to find because they are elusive; found only in remote places; or encountered where they should not be found.

Giant Ibis at dawn, Northern Plains, Cambodia

The 'Critically Endangered' meaning of rarity is the one that should grab most of our attention. In many places (like in Indonesia's lowland forests), hunting, trapping and the wildlife trade are now among the biggest threats. Some economists used to advance a theory that 'trophy species' (like tigers) would rarely be hunted or fished to extinction in the wild, because the cost of so doing would increase dramatically the closer to zero the population became. Then some other economists turned this theory on its head, demonstrating with a different logic (and using evidence) that as the population numbers diminished, the 'trophy value' dramatically increased, meaning even more money and effort were invested to catch the final wild specimens (extinction being the dismal endpoint).

Trophy species (see also Chapter 16) are status goods whose value is wrapped up in subjective meanings and identity (in the case of hunting trophies, in such things as masculinity and wealth). Birders who wish to add rare birds to their lists for their rarity value are in one sense like trophy hunters who shoot tigers in the wild and hang their skins on the wall. But of course, they are fundamentally different in that they do not try to kill the birds they find. Hopefully, instead they contribute to the survival of rarities by providing support and incentives for protection. If birders rather than the hunters or trappers are the trophy hunters, the dismal logic may be reversed.

In the case of the Sam Veasna Centre in Cambodia, significant revenue comes from running guided tours for birders to see the Giant Ibis, and much of this revenue ends up with the local villagers that help protect these species. In a recent (June 2020) edition of the journal *Birding Asia*, the Chairman of the Oriental Birding Club raised the alarm that, with the termination in 2020 of overseas travel due to the COVID-19 pandemic, the local conservation efforts had lost a major source of funding, further throwing the future of the species into doubt.

When a birding tour company advertises a special trip to see a very rare bird, the prospective customers, eager to get a hand on the trophy, line up. I once asked a guide how it felt always to be confronting habitat loss and looming extinctions, on a daily basis.

He gave me an odd look: maybe he had mixed feelings about extinction birding. As a bird lover, he shares the dismay of observing the potential decline of species richness. At the same time, the growing number of critically endangered birds in ever diminishing habitats is good for business, as it means a higher premium for his knowledge of where to find them and for his skills in succeeding.

Many professional birding guides invest considerable effort in scouting new sites where such birds are accessible to the birder. In the process, some make important discoveries of new populations, perhaps even new taxa to add to the checklist. Such discoveries are often followed by efforts to protect the population. Often, a certain amount of secrecy is advised in advertising its whereabouts (that is, until measures have been put in place to secure and protect the birds). Publicizing the location for other birders also attracts the trapper seeking to turn a profit in the caged bird trade – indeed, eBird has protocols to deal with this possibility.

Birding intersects with and affects the natural world in various, often paradoxical, ways. The professional birders who scout the field and make these discoveries are contributing to science, advancing their business interests, encouraging conservation and providing a valuable service to people like me, who egg them on in our quest for birding trophies. Hopefully, this is a virtuous circle. By placing value on rarities as living creatures, rather than as trophies in a glass cabinet, we may be helping to avert the endpoint of the dismal logic of trophy-hunting, even if, in some cases, what remains is an impoverished, pale imitation of how nature once was, now preserved in enclaves and fragments for our benefit as well as for the benefit of the birds. But such is the one of the better outcomes for nature in the Anthropocene.

CHAPTER 16

Trophy Birds

To a birder, all species of bird are equal in one important respect: they each have the same value as an entry on the life list. But in other respects, birders do discriminate, albeit in ways that make sense only to them. The most basic form of discrimination is between birds we have already seen and those that are lifers – new birds, never before encountered. The excitement of a lifer is something only birders experience when a bird comes into sight. A rare, elusive bird that poses a particularly tough challenge for the birder is often referred to as a 'mega'. Often these birds are also spectacular, like a bird-of-paradise, but this need not be the case – some may be just LBJs. Every mega, regardless of appearance, is prized like a trophy.

I have a number of trophy birds on my list and I am not averse to bragging about them when conversation with other birders turns that way. Often, it is the circumstance of the sighting as much as the charisma of the bird that confers the bragging rights. One such in my own case is the Gurney's Pitta, a spectacularly beautiful bird even for a pitta, all of which are gorgeous. It is now considered to be extinct in Thailand, but a population still exists in Myanmar, albeit seriously threatened by habitat loss.

For a number of years, the Thai population survived in very small numbers at Khao Nor Chuchi, near Krabi in southern Thailand. Its forest refuge was nearly all cleared (mainly for palm oil plantations) by 2011 when we visited and were fortunate to find a calling bird in the tiny forest reserve that remained. By then, this bird may have been the only known surviving male of the Thai population. Two females from a successful breeding event in 2008 were last seen in 2014, which is when the male was also last sighted.[82]

In previous years, birders wanting to see any of the remaining birds would visit a local farmer, who hand-fed the pittas and would entice them to appear out of the forest for a fee (often followed into the birder's line of site by the beaters, who had helped urge the birds to the feeding station). Our encounter was not manufactured in this way. We came across it while it was engaged in what seemed to be a territorial singing contest with a nearby Malayan Banded-Pitta, which was also in view, across the other side of the trail.

82 Philip Round, 'Gurney's Pitta in Thailand – from rediscovery to extinction in just 28 years,' *Natural History Bulletin of the Siam Society*, vol. 60, no. 1, 2014, pp.3–8.

The disappearing Gurney's Pitta, Khao Nor Chuchi, Thailand, 2011

Apparently, one of the surviving Gurney Pitta females during this time period cross-bred with a member of this closely related species.

Hardcore birders will expend huge amounts of time, expense and effort to try to collect such trophies. Sometimes this involves a special trip, just to see that special bird. This was not the case with the Gurney's Pitta, as the trip in question was seeking to see many other birds in that part of Thailand, at a number of different sites. We did not have especially high expectations for the Pitta, but we were ecstatic to come across it during our walk through that patch of forest.

But many trophy bird expeditions are very much focused on finding just one particular species, surviving in an isolated population in some remote inaccessible location. I have already described one, the Tragopan trek, in Chapter 4. The two I focus on here are both in Australia: first, the Black Grasswren and second, the Orange-bellied Parrot. The former is a charismatic member of the grasswren (*Amytornis*) genus in the family of Australasian Wrens, all of which are little gems. It is listed as Near Threatened by the IUCN on its Red List due to its restricted range and threats to its habitat. The latter is a member of the *Neophema* genus of Old World Parrots, all of them Australian, and it is Critically Endangered. It is perilously close to extinction and a leading symbol of the country's extinction crisis due to regular media reporting on the heroic efforts being taken to bring it back from the brink. It helps, too, that the bird is a little stunner. For several years now, the population surviving in the wild has been hovering around 50 individuals. For the birder, rarity of this kind sets up a desperate race against time. Dare I say it, but if the species were to go extinct in the wild, my trophy would not dull, but shine brighter.

Remoteness and inaccessibility were factors in heightening the challenge in each of these two cases. Fortunately for us, modern technology helped us out. Both expeditions – if that is the right word – involved boarding aeroplanes with not nearly enough propellers

and heading for a remote landing strip in the outback. Both were part of organized birding trips, offered as 'optional extensions' to a longer tour (principally because they added a considerable amount to the overall cost).

On the trip that climaxed with finding the Grasswren, we had progressed by stages down the highway from Darwin in the Northern Territory to Kununurra, just over the Western Australia border. From there, our extension was a relatively short hop up onto the Mitchell Plateau. We were joined by some other birders who had made the long flight north from Melbourne just for the rare chance to see this one bird (such was the charisma of this bird and such, also, was the reputation of our guide for hitting his targets). It was nice to know that I wasn't the maddest one on that plane.

Not only did we have to get on a plane (only one propeller) and alight on a rough-and-ready, dusty landing strip, we then had to climb into a helicopter that lifted us up onto the

Mitchell Plateau proper. Up there is a camping site, which is also accessible by four-wheel drive – but it takes days to drive in, hence the aeroplane and the helicopter. We took off from Kununurra early, into a sky that was tinged pink with the dawn. Below, the landscape looked like a Cezanne painting in the early morning haze. The helicopters were waiting at the landing strip, it all went very smoothly, and we were soon clambering over the rocky landscape in search of our bird.

According to trip reports, the tension is always high as birders head for sites where the Black Grasswren is known to occur. Each year there are likely to be bush fires and known territories are burnt out, reducing the population or driving the birds to new areas. We were fortunate. After a 40-minute scramble over the rocky terrain, we found a pair. Their appearance is handsome if understated, with chestnut mantles, the male a black chest and belly and the female chestnut all over, except for a pale throat and black head and tail. Both male and female display striking white striations flowing from the forehead down the nape and across the throat and upper breast. When excited, they show off with duets, posing together in full view and flying from rock to rock. We got the full show.

There were some other goodies up there as well, including the regionally endemic Kimberley Honeyeater and a very smart subspecies of Partridge Pigeon, distinguished by its yellow face, rather than the red face of the lowland bird. We were a happy band as we clambered into the helicopters to be taken down the escarpment to our waiting plane. That was what I call a good day's birding.

Grasswrens have their own Facebook page for birder fans, with around 1,500 members. They are all inhabitants of the Australian outback and the biggest trophy for a birder is to have seen all 15 of them (tantalizingly, the number keeps growing as more taxonomic

Black Grasswrens

Short-tailed Grasswren

research is done, resulting in splits). To tick them all off you would have to travel a serious number of outback kilometres, into some really remote places, and it is the ambition of many hardcore Australian birders to do just that.

The lure of grasswrens is such that, not only was I eager to go on this mad dash, but also, on my own, I later spent a week in distant, remote Mount Isa, a mining town in Queensland, to look for two others – I was fortunate to see them both. On the morning that I found the Carpentarian Grasswren, in the middle of nowhere down a mining road, I bumped into that same guy from Melbourne who had boarded our plane on the Black Grasswren trip some years earlier. I later read his Facebook post – it took him and his two companions another six or seven hours to find the bird. That's what grasswrens do to you.

I was also crazy enough in 2019 to go on a seven-day, 3,500-km trip down the dirt roads of the outback of South Australia, Queensland and New South Wales (in the midst of one of the worst droughts in written records) to try to see six more of them. I bagged five. One of them, the Short-tailed Grasswren, has one of the least apt names of any bird – look at that tail; but then go and check out the other grasswrens, which have even longer ones. That these grasswrens were still out there, despite the extreme conditions and the threats these posed to their existence, was somehow a hopeful sign. They are clearly tough little Ozzie battlers: trophy birds, all of them.[83]

Despite the allure of the Grasswren, I might just give my trip to see another Australian battler the pride of place in my virtual trophy cabinet. This adventure was another optional add-on with the same intrepid birding guide who took us to the Black Grasswren site, this time on a trip to see all of Tasmania's endemics. The destination was the remote, isolated Tasmanian south-west wilderness, where the last Orange-bellied Parrots hang on at their one remaining breeding site. The birds breed on heathland, where they feed on button grass and build nests in small copses.

83 For more on my grasswren adventures, check out my blog: http://anthropocenebirder.com

Only a bit bigger than a budgie, Orange-bellied Parrots migrate north after the breeding season, up the west coast of Tasmania and across stormy Bass Strait, wintering on salt marshes and paddocks in southern Victoria (they used to range further afield in mainland Australia, but not anymore). Up to the mid-20th century, the Orange-bellied Parrot was not uncommon in its range, experiencing good breeding success. Then, the population declined catastrophically for reasons that are not entirely clear but include destruction and fragmentation of habitat combined with trapping and predation on the winter feeding grounds.

The breeding site is accessible by a long trek into the south-west wilderness, for which tents and survival gear are necessary – but fortunately there is also a landing strip. Melaleuca was the home for 50 years of Deny King (1909–1991), miner and naturalist, who built a house there, worked the tin mines and studied the local flora and fauna. His mining unearthed fossil remains of an extinct Banksia species, *Banksia kingii*, and he discovered several new living plant species including a Protea, often known as King's Holly. He also played a key part in preserving the breeding habitat of the Orange-bellied Parrot. His property and surrounding landscape are now part of the Southwest National Park and the Tasmanian Wilderness World Heritage Area.

The day before we were due to fly to Melaleuca, we got a call from the charter company to say that the prospects were not good due to gale-force winds. Later, we heard that the winds might drop by mid-day, allowing for a safe flight. We were lucky and got the thumbs-up at the last minute. On this occasion, we had two propellers so, despite the weather conditions, I was quietly confident. We pitched and bumped as we flew laboriously west into the teeth of the gale. Down below, we saw evidence of the logging of old growth forests wrought by the state-run forestry authority, a conservation battleground over several decades. The landing strip came into view and we roller-coasted down in the buffeting gusts, banking at the last minute in a stomach-churning manoeuvre to hit the white gravel and skid to a halt.

A permanent staff of conservationists is present at Melaleuca in the breeding season, stocking the feeding stations, checking the nest boxes and monitoring the parrots. Of course, in those circumstances we got close-up views of a good number (the first feeding stations were just off the end of the landing strip). We also came across groups of them feeding in the natural vegetation as we walked around. They are beautifully elegant little parrots, bright green and yellow, with blue in the wings and in a bar across the forehead. Males have a slightly larger orange belly patch than the females.

The bird's highly specialised habitat, its stubbornness to try new places and its hazardous migration route marks it down as a species whose adaptations seem to have led it down a blind alley to extinction. But undeniably, the proximate reason for its current dire straits is human disturbance and transformation of its habitat. More precisely, I should say that European human invasion is the cause of its troubles, starting in the 19th century; before that the bird seems to have lived in harmony for thousands of years with the aboriginal population and their lifestyle. Tasmanian Aboriginals, or Palawa, were extinguished as a distinct ethnic group on their own lands in the 19th century. Most contemporary historians describe this as a genocide, undertaken at the hands of the European settlers.

Knowing that our recent way of life and how we treat the natural world is the cause of the near-extinction of the Orange-bellied Parrot, the least we can do is to give the bird a helping hand.[84] As well as doing this for its own sake, publicity about the bird's fate,

84 *National Recovery Plan for the Orange-Bellied Parrot*, Australian Government Department of Environment, Land, Water and Planning, 2016.

Orange-bellied Parrot

Eastern Ground Parrot

including regular media reporting on the battle to save the species, raises public awareness of the extinction crisis in Australia, where nine birds have gone extinct since European settlement.

It is hard to describe the feeling of being in the presence of all the last remaining wild members of a species that is on the very brink of extinction in the wild – a sense of privilege, relief that we made it in time, and a good deal of sadness. In one sense, the Orange-bellied Parrot is no longer extant in the wild given that the nesting area is patrolled and that the survival of the species from year to year depends on the release of captive-bred birds. They do, however, struggle through the same cycles of migration and breeding in the wild that their ancestors have done for countless generations. But we could be in no doubt from visiting Melaleuca that the survivors now depend in part on humans to continue to exist and to reproduce. Birders are having to get used to a lot of this kind of birding in an age of extinctions, ostensibly in the bird's natural setting but, in reality, providing an experience much like going to the zoo. Birders' rules of what can be counted (Chapter 14) meant that I could legitimately add it to my list. But the triumph that this trophy celebrates, it has to be said, is bitter-sweet.

To remind me that this was a wild place, and that I saw some 'really' wild birds, I am thankful that we also saw some others out there, especially the Eastern Ground Parrot, another stunner (and a rarity) and, so far, seemingly thriving at Melaleuca without a helping hand. This species had eluded me for many a year despite several efforts to find it at a regular site on the mainland, not far south of Sydney on the eastern escarpment of the Great Dividing Range. It is on the Red List as 'Near Threatened' and this Melaleuca individual is also in my imaginary trophy cabinet.

CHAPTER 17

Birders and the Species Problem

I was in my living room in Canberra when a commotion in the bushes drew me to the window. A large, winter flock of small birds was passing through my garden. The small trees were alive with them, calling, hanging upside down on the branches, flitting back and forth, darting down to ground level and then to shelter in the bushes as the flock moved through. The spectacle of sound and movement was compelling, spellbinding. I dashed for my binoculars. What species were they? Could I add something to my garden list? I tried to fix on the birds one by one through my lens: Silvereye, fairywren, more Silvereye – was that a Yellow-rumped Thornbill? – another fairywren; then they were gone. I wished them back, not because I had perhaps missed a species, but because I had missed some of the fun

Silvereye in a rose bush

of the flock. I had done what all birders do: looked for the species, not just at the birds. And on this occasion, I regretted it.

Flocking is a form of bird behaviour that produces many spectacles, some much more dramatic than this, such as the sight and sound of a cacophonous mob of squawking Sulphur-crested Cockatoos launching themselves *en masse* from the top of a gum tree, swooping low overhead as if on a kamikaze mission; a skein of honking geese stretching across the sky as it passes majestically overhead; the explosion of a swarm of Common Starlings moving as one in a fluttering, zig-zagging phalanx over the rooftops, until settling again on TV aerials, rooftops and leafless winter trees.

A feeding flock of small passerines in a subtropical or tropical forest is one of the great birdwatching spectacles. I learnt this early as a birder, birding in the forest of Tai Po Kau in Hong Kong. I was off trail, clambering through the trees up a steep slope, when a multi-species flock suddenly appeared. So intent were they on feeding, they took no notice of my presence, passing within feet above and below my line of sight, some of them buzzing and flitting around my head. It was spellbinding, and I had the good sense on this occasion to leave the bins hanging and just to take in the sounds and the sights of the flock all around me.

Such flocks are a source of many of a birder's ticks in a forest. The appearance of a mixed flock containing 10, 20, 30 different species is a much-awaited moment of drama. Mostly still and quiet to our senses, the trees suddenly come alive as different species of bird, of different shapes, sizes and plumage, some near the ground, others in the lower story and yet others in the treetops, appear all around in a frenzy, darting through, calling, fluttering and furiously feeding on the disturbed insects. This is the birder's big moment, when eyes search frantically for signs of positive ID amidst the movements in the branches; when sharp-eyed fellow birders and the guide call out species names and others look desperately for a confirming glimpse; and when panic and fear take hold in case something special on the target list is missed, when it is actually there, in full view – but not in my bins, which are pointing at something else as it disappears behind the leaves.

Looking through the binoculars in this kind of situation often misses much of the spectacle, as in the case of my Silvereyes. It also doesn't guarantee identifying many of the individual birds, which flit in and out of the narrow field of vision offering only frustrating half-glimpses. Matching the challenge of compiling and completing the list, in other words, interferes with the pleasure of seeing the birds. It can even turn such pleasure into stress as it subjugates enjoying a visual and aural feast to the thirst for a tick. Watching a flock as a birder can be both a highpoint of the thrills of birding, but also the epitome of its disenchantments.

But for nearly all birders, I am sure, identifying species and listing are so much tied up with birding as an activity that all of the above simply misses the point. Birding is a challenge, so it ought to be a bit stressful; bird identification is a skill and requires study and practice, entailing all the satisfaction as well as the frustration of turning ignorance into knowledge, transitioning from novice to expert. The harder, the better. If it's just 'nature' that grabs you, leave your bins at home, take your deckchair into a grassy meadow, listen to the buzz of the bees and the trilling of the Song Sparrows, and doze off in the sunshine.

No one who is a birder has just chosen birds at random as their units of observation. So surely, we must like them for what they are? But if as a birder we reduce birds to two primary, complementary lists of species – the ones we have seen and the ones we have not – we are doing something that does not stem obviously from a love of birds, but from something else: the challenge of the chase and the lure of listing. Birds (rather than, say, butterflies or beetles) are the ideal subject for our quest to grow the list (or lists): accessible, ubiquitous and not so hard to differentiate and identify in the field as to make it an impossible task; not so many that the challenge of seeing a whole lot of them is infeasible, or so few that it is no longer a challenge; and so on.

Birds plainly fit the bill. Steam locomotives shared exactly these qualities in my youth (like birds, they also required one to be outdoors and to travel to new places). Before the perfection of field binoculars, for some bird enthusiasts the object of desire was birds' eggs, which also shared all the right features for nature lovers who liked identifying, collecting and cataloguing things. Egging is illegal these days and steam locomotives are nearly all gone, so we are left with birding.

There is nothing odd or unusual about having mixed motives, some of which might be a bit contradictory. It's just that listing can get in the way of looking at and appreciating birds for what they are. As I point out in other places in this book, most of the time birders don't actually look *at* birds, they look *for* bird species, because they are what comprise the list. Missing the spectacle of the flock in pursuit of the names of the individual species is just one way in which this focus, this point of view, can distract from what is in front of us. Another is that once we have got a reliable ID we hurry on in search of the next species, rather than linger and look more closely. We are clearly not so much interested in what the bird is doing and how it behaves as what it looks like and what it is called. Only if we are certain that there is nothing new for the list to be found within the field of vision can we relax enough actually to watch birds going about their lives, rather than look at them just to identify the species.

This depiction of what birders like doing is a bit of an exaggeration, of course. If we are looking for a special target bird to fill a gap in our list, most of us hope to see it in as much detail as possible as it goes about its business. We dwell on it, watch it feed, try to track it through the foliage or on the ground and really try to get acquainted with it. But I recall the time in China when a group of us found a pair of very rare Chinese Crested Terns, sitting quietly together in the shallows amidst a flock of other terns. The birds were distant, so the fieldscope was put to use. The first to look was a big lister for whom this was a target. He identified them speedily, punched the air in excitement and handed over the scope to the rest of us.

After we had all had taken our first quick glances so as to record the tick, most of us took extra, longer looks – the birds were preening, communing, enjoying the fresh water from a stream as it met the ocean, and generally having a nice quiet time. We stood around sharing our reflections on the birds and their behaviour. Our companion who had taken the first look stood by with a satisfied look but was not so keen to indulge in a second or third session at the fieldscope. He had got what he had come for. And there was a bit of him in all of us, because when someone spotted another bird of interest out on the mud, we quickly and eagerly turned the scope onto it.

One of the ironies of all of this is that our unit of observation, our fixation, the species, isn't actually a fixed object. Birds quite clearly know their own species when they encounter a member of it. But we can't 'know' like birds. For us, naming a species is a product of a classification system that taxonomists have imposed on the living world of avian variety.

Variety among birds comes in all sorts of wondrous, visible and not so visible forms – colour, size, habitat, song, call and behaviour, nesting, feeding, mating, flight and so on. Species are only one category which we might use to sort and classify these differences. Can a birdwatcher observe and appreciate all the dimensions of this variety without putting a species name to everything they look at? Yes, but only up to a point. Knowing the species is part of the homework as well as the fieldwork, and this homework can lead one down all sorts of paths of discovery, after which we may appreciate birds even more. Delving into the precise nature of the differences that identify species can be a fascination in itself and is one of the attractions of birding.

But lots of people who enjoy looking at birds actually do manage to get by without the compulsive urge to give everything its proper species name. Nearly all of us, birder or non-birder, get to know the correct common names of our most-often encountered backyard birds. Even more know the local, colloquial names. But for many bird lovers out with their dogs, it's good enough to say: 'Listen to that thrush!' or 'Look at that eagle!'. Everyday names like 'sparrow' or 'duck' get us a long way in appreciating the richness and variety of the world of birds. Being more scientific about the names we use is not a bad idea, but not always essential. The fact that terms like 'duck' and 'eagle' do roughly correspond to taxonomic categories like 'family' and 'genus' is important, but beside the point. Tennyson in his eponymous poem didn't have to name his eagle as a species or a genus (either in English or in Latin) for him to take in so much about it; nor do we in order to appreciate the poem and, as a result, acquire insights better to appreciate eagles.

Indeed, the biggest irony is that so similar in appearance and behaviour are many different species of eagle, sparrow, thrush, or tern that 'variety' ceases to be the right word at a certain point – or at least variety as it presents itself readily to the eye and to the ear. This is the kind of variety that best reveals itself in the library or museum, where drawers full of bird skins allow the ornithologist to take measurements and to look minutely at every feather; or that is evident in the test tube or Petrie dish, where laboratory scientists isolate DNA from samples; or that can be deciphered from the sonogram of the recording of a song.

As birders, we wouldn't end up bothering about some of the differences that exist if taxonomists didn't first tell us about them. In the field, many bird species are, to all intents and purposes, indistinguishable by their appearance and their song or, more precisely, the apparent differences are only small and very particular. The Chinese Crested Tern is mostly reliably distinguished from some other species of tern by the black tip to its yellow bill, but otherwise it is pretty much identical. For the birder, it is fortunate that this stands out to the eye.

Ironically, there are some differences that we can readily observe that do not register among the features that differentiate species. Some species include birds that are different morphs. For example, the Long-tailed Shrike is a handsome bird with a grey head, chestnut back, black and white wing feathers and white underparts. It also has the characteristic shrike's black mask over its face. But there is also a fairly common 'dusky' morph that is all iron grey and black. This melanistic variety only occurs in parts of the species' range. In my early edition of a field guide to the birds of Hong Kong, it is illustrated and named 'Dusky Shrike', but correctly not listed as a separate species (although it has been listed as such in the past, before taxonomists properly sorted it out). Melanism is a genetic mutation not uncommon in nature which, in the case of one subspecies of Long-tailed Shrike (*Lanus schach schach*), is relatively common in the population.

Much more common is sexual dimorphism, where the male and female of a species are very different in appearance. But this, too, is an incidental form of variety to the birder, even though the differences in appearance can be very dramatic, including plumage and size. Everyone who has visited an urban park or zoo knows how different the male Indian Peafowl is from the female (most know them by the popular name of 'Peacock'). But of course, birders have to take note of this form of variety because we can tick a species from seeing either male or female. But it is only one tick: the species is the only difference that matters to us.

Habitat and food types are an important distinguishing feature among some near-identical species. Sometimes, given that speciation is strongly influenced by isolation, it is the geographic location that can be the key piece of information, as many look-alike, closely related species tend to be geographically separate, occupying distinct ranges. But birders beware! If these ranges overlap, there may be interbreeding (hybridization) and 'intergrades', that is, birds that are neither one species nor the other – or, if you like, both. Hybridization among different species of bird in the same family is a common phenomenon and may lead to fertile offspring. Most birders would shudder at the idea of ticking two species if we are certain of the nature of the hybrid, but it seems pretty logical to me (no fear, fellow birders, I'm only kidding!).

The birder in me might find all this frustrating, but the bird lover in me couldn't care less – as when we saw a Sooty Grouse (I think) in the mountains inland from Vancouver. The Grouse and its two chicks were a highlight of the day, giving us terrific views. The mother stood defiantly and proudly on a rock defending her brood and watched us warily,

A grouse with no name, Manning Park, British Columbia

while the chicks ran around happily and somewhat recklessly right in front of us, doing what youngsters will do.

Not so long ago, the Dusky Grouse and Sooty Grouse were considered to be subspecies of Blue Grouse, but the ornithological community decided that they were actually two species. Roughly speaking, those west of the Rockies in Canada and north-west USA were designated 'Sooty'. As to distinguishing field marks, they are subtle and few. In fact, this bird was very probably a hybrid, because we were in 'no man's land', the zone of indeterminacy, both east and west, but neither. There, the two species (formerly, subspecies) cross-breed. 'Blue Grouse' is no longer on the taxonomic list or on my database (other than as a footnote) so, short of taking a bit of a punt on which it was, I had nothing to tick.

Actually, the colour of the banding on its tale indicated a key field mark of a Sooty. So, a birder would tick it as 'Sooty' because that field mark is highlighted in the field guide. Birders look for species that are illustrated and described in the field guide, so whether or not it is 'really' a member of one or the other species (or both) is pretty much irrelevant once a few key field marks that are taken to be the key identification features have been confirmed.

Hybridization can, in somewhat rare circumstances, mean the extinction of a species. In the Mallee country of South Australia and neighbouring Victoria, the Black-eared Miner is in danger of going out of existence as a distinct species because the closely related, much more numerous Yellow-throated Miner is invading and taking over its habitat. This is probably because of human-induced changes to the habitat. One theory is that the Yellow-throated Miner preferred more open wooded areas, while denser Mallee woodland was preferred by the Black-eared Miner. Tree clearance and the grazing of sheep and cattle in the Mallee following European settlement have thinned out and diminished many of the densely wooded areas. Much of what is left is now occupied jointly by both species, and the smaller populations of Black-eared Miner are being overrun.

Distinguishing field marks are quite subtle, so the birder has to decide for themselves whether a bird seen in a flock of hybrids is 'actually' a Black-eared or a Yellow-throated. Keen birders who enter this habitat in search of the rare Black-eared Miner can refer to a checklist (extracted from a peer-reviewed article on the topic) of key distinguishing field marks, from which a certain number should be identified to claim a tick. How pale is that rump? How black is that moustache and that cheek patch? And so on.

Upon seeing that Black-eared Miners, given the opportunity to hybridize, give up their purported identity, a group of birders is quite likely to embark on a debate about what should count as a 'real' species (although, mostly, we just throw up our hands and leave it there). Among scientists there are broadly three main species concepts:[85]

1. The *biological* concept refers to a group of organisms that can produce fertile offspring to perpetuate the species as a unique group with its particular morphological features (that is, forms such as shape, size, colouration and so on). Members of the group live geographically contiguous lives and they have distinct calls and other characteristic behaviour that normally mean that mating takes place only within the group (which is not to say that, in not-so-normal conditions, hybridization cannot occur).

85 Marc Ereshefsky, *Species*, Stanford Encyclopedia of Philosophy (Fall 2017 Edition) accessible online; Jody Hey, 'Why should we care about species?" *Nature Education,* vol. 2, no. 5, 2009.

2. The *phylogenetic* concept places the emphasis on genealogy: a species of bird is defined by a group's unique ancestry, its place on the 'family tree' of all bird species. DNA analysis is critical to applying this concept.
3. The *ecological* concept refers to a group that is uniquely adapted through evolution to a particular ecological 'niche' – for example, the Cactus Finch, one of 'Darwin's Finches' on the Galapagos Islands, has a distinctive beak adapted to pierce the hard skin of cactus leaves to provide it with a unique food source not available to the other ground-finches on the same islands.[86]

These three concepts are not mutually exclusive. Morphological traits are inherited, so phylogenetic analysis serves as additional evidence to the significance for species identification of these inherited traits. Habitats shape adaptation through genetic variations that enhance fitness – different shaped beaks, longer legs and so on. The concepts generally line up together: a species of bird is a set of reproductively isolated, genetically identifiable, look-alike (and sound-alike) birds which occupies particular ecological niches and whose morphological features and ways of life are passed down through the generations.

While taxonomists divide themselves into camps and argue heatedly about all this, I am not keen on following them down all their rabbit holes. But you can see why they argue so much. Phylogenetic analysis (which is relatively new, and very fashionable) can generate discovery of a multitude of new species based solely on the evidence of genetic differences, although the populations exhibit no morphological differences whatsoever. These are sometimes labelled 'cryptic species' because their differences are hidden from us or, if apparent, quite small. Speciation can happen when populations have been geographically isolated on tropical islands in very similar habitats for many thousands of years (presumably, the birds concerned don't like flying over water). For the time being, nothing happens to produce significant morphological variations, but genetic analysis shows they are different. In this way, what were once 'lumped' as subspecies get split into many species.

As a birder, I am not going all-in for applying a phylogenetic approach to the exclusion of accounting for actual differences that I can see or hear. Indeed, the prospect of a whole new suite of cryptic species, identified solely by using modern DNA analysis has, in one sense, made birdwatching a relic of a previous, misinformed era. Thankfully, the time is yet to come: a pluralistic approach to species confirmation seems to be the broad scientific consensus for the time being.

A source of unity in all of this is that each of these concepts in modern biology assumes the underlying theory of evolution, including inheritance of features, natural selection and adaptation. Essentialist versions of the concept, such as those found in creationist theories, are rejected. But in case we think Darwin is a good place to look for a clear answer to the species problem, it's worth taking note of something that he wrote about the concept in a letter to a scientific colleague:

> It is really laughable to see what different ideas are prominent in various naturalists' minds, when they speak of 'species'; in some, resemblance is everything and descent of little weight – in some, resemblance seems to go for nothing, and Creation the reigning idea – in some, sterility an unfailing

86 Jonathan Weiner, *The Beak of the Finch*, New York, NY: Random House, 1994.

test, with others it is not worth a farthing. It all comes, I believe, from trying to define the indefinable (24 December 1856; in F. Darwin 1887, vol. 2, p.88).[87]

To Darwin, the important fact was variety, which comes in many forms through inheritance as creatures adapt and evolve (and cross-breed, as in the case of cage-bred pigeons, which Darwin studied closely). It was not clear to him (and it still isn't to us) that amidst this variety we can pin down the species as a particular group of organisms that unambiguously presents itself fully formed at a point in time. 'Speciation' happens, and we know a great deal about how and why, but it is a process, not necessarily producing a fixed object.[88] The species boundaries can be fluid, not fixed, and are continuously subject to change due to hybridization and to genetic mutation, taking place partly endogenously but also under the continuous influence of changing external conditions, some long-term spanning millennia, such as climate change, volcanic activity and ecological interactions with the evolutionary paths of other species; others more immediate, such as changing food sources, the effects of human settlement and extreme weather events.

Our difficulties in demonstrating that species are hard and fast 'things' in nature do not mean that the efforts to classify organisms into a hierarchy of defined groups or 'taxa' – orders, classes, families, genera, species and subspecies – is not valid or useful. But not surprisingly, given all the above, taxonomic decisions (placing particular groups and populations of birds into a distinct set in one of these categories) can be fraught and contested.

The IOC is one of the two principal worldwide authorities that oversees the standard avian taxonomic order (the other is the *Clements Checklist of Birds of the World* under the auspices of the Cornell Lab of Ornithology). IOC describes the concept of species that it follows in this way:

'The IOC World Bird List adopts a modern version of the Biological Species Concept with increased emphasis on monophyletic evolutionary lineages'.[89]

A 'monophyletic lineage' is a core concept in phylogenetic analysis and refers to a group of organisms (or 'clade') that comprises all the descendants of a common ancestor. To trace back these lineages, DNA analysis is used, deploying techniques that are themselves often contested. Observable features in the field or in the museum, such as form, appearance and song are also part of the data that are evaluated.

When dealing with specific cases where new research is reported proposing changes to the existing taxonomic list, a consensus is sought by committee. Scientific judgement is exercised, and votes are taken. However, the IOC committee and the Clements committee don't always agree. IOC and Clements recognize different numbers of species (IOC's May 2019 version had 10,896, while the then-current Clements version contained 10,585), many with differing common names and occupying different places in the taxonomic order. Moves are under way to try to find agreement on a unified process and a single avian taxonomic list (there was 'a vigorous Round Table discussion at the 2018 International Ornithological

87 Quoted in Ereshefsky (op. cit.), p.30, from a volume of the published Darwin letters.

88 Peter R. Grant and B. Rosemary Grant, *How and Why Species Multiply: The Radiation of Darwin's Finches*, Princeton, NJ: Princeton University Press, 2008.

89 IOC World Bird List, 2019.

Congress…' on the subject).[90] Another committee has been set up (I am not holding my breath).

For most birders, the scientific debates over what is a species and over the technical problems of taxonomy are peripheral and incidental. But we usually pay some attention because the taxonomic order is the basis of our lists and the main organizing principle in our field guides. In fact, most birders probably find much of it pretty tedious and confusing – if only they would make their minds up! Once we have decided which list we want to follow – IOC or Clements – we birders mostly just follow its mysterious ways.

As pointed out earlier, even when the ornithologists seem to have made their minds up, we are left with much to puzzle over in the field, trying to spot different species. As I write this, I have open in front of me a field guide to the birds of Peru.[91] I am looking at the first of 41 colour plates, six or seven birds to each plate, illustrating members of the New World tyrant flycatcher or *Tyrannidae* family of birds. That's nearly 300 species. Peru is home to most of the *Tyrannidae*, but all told in the Americas there are nearly 450 species, grouped into about 100 genera. The first plate in my Peru field guide is a good example: six tyrannulets, five of the *Phyllomyias* genus and one of the *Mecocurculus* genus, each subtly different but all remarkably similar at first glance. On the score of appearance at least, these look like distinctions without a difference, but the text points out other differences (call and song, perching and feeding behaviour, habitat, range and so on). Each page of six or seven illustrations and accompanying text repeats the same story.

On the one hand, the overall common resemblance among many of these birds, especially those in the same genus, is what first strikes one but, on the other hand, the subtlety and complexity of variation, once it is pointed out, is bedazzling. It is astonishing and miraculous that in Peru all those look-alike, greenish-brownish-greyish birds, most with a couple of stripes on their wings, flitting about catching flies amidst the branches, actually comprise hundreds of distinct species, each with their own way of life and their own ancestors, stretching back for tens of thousands or millions of years. This is a matter of wonder but, for many birders (especially world birders) it is also a source of frustration and perplexity.

In South America, tyrant flycatchers are only the beginning of a birder's problems – there are also scores or hundreds of superficially look-alike hummingbirds, antbirds, woodcreepers and so on. Other parts of the world also have their notorious look-alikes, for example the *Phylloscopus* warblers in Eurasia (tiny, greenish-yellow birds with (most of them) one or two wing stripes, mostly inhabiting the tops of tall trees) and the cisticolas in Africa, LBJs down in the long grass, often named for their song because that's the only distinguishable feature: Whistling, Trilling, Chattering, Bubbling, Rattling, Churring, Tinkling, Wailing, Winding, Chirping, Croaking, Melodious…. One, very unhelpfully, is named Singing Cisticola. All these look-alike families have seriously challenged the imagination and creativity of their discoverers when they came to give them names – two of my favourites are in the *Phylloscopus* family, namely Greenish Warbler and Two-barred Warbler. Thanks a lot!

Species identification in all of these cases demands a high level of expertise and, if you are travelling from continent to continent in pursuit of thousands of species, you are unlikely to be expert enough. Rising successfully to the challenge of knowing even a modicum of what to look for in order to differentiate so many newly encountered species demands a

90 The quotation is taken from the preamble to the latest update of the IOC checklist (as of December 2020), which is accessible on the IOC website.

91 Thomas S. Schulenberg *et al.*, *Birds of Peru*, Princeton, NJ: Princeton University Press, 2007.

Rattling Cisticola, Lake Langano, Ethiopia

considerable intellectual feat. Learning the different songs and calls is critical, but they too are so many variations of a few themes. On a birding trip, I often go around in a semi-fog of half-knowledge as I look to tick off new species. I may see and hear some of these species several times over, when familiarity kicks in and I begin to feel more at home. After several trips to the relevant region of the world, sorting out species of tyrant flycatchers becomes a lot less forbidding as a result. But variety and novelty are what world birders are after, not familiarity. Once we get to know a bird really well, we are less interested in it.

At some point, each birder has to make their own personal compromise with their incomplete knowledge. At first, I was infinitely frustrated at how much I missed, at what I didn't 'see' even though I was looking straight at it. Over the years, I have learnt a lot and improved my ID abilities. But in the case of cisticolas, I readily admit defeat. I mostly rely on the voice of the expert guide to confirm an ID and take solace at just looking at the birds in all their spectacular, infinite variety while, along the way, picking up enough know-how to limit the 'dips' to a decent, acceptable number.

Indeed, there are aspects of species identification in the field that I find tedious and unappealing. This is a dangerous admission to make as a birder, but it happens every time we take out our scopes to scan a mudflat teeming with look-alike, dull-brown waders. To many of my companions, this is a highlight. Collectively, waders are a beautiful and wondrous spectacle but individually, they are not only pretty similar, but they are also usually so far away. Rarely is there a new species for the life list, because most waders have a very wide range and are seen repeatedly by travelling birders. But nearly all my companions eagerly engage in friendly competition to be the first to name a species, each of them calling out their IDs, sometimes challenging each other and engaging in heated debate.

Worse still are gulls. Of the hundreds of wintering gulls on the mudflats of Swansea Bay, 99.9% will be from a few, familiar species, but amidst them there may be a vagrant, perhaps a Mediterranean Gull. Winter plumages are pretty jaded and lose many distinguishing features and, just to make it harder, gull plumages don't really develop their distinctive features until individuals are a few years old. For some birders the challenge is irresistible, and they will spend hours trying to pick the odd one out. Even among hardened birders, the top gull experts are considered a bit extreme, treated with awe and wonder. Me, I mostly just enjoy watching the comings and goings and the rest of the carry-on in the flock. To my mind, my fellow birders, looking for anomalies of plumage, size and so on amidst the flock, are not really looking at the birds.

Thankfully, in my experience, all (or nearly all) birders will also come together to spend time during a day in the field when something really special, as a pure spectacle, is in the offing; when the object is not to strain to identify a species but to just enjoy the birds. These are often my most memorable highlights. We will just sit and watch and, in the process, get a good look at birds, individually or in groups, feeding or displaying. Very few birders (and ornithologists) that I know, even the most avid and relentless listers, would stand up the chance to stand or sit still for a while to see manakins displaying at a lek, or a bird-of-paradise doing its dance, or a mob of parrots at a salt lick. Most often, these occasions happen when our schedule sets aside an hour or two at a hide or in front of a feeding station. And artifice will often be involved – for example, hummingbird feeders stocked with sugar water. Occasionally, and magically, we come across such an opportunity just in passing, in the forest. Feeding flocks, including those accompanying ant swarms, are perhaps the best and most memorable such birding episodes.

But on many trips, these are brief interludes amidst the relentless quest for new species. This may require walking through the forest where the local guides know the lay of the land, listening for calls and playing a recording to try to attract a target bird to fly in for a look. That look is often fleeting, as the bird shoots off as soon as it sees us lift our bins. When I started birding on overseas trips with groups of birders and a guide, I occasionally thought, as we walked through the forest and especially when we headed back to the bus to set out for the next birding hotspot, that it would be nice just to stop where we were, stand quietly and unobtrusively, listen and look about, and wait for what might turn up. I soon gave up voicing this, as it got me some strange looks. Apparently, this was not the way to add to the list – we had to get to the next site or trudge on around the next bend in the trail.

I became increasingly reconciled to this way of birding, because that's the way to see a greater number of species. But this can sometimes get pretty dismal. I have a picture in my mind. We are in Madagascar, and our group has had a successful day, seeing all the target birds and getting some great looks in the process. Walking slowly back, contented, late in the afternoon, we cross paths with another birding group, going in the opposite direction. Greetings are exchanged. They have so far failed to find the Brown Emutail, which we watched earlier for several minutes flitting around in some bushes and calling. Etched on every one of their faces is boredom, frustration and weariness. On the leader's face in addition, there is anxiety and even desperation. His tone is one of resignation. They march slowly off and disappear down the trail. Perhaps they are still out there.

As always, it's a matter of balance, of taking the rough with the smooth. Our day of new birds and great views in Madagascar was memorable, the result of a fortune-blessed, well-planned quest for a realistic target list. Some afternoons, who knows why, you might see next to nothing. Quite probably, that long, futile search for the Emutail is etched in the memories of those birders, a war story to retell with shaking head and wry smiles, as the listening fellow birders nod in mutual sympathy and recognition.

But seeing new species in the field and how unique the vast majority of them are, even in subtle ways, can be both exciting and amazing. Learning and trying to rise to the challenge can also be rewarding. A memorable experience of this was on Emei Shan in Sichuan Province, one of China's Four Sacred Buddhist Mountains, with monasteries, temples and shrines from top to bottom. Pilgrims, not birders, do it from bottom to top, the most ardent on foot, using the ancient trails (although the vast majority of visitors use the modern roads and cable cars, stopping briefly at the principal temples to take selfies).

Our descent was some 2,500 m (the peak is just over 3,000 m above sea level). The walk, birding all the way, took two days, pausing at the occasional noodle shop, with an overnight stop in a monastery halfway down (the less said about the accommodation arrangements, the better). As we slowly descended the trails and steps, we came across four different species of 'spectacled' warblers (White-spectacled, Martens's, Alström's and Bianchi's), each almost identical but for their songs, their populations differentiated and separated by altitudinal range. Preference for different habitat and the female's recognition and appreciation of the male's territorial songs keep the species apart. These four were among 11 *Phylloscopus* warbler species encountered on that descent (including, of course, the Emei Leaf Warbler). I had been exposed to an education in speciation and in species identification (and, of course, I needed an expert along to help me out!).

Both before and after encountering these birds, ongoing research has resulted in a complete reordering and renaming of these and some closely related little green jobs. When I saw them, my out-of-date field guide lumped three of them as Golden-spectacled Warbler in the genus *Seicercus*, but apparently not so – this species name has disappeared from the list and alas, poor *Seicercus* has dropped off the avian family tree altogether. Fortunately, the downloads of taxonomic updates into my database have dealt with all this seamlessly, without need for my intervention.

As memorable as that birding experience was, equally, some of my best birding days have happened when I knew (or I was at least 99% certain) that I was not going to be coming across any new species. This is the quite different pleasure of birding in familiar places, or in places with familiar birds. I still want to identify what I see and, for the most part, I can (without help). But it is no longer a compulsion to look for new birds around every corner. Sometimes, on that kind of day out, I don't bother to record the list at all. On coming across a flock, it's great just to put the bins down and take it all in; or upon seeing a pair of birds building a nest or feeding young or trying to distract and ward off a predator crow or magpie, to stop for 20 minutes and just watch.

The more I do this, while the growth of the list may slow down, the more birding becomes less like hard work and more like leisure. Then, the more I connect with nature, the more of it I enjoy. But back home in the armchair, I also delight in sifting through the taxonomic details in the latest IOC or Clements list updates and (especially in the case of splits) seeing them appear as amendments to my life list.

CHAPTER 18

Extinction Birding on Norfolk Island

Over the Christmas of 2018, I spent a week on Norfolk Island, a tiny dot on a map of the Pacific Ocean, 1,700 km north-east of Sydney, 1,100 km north of Auckland and 700 km south of Noumea. Norfolk Island is a territory of Australia, inhabited by about 1,600 people, plus a visiting tourist population at any one time of around 500. The main island occupies 35 km^2 of volcanic outcrop. Much smaller Phillip Island is just off to the south. The climate and natural vegetation are subtropical. Traces of settlement by

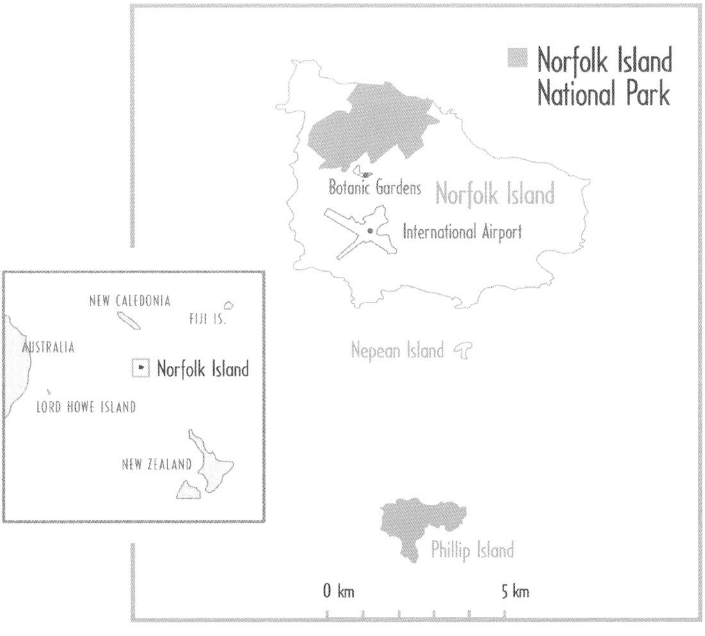

Polynesian islanders have been found dating back some 800 years, but Captain Cook, who landed briefly in 1774 and reported its potential for resource extraction, found no signs of them; it appears they had long gone.

European settlement dates from 1788, not long after the First Fleet landed in Sydney Cove. A ship and some transported convicts were dispatched to establish a settlement. The island was prized as a possible source of tall timber for masts and of flax for sails to keep the British Navy sailing the high seas. The Norfolk Pine actually turned out to be unsuitable, but other reasons for raising the Union Jack on these remote islands were found, first to house the most recalcitrant of transported convicts and, after that ended in 1855 and the convicts left, to re-settle the descendants of the Bounty mutineers and their South Sea Islander wives from Pitcairn Island in 1856. Fletcher Christian was the most famous of these mutineers (thanks, in part, to the screen depictions of Errol Flynn, Clarke Gable, Marlon Brando and Mel Gibson). 'Christian' remains one of the most common entries in the local phone book which also, uniquely, lists some of the residents by their nicknames.

This remarkable history, along with the heritage of landscape, language, customs and buildings that mark it, make Norfolk Island an enticing tourist destination. For me, the added attraction was the existence of a handful of endemic birds, plus large populations of seabirds using the cliffs and the island's wooded areas for nesting. Ecotourism and the island's natural beauty are key selling points for the island's tourist industry, more so than wild beach parties and cool poolside bars – there are only a few small beaches and the surf is not great. The climate is subtropical, and the native flora (most famously, the Norfolk Pines) are ubiquitous on the island.

Oceanic islands such as Norfolk are both hotbeds of endemism but also hotspots of extinction. For these reasons, many of them are magnets for birders who want to add endemic birds to their life list before extinction removes them from the wild. Almost universally, human encroachment and settlement on remote islands in the past two or three centuries have been ecologically devastating. The archetypical island avian extinction story – the fate of the Dodo – is a case in point. It does not take long on a relatively small island to eat the tastiest and most easily caught wildlife to extinction, or to chop and burn down

Colonial-era government buildings and Norfolk Pines

a forest that was the only home to a few thousand members of an endemic population. Just as destructively, invasive species that arrive with human invaders (such as rats and fast-growing weeds) can very quickly decimate the native flora and fauna.

However, on such an island (if it has been settled by humans) what is being lost eventually gets noticed, first of all because it's in everyone's backyard and second, because scientists, tourists and other enthusiasts from outside raise the alarm. Increasingly, islands like Norfolk are a focus for intense conservation efforts. Once the mind is concentrated in this way, it is not impossible to ring-fence a small, surviving population of birds in a preserved, remnant habitat such as a forest patch that is designated as a National Park, and to launch a concerted effort, by a variety of means, to rescue it from extirpation. This has happened on Norfolk Island. What we now experience is a delicate equilibrium between past and current human activity and the remaining fragments of a natural world in which, for the time being, complete destruction of the indigenous wildlife has been forestalled.

The visiting birder to Norfolk Island focuses mostly on the nature reserves with their remnant populations of endemic birds, plus the seabirds soaring over the spectacular cliffs. The counterpoint to this is, of course, the impact of human settlement, a story of destruction, modification and innovation that has led to the current state of the landscape, including the transport infrastructure, the cultivated fields and the treeless pastures. When birders and other tourists visit the island to admire the wildlife, we become part of that story. We are drawn in quickly to the island community and its history. We hear the origin story from islanders as a personal one – how their ancestors set about carving out a living for themselves and their descendants from the land and its resources. And we can see and comprehend the totality of the results on just one morning drive – an island made fit for human habitation and commerce but, in the process, denuded of its pre-human life supports.

I rented a holiday cottage, complete with hire car waiting for me in the parking bay. My landlord, a member of the extended Christian family, told me that his grandmother told him stories that she first heard from her grandmother, who was among the original Pitcairn settlers: '...I looked into her eyes as she told the story, and those eyes had looked into her grandmother's, who was there when it all started'. Norfolk Islanders express pride in their roots and in their culture and have a strong sense of identity, including their own Creole language, still spoken by a few who want to keep the language alive. And many of them now include in their attachment to the island their pride in the uniqueness of its flora and fauna, and their wish to preserve what is left.

One of the first things many visitors see when they arrive on Norfolk Island is the airport runways, without which their visit would probably not have been feasible. Unless you are on one of the Pacific Island cruises that occasionally stops by for a couple of days, the island is only accessible for longer-stay tourists by plane – there is no harbour and it's several day's sailing from any population centre. The Norfolk Island airport can take international jet flights, boasts two runways and occupies a big chunk of land. It was built as a military installation during the Second World War, requiring levelling of a number of hills, uprooting many trees and the laying of copious quantities of bitumen. By some accounts, the locality was a remaining refuge of the Norfolk Triller, the now extinct, endemic subspecies of the Long-tailed Triller, last recorded in 1942. Of course, this is not the whole story of the Norfolk Triller's demise: loss of the island's lowland forests had already occurred on a larger scale, and the invasive Black Rat most likely sounded the birds' death knell.

While the modern airport now provides a bitumen and concrete symbol of the effects of settlement, things got started much earlier. The first convict settlers and their keepers in the early 19th century cleared land, quarried stone, put up some impressive buildings and did a pretty good job of eating much of the nesting seabird population into local extinction. In the same ways, they hastened the extinction of some endemic land birds. Clearing of land continued as more settlers arrived. As always, foreign plants and animals invaded with the humans. The earlier Polynesian settlers probably had already brought the Polynesian Rat. Cats arrived as pets with the first European settlers. Black Rats, which have proven to be a very efficient destroyer of local birdlife, came ashore sometime in the 20th century. Many non-native birds were deliberately introduced and thrived, including European Blackbirds, House Sparrows and Crimson Rosellas. The latter have outcompeted the native parrots for nesting holes.

Goats were introduced very early to Phillip Island, a few kilometres offshore, to provide game for the bored British officers. Pigs and rabbits were also landed there. Goats and pigs were gone by 1900 and rabbits by 1986. By then, nearly all the trees were also gone (Phillip Island was once densely forested, but now it is almost bare) and up to 2 m of soil had been washed from the surface. Europeans also brought numerous plants to Norfolk, some deliberately for cultivation and decoration, others accidentally. Many are now taking over from the local vegetation. These invasions are ongoing, the latest arrivals including Argentine Ants and several exotic plant pests and diseases.[92]

The visitor arriving by air can readily appreciate habitat loss on the island just by seeing the extent of agricultural land and human settlement from the plane as it lands. The island was once mostly forested. Unlike some other colonized oceanic islands, agriculture and land clearance on Norfolk were ultimately driven less by export markets for local produce than by subsistence needs. An exception was a Kentia Palm seed business, with several plantations on the island (the seeds are used worldwide in the horticultural industry). Kentia Palm is an endemic of Lord Howe Island, another Australian territory 1,000 km to the west of Norfolk Island. The first plantings on Norfolk Island took place in the 1880s.

Driving around the island, pasture is the dominant land use and contented cows roam everywhere. They have right of way on the narrow roads. Just as ubiquitous are feral chickens (we should call them Jungle Fowl on our taxonomic list now that they are running wild). Settlement is scattered – everywhere is ex-urban, but without the city. The National Park, occupying about one-tenth of the island, is the only place where you won't see a house and a road in the landscape if you scan in all directions. A shopping centre catering for visiting tourists is located on a couple of streets in the centre of the island, not far from the airport.

A number of the island's indigenous plants and animals are shared with other Pacific Islands in the region, but there is also a high level of endemism. There are over 40 endemic plants, out of a total of over 180 indigenous species. Eight have gone extinct.[93] There are over 60 endemic species of land snails – six of them have gone extinct. Two native bats have gone extinct. As to birds, there are around 40 resident land and freshwater species, 12 of which are introduced. More than 20 species of seabirds either nest on or visit the islands – petrels, boobies, shearwaters, terns, gulls, frigatebirds, tropicbirds and noddies. Some that used to nest on Norfolk Island are now locally extirpated due to human impacts, including

92 *Norfolk Island. Protecting an Ocean Jewel*, Fairfield, Victoria: Invasive Species Council and Island Conservation, 2017.

93 There are also about 430 exotic plant species on the island.

predation by invasive mammals. Some that are no longer found on the main island can still be found nesting in small numbers on Phillip Island.

Four endemic land bird species have definitely gone extinct: Norfolk Kaka, Norfolk Pigeon, Norfolk Ground Dove (all relatively large, easy to catch and edible) and the White-chested White-eye. So, too, have three endemic subspecies: Tasman Starling (the other subspecies, on Lord Howe Island, is also extinct); the nominate subspecies of Island Thrush (*Turdus poliocephalis poliocephalis*); and the aforementioned Long-tailed Triller. Four endemic bird species are still classified as extant on the IOC checklist – the Norfolk Island Parakeet, Norfolk Island Gerygone, Slender-billed White-eye and Norfolk Robin. Until very recently, the endemic White-chested White-eye was also on most taxonomic lists as still surviving. Some people continue to hope it may turn up after over 25 years of no records, but so far to no avail.[94]

There are also endemic subspecies of the Australian Golden Whistler and the Grey Fantail. The first is a possible future split – unlike other golden whistlers, male and female look similar. The subspecies is described as 'hen-feathered' – males have given up on expending the extra energy needed in order to look bright, crisp and smart in their yellow, black and white outfits. There have been numerous recent splits in the golden whistler complex, particularly of formerly designated subspecies on other Pacific Islands, but this one has yet to be accepted. The island's very own owl, known locally as the Norfolk Boobook, is a subspecies of the Morepork (the nominate subspecies is found in New Zealand). The Norfolk Boobook population was reduced to one female in 1986, but in a last-minute rescue effort, an introduced close cousin from New Zealand successfully mated.

Most visiting birders have little trouble finding the surviving endemics. My lodgings were on a road out of town that turned into a dirt track that trailed up the hill to one of the entrances to the National Park. In my garden, a fantail showed on the first evening and I could hear gerygones singing. A Norfolk Pine at the bottom of the garden held a pair of White Terns, one always present, brooding on an egg in an elbow of a branch, the other off

Australian Golden Whistler, Pachycephala pectoralis xanthoprocta

94 Guy Dutson, 'The ghost birds of Norfolk Island', *Australian Geographic*, 22 December 2010.

fishing. The chick hatched on my second-last day. I was up at the crack of dawn on the first morning, woken by the Jungle Fowl crowing at around four in the morning. I was lucky enough to see all the endemics except the Boobook before breakfast.

One of the reasons this result was possible is that the target species are all inhabitants of the original subtropical forest which, once ubiquitous across the island, is now mostly confined to the National Park, a small, well-protected area in the north of the island. It contains a mix of indigenous deciduous and evergreen trees, with Norfolk Pines towering above. Parts of this forest are degraded by invasive species, although work is proceeding to mitigate this. The park area is centred on the island's two biggest hills, Mount Bates and Mount Pitt. Good birding can also be found in the nearby Botanical Gardens.

In other words, here is a case where the modern birder is favoured both by human settlement – making possible the easy accessibility of the remaining forest – and also by the conservation efforts, which have halted habitat destruction just in time. Ironically, in places like Norfolk Island, there is often a birder's sweet-spot of accessibility, vanishing habitat and not-quite-extinct populations. For the birding rarity-chaser, there are easy pickings. Walking a few trails in a relatively small patch of protected forest usually results in finding the target birds. Human efforts to conserve these remaining populations, such as aggressive rat eradication, close monitoring of nests, provision of nest boxes and, in the case of the Norfolk Island Parakeet, captive breeding and releases into the wild, not only preserve the population but may also help habituate birds to a human presence in the protected areas.

Norfolk Island is only one example of a number of places that I have encountered where birders benefit from impending extinctions because special efforts are made to protect the remaining birds, often in relatively small fragments of suitable habitats where we can easily find them. As I described in a previous chapter, in such destinations we go extinction birding. Birders often come away from a visit to such a destination with a self-satisfied feeling that their presence has contributed to the conservation efforts. These may be part-funded by tourist revenue, while the benefits of ecotourism are a strong argument made when seeking government resources for conservation. The island's human inhabitants have recently played a big part as willing volunteers in the conservation programmes.

But this conjunction of human effort and conservation success was preceded by a sorry record of human-induced extinctions and is still accompanied by continuing threats. The main damage has already been done even if, for the visiting birder, it all now seems to be good enough for them. On Norfolk Island, this is not to belittle the dedicated local volunteers and park rangers, the researchers, the NGOs and the government officials who are fighting to hold back the tide. Among the endemic birds, the Norfolk Island Parakeet is the iconic symbol of this effort. Twice in the past 30 years (most recently in 2013) its numbers have declined to just tens rather than hundreds. In the latest crisis, careful location of nest boxes and human-made nest hollows, measures to dissuade competition from the invasive Crimson Rosella and redoubled efforts at rat eradication, have succeeded in reversing the decline. Hopefully, this much-observed and protected population will remain intact. The accompanying image is testament to the care that is being lavished – the ID band on its leg is clearly visible.

My landlord told me with evident pride that the week before, he had seen a couple of Green Parrots (as the locals call them) flying over my holiday cottage. I spotted them one evening from the verandah. He took me to his landholding on the other side of the

Norfolk Island Parakeet

White Tern with chick

island, close to where he was brought up. He led me down a forested gully infested with invasive plants, where he used to play with his boyhood friends. He was halfway through clearing the weeds and exotics, but the tangle was still formidable. He planned to build a house on the land for his family, and this was to be their native garden. We watched as the White Terns and Black Noddies wheeled and squabbled overhead, coming to their nests and feeding their chicks in his trees.

Later, I spent time on the cliff tops watching these and other seabirds riding the wind, many with their beaks full of tiny fish, soaring over the cliffs and heading inland. A vagrant White-tailed Tropicbird was an unexpected bonus. In the evening, huge rafts of Wedge-tailed Shearwaters gathered on the ocean as dusk approached, ready to head inland to their nesting holes and hollows amidst the trees. I made numerous visits to these sunny, windy clifftops during my short stay: the birding there was magical, the ocean vistas spellbinding. The endemic ticks were a buzz, but these excursions were the highlights.

Ironically, Norfolk's resident human population is now facing what they see as an existential crisis of its own. Its unique system of local self-government was abolished in 2016 by the Australian Government due to a local budgetary crisis. One plan that the local government hatched to rescue their budget before the takeover was to set up an offshore tax haven. Perhaps this was the final straw for the politicians and bureaucrats in Canberra, who decided to integrate the local administration and economy once and for all into the rest of Australia. A local system of taxation and service provision run by a locally elected body was supplanted by a district administration supervised from Canberra. Norfolk Islanders now pay federal taxes and receive federal benefits. Perhaps a silver lining is that biosecurity measures will improve, and more resources will be available for conservation, but this can't be taken for granted.

There is a local opposition movement, including a 'tent embassy' set up by local protesters in the grounds of one of the colonial-era government buildings, and a petition to the United Nations. The tent embassy is a replication of one that was set up 1972 in front of Parliament House in Canberra by Australian Aborigines and is still there. It is a symbol of their protest and resistance. The Norfolk Island version is more modest, has the same purpose and also occupies government-owned land. When I visited, I read the signs and the posters, although no one was in the tent. Norfolk Islanders believe that their original rights as settlers, granted by the British Crown, have been usurped and their special history disrespected. They believe they are unique and have had their island life supports taken from them. On Norfolk Island, more than the endemic wildlife may be under threat of extinction by invaders.

Site of the tent embassy

CHAPTER 19

Slow Birding in Grenfell

Grenfell is a typical Australian small country town of some 2,000 inhabitants – along the wide, spacious High Street which takes traffic through the town, there is angle parking; a Chinese restaurant which has been there as long as anyone can remember; three pubs, one of them boarded up; the old Rural Bank building empty and up for sale; and two pie shops, one of them attached to a small restaurant. Signs of the times as the town adapts to the 21st century are the shuttered department stores, a few boutiques and arts and crafts shops and the aroma of espresso coffee from a recently opened café. Close by, gracious pre-Federation era homes with well-tended gardens are occupied by retirees enjoying their quiet retreat. On the fringes of town, grain silos and ribbons of agricultural machinery and car sales yards line the two main roads in and out of town. The railway tracks, freight yards and the heritage-listed train station are mostly silent.

Tourism is increasingly important – hence the city-style coffee and the boutiques. A relaxed day's drive due west of Sydney and a few hours from Canberra, Grenfell's main claim to fame is its history. Many fine old buildings with covered verandahs line the main street, which is distinguished from others like it by its elbow-like bend halfway along. The long-deserted goldfields nearby were the birthplace of Australia's favourite bush storyteller and poet, Henry Lawson. A full-size diorama in the main street plays recordings of some of his most popular bush ballads when you press the buttons. Further along, a life-size statue sits on a wooden bench, pipe in mouth; tourists sit next to him and take selfies. In the off-season, this bench is the favourite seat of a bearded young man, contentedly smoking something in the morning sun. He greets me as a welcome stranger – I am there as a tourist, a birder in search of parrots and other birds in the surrounding countryside.

Bank building: 'For Sale'

The land around Grenfell is largely agricultural – wheat and sheep are the main staples. But the dominant feature in the landscape, seen from all directions, is Weddin Mountains National Park, an outcrop of eucalypt and pine wooded slopes rising 400 m from the wheat fields and paddocks, some 15 km south and west of the town. Just to the west again is Bimbi State Forest, an open Cypress Pine woodland, once logged but now quiet. Local roads through the agricultural lands are typically tree-lined, including many stands of fine, mature eucalypts such as Red Gum, Grey Box and Yellow Box.

In sum, within a short distance of Grenfell is excellent habitat for parrots, raptors and a good variety of passerines such as robins, thornbills, honeyeaters and finches. The district used to be a good place to find Bush Thick-knee, although latterly foxes and other invaders have decimated the local population, which is probably extirpated. Most visitors to the National Park head for the campground on the western side and climb up to see Ben Hall's cave. Ben Hall was, as the Grenfell tourism website puts it, 'one of Australia's most revered bushrangers' (Ned Kelly would probably win the popular vote). He used the cave as a hideout in the 1860s before being tracked down and shot dead by the police in 1865. Legend has it that his stash of stolen treasure is still buried somewhere on the slopes of Weddin Mountains.

A web search has dug out a very handy birder's guide to Grenfell and its surrounds, a sign that every possible niche is being explored to be helpful to visitors. I have come for a short stay of three nights. My host owns a converted nunnery on the High Street, now a B&B, that he has renovated and furnished to reflect not only the building's religious background and its colonial-era origins, but also his exotic taste in art and artefacts, indulged during a lifetime of travel. The dining room contains period furnishings and a splendid collection of silver chafing dishes and crystal decanters. Stained glass windows have been restored and one of the bedrooms is in the old chapel. In my room, a large Kilim carpet covers the floor. Furnishings include a vast four-poster, a Chinese altar, a huge Russian Orthodox candelabrum and a selection of religious paintings. Fortunately, the room also has material comforts – a fridge, kettle, wine glasses and a good heater (it is mid-winter and frost is on the ground each morning).

Armed with my Grenfell bird guide and a record of recent eBird sightings, I set out each morning as the sun begins to melt the frost, fortified by a gourmet breakfast and, after a brief stop on the High Street, armed with a sausage roll and a sandwich from one of the pie shops. By the third morning, I am welcomed in the shop like an old friend. My first morning is spent birding along the dirt road adjacent to Bimbi Forest and in the lee of Weddin Mountains to my east. Between the road and the mountains, the wheat fields are green and dotted with the remains of dead kangaroos (maybe they were culled – farmers and animal welfare advocates in Australia argue incessantly over this practice). On the other side of the road, the State Forest woodland comprises scattered trees with patches of open grassland and, as I climb from the car, it is immediately obvious that this is prime habitat. Flocks of Eastern Rosellas, Eastern Bluebonnets and Red-rumped Parrots shoot from tree to tree across the open ground. In a roadside gum tree, a small group of Australian Ringnecks feed quietly. Galahs and cockatoos are about, their calls ringing through the tress. Clambering through the barbed wire, in quick succession I come across Red-capped Robin, Flame Robin, Hooded Robin, Jacky Winter and Eastern Yellow Robin. Little flocks of Yellow-rumped Thornbill flit across the ground. A Southern Whiteface appears briefly.

Eastern Bluebonnets

All of these birds (and others) are comfortingly familiar. I had not really known what to expect, and the ringnecks and bluebonnets were a pleasant surprise. The robins are everywhere, their bright plumages catching the eye. A couple of hours pass pleasantly as I watch these birds one by one, still in sight of my vehicle. Later, I head to another dirt road, a stock route along the eastern edge of Weddin Mountains. The highlights here are several groups of both White-winged Chough and Apostlebird, performing their antics. Again, the abundance is striking. I sit and watch out of the car window for I don't know how long, at Apostlebirds hopping about, clambering onto logs, sitting around in groups and generally carrying on with their very active social life. Later, on the way back to the main road, a small group of preening Gray-crowned Babblers show themselves on a perch. Without getting out of the car I watch as, undisturbed, they pass the time of day together. A brief stop at a roadside lagoon on Emu Creek turns up ducks and cormorants and, perched on a fallen tree in the lake, a serene, statuesque, Yellow-billed Spoonbill (but no sign of Emu).

So ends Day 1, productive and full of delights. No ticks, but no worries: I am replete, looking back on a perfect day's birding. A dinner of sweet-and-sour in the Chinese restaurant (Australian Chinese, that is) with a cool beer is an appropriate finale. I want to use the term 'slow birding' to describe this day, although I saw plenty of birds, with rarely a dull moment. In normal birding parlance, 'the birding is slow' means there is very little bird activity. But in this case, it was my pace that was slow and relaxed, and above all I wasn't compulsively chasing anything, but leaving time for just enjoying the setting and watching the birds. Indeed, I am not the only birder who has recently found more satisfaction in this kind of birdwatching.[95]

95 Madison Audubon, *Slow Birding*, 21 September 2020.

Grey-crowned Babblers

Yellow-billed Spoonbill

True, there are still a couple of big gaps in my list of possible parrots – Superb Parrot and Turquoise Parrot, the least common and (of course) the only two possible lifers on the list – but tomorrow is another day; surely, they'll turn up somewhere. And I have a cunning plan. I will spend the first part of the day on some other back roads on the eastern edge of Weddin Mountains, and in the afternoon follow some leads in the Grenfell bird guide and visit some recommended spots for Superb Parrot on the other side of town.

In fact, the next morning draws a blank so far as my parrots are concerned, the highlights being a close-up of a Brush Bronzewing, a good number of Australian King Parrots' and a couple of Speckled Warblers. Not bad, actually, each of these birds are well worth a close look – and still I am in no great hurry. The afternoon sites are on the other side of town and comprise roadside eucalypt stands situated amidst agricultural land. The first two draw blanks. By the time the third site is reached, it is late afternoon. The sun is getting lower and the light is beginning to glow with its evening warmth. Superb Parrots are swift in flight, long-tailed, slender and vivid green, with a golden front and throat, and red trimmings. They have a distinctive cackling, bubbling call. From a distance, one flock seems to fit the bill, and it lands in a dead roadside tree. Sure enough, they are Superb Parrots, and they ignore me as I walk up to the tree, preening as they ready themselves for the evening roost. The light is fading fast, and they are silhouetted against the sky. Suddenly, the flock takes off as if one, and the birds join others in a wooded area further down the road. There, they settle in as the dusk rapidly approaches and I follow and quietly watch, taking photos.

If you want to find a particular bird in its customary habitat, there is no substitute for local knowledge. The Grenfell birder's guide map, giving directions to six signed 'Bird Walks' in the district and highlighting the species to be expected at each, is a case in point. I

Superb Parrots

found the Superb Parrots exactly where they said I might. But an even better illustration of the value of local knowledge on Day 3 leads me to my other main target. I am back where I started, on the dirt road beside Bimbi Forest – eBird reports suggest this is a likely place to find Turquoise Parrot, a small, delicate grass parrot of the *Neophema* family. Again, I climb over the barbed wire, leaving my car on the side of the road. As I walk through the trees, I notice a vehicle pull up, from which appears a man and his two dogs. He looks in my car and scans the trees. The dogs inspect the tyres. I holler and make my way over, acting friendly but wondering if that is the right attitude to take. Indeed, it is – a local farmer wants to make sure I have not had a breakdown.

After greetings, we get straight to the point as he notices the bins around my neck. He knows where I might find Turquoise Parrots, and he gives me exact directions – drive down the road, over the first gully and through the open gate further along on the right; park, turn back on myself, and the parrots can often be seen in a paddock between the road and the gully as it winds into the forest. He is an enthusiast and reminisces back to the time when he used to come across Bush Thick-knees in his paddocks, before the foxes finished them off. He hasn't seen one in years. His dogs are just as friendly as he is, and we part on good terms.

I park the car by the gate and wander in. No luck, apart from a Striated Pardalote in the treetops and some more robins, so I follow a trail, straight as an arrow, deep into the forest, which is mostly open and airy (this is a State Forest, and the trail is to facilitate extraction of the wood – although it seems hardly used). Common birds offer plenty of entertainment, but again, no luck with the parrots. I walk back and try the paddock one more time. As I approach the gully, from behind me a flutter of wings disturbs the air low over my head and a small green parrot shoots by, followed by several others, landing together in a tree. I instantly feel this is my target. Creeping closer, my instinct is confirmed by a closer view of their yellow bellies and blue wings. They drop down to graze, and for the next 20 minutes I creep from tree to tree for cover as I follow them across the paddock. As they feed, their

Turquoise Parrot

wary eyes are on me, but they seem not unduly disturbed. They are stunning: tiny bundles of bright green, electric blue and vivid yellow, with a tiny red patch glowing on the wing. Suddenly they take off and, looking up, I see them join a passing, much larger flock of the same species, maybe 40 birds altogether. They disappear together into the forest in a buzzing whirl of colour. I wander through the paddock again, dazed, elated and thankful.

Mission accomplished! Grenfell has welcomed me as a birder and generously given up its treasures. I have experienced something of the steady life of this country town and been fortunate enough to light on some first-class birding. The pace has been relaxed, the rewards have been high – not just the two new lifers but also close, prolonged views of these and many, more familiar species. Next morning, as I do some last-minute birding before hitting the road, I get a further dose of the locals' warmth and friendliness, albeit this time with less fortunate results for my birding. I have stopped my car by a stand of trees and have spotted a pair of Superb Parrots feeding in the grass. As I walk quietly along the road to get a better view and a photograph or two, a local farmer pulls up for a chat, dogs barking in the back of his clanking truck. The parrots flee the commotion, but I put on a brave face and we talk about the birds he sees on his property, and about his dogs. I feel no irritation. The openness of the local people, including their pleasure in sharing with visitors their knowledge and love of the area, is its own reward.

The trip lasted four days including travel (leisurely, along the back roads, with occasional stops to scan the paddocks and trees). There were the thrills of seeing two terrific new birds of one of my favourite set of families, the Old World Parrots. But the whole experience was much richer than just bagging a couple of lifers. For this visiting birder, Grenfell – the place, its people, the landscape and its parrots – are equally memorable parts of an inseparable experience: a long weekend of slow birding at its best.

CHAPTER 20

Final Thoughts

As a birder, I have lived through decades that may be looked back on as a Golden Age of birding. Technological advances and globalization have enabled the development of new forms of birding, including world birding. Growing popularity of the pastime has coincided with new levels of knowledge and expertise on how and where to find birds, assisted by advances in human communication, both real and virtual. Birding tourism, both within national borders and internationally, has boomed, providing a stimulus to protecting and conserving local habitats, and promoting and supporting community and government efforts to remove threats to birds. The result is a sophisticated, worldwide birding support infrastructure that has immeasurably expanded our birding opportunities.

But these decades have also been those during which we have come face to face with the limits to our continued, restless exploration and exploitation of the planet and its natural resources. The growing climate crisis due to human-induced global warming, coinciding with an alarming decline in biodiversity and a looming mass extinction event, have broken into the public consciousness, even if many who wield the levers of power profess to disbelieve what is happening before their eyes, or dismiss its significance for the future of the planet and for humanity.

And now, as I write this in December 2020, we are struggling to cope with a global pandemic that has to all intents and purposes shut down worldwide travel. From this perspective, I look back on my own globetrotting as a birder and wonder whether that kind of activity will ever be possible again. The Golden Age may already be over. But this is not the time or place for me to speculate about the future; indeed, by the time you read this, whatever I write now about the future of birding is probably going to leave me with egg on my face, so unpredictable is the course of this crisis.

So, I will mostly steer clear of prognostication. But I cannot miss the chance to draw parallels and to point out that the pandemic, with its source in a coronavirus that crossed from wild animals into humans with such devastating effects, has its roots in the same escalating intrusions by humans on wild habitats that I have been pondering throughout this book.[96] This is not to say that birders are in any direct way a significant part of this particular problem. We intrude on wild habitats, but not in a way and at a scale that is likely directly to result in species-crossing infection events. These have their origins in much larger-scale phenomena accompanying the spread of human settlement on the fringes of wild habitats, such as bush-meat hunting and the domestication of more and more species for commercial gain, either to add to the human food chain or to the stocks of medicinal remedies. And world birders are only a very small part of the constellation of indirect facilitators that result in the spread of novel viruses across the globe, once the disease has been let loose on the human population by these other forces. Nonetheless, we are a part of it.

So, the good times may be coming to an end. The continuing destruction of habitats and the increasing levels of threat to ever more species, if left unchecked, could shortly reduce life on the planet to a pale shadow of its current (much less its former) state. The irony, or tragedy, of all of this is acute: just as birders gained the means better to engage with and enjoy the whole world of birds, so that world seems to be falling apart. We can dip into our pockets (if they are deep enough) to pay the additional costs of post-pandemic world travel and we can do something towards a 'fix' for this and future pandemics through advances in science and technology. But the alarming and accelerating decline of wildlife (aside, that is, from viruses and bacteria) is another matter. Money and technology alone may not be enough.

We have seen the extinction crisis coming for a long time. Even on our local patches, the 'Backyard Bird Count' and its various versions in different countries, when everyone is encouraged to spend a few hours naming and counting the birds in their back garden, has turned from being a celebration of our enjoyment of birds into being a dismal record of their decline and disappearance. We clutch at the good news that a few species are thriving as environmental conditions change, but the signs are clear that, overall, these changes are doing more harm than good.

Birders as a community are, at one and the same time, acutely aware of some of these threats to birdlife and are more and more motivated to celebrate what remains. In North America, for example, they can still enjoy the spring migration at key hotspots, where birders gather in their thousands and marvel at the spectacle of up to 40 species of warbler congregating at the same stop-over refuges that they have used for millennia; or they can visit Hawk Mountain Sanctuary in eastern Pennsylvania and watch the raptors streaming overhead on a good migration day.

That these spectacles are still accessible in the modern age is due in no small part to a century plus legacy of conservation. Everywhere a birder goes, nature reserves are key birding locations. These days, every nature reserve seems to house its vulnerable or endangered species. Many are public, but an increasing number are private. Both depend on voluntary contributions and paying visitors, such as birders, to keep them going. Many are prime birding destinations, where all the tricks of the trade that bring birders close to birds so they can see them can be brought to bear.

In these and other, less protected places, the phenomenon of extinction birding has become a significant part of what many birders do, particularly world birders. They chase

96 Josef Settele, Sandra Diaz, Eduardo Brondizio and Peter Daszak, 'COVID-19 stimulus measures must save lives, protect livelihoods and safeguard nature to reduce the risk of future pandemics', Intergovernmental Science-Policy Platform on Biodiversity and Ecosystem Services (IPBES), 27 April 2020.

rarities, most notably birds that are on the verge of extinction. Some of these birds are in desperate straits and may actually go extinct, but many are for the time being kept more or less safe in refuges created for the purpose, spurred on by the conservation movement, reliant on advances in conservation science and sometimes supported by the economic proceeds of avian tourism.

For the most part, birding and conservation have a symbiotic relationship – good for both the birds and also for birders. But while extinction birding gets me lots of ticks, many of them leave a bitter taste. The remaining refuges are a hollowed-out version of the natural world that once existed. They are, in one sense, a weak substitute for more radical, holistic efforts to conserve the richness and diversity of the natural world. And with climate change, the very idea of preservation-in-place of vulnerable species is being seriously challenged. The smaller and more confined to refuges is the surviving population of a species, the greater the loss of genetic diversity and chances of survival, particularly with rapid changes in climatic conditions. Unless climate change is arrested, the right climatic and habitat conditions will, in relatively short order, move somewhere else, where there is little or no protection. Many birds, especially migratory ones, will not move fast enough with the changing climate as they seek out their winter and summer habitats. They will arrive at the wrong place, at the wrong time, as the seasons move and as local weather patterns and climate change.

The very concept of extinction birding expresses a looming tragedy. The extinction of any species is in each case a catastrophe, for which in the current age we bear the great bulk of the responsibility. Extinctions are not new, of course, but the contemporary mass extinction rate is of an entirely different order to the underlying rate of extinction. It is sudden, massive and caused by humans. Multiple forms of life, evolved into species over millennia by the struggles for survival and procreation by individual members of successive generations, are being lost forever in the blink of an eyelid. Not only these species' cultural heritages, but also the individual strivings of millions of individuals across many generations to reproduce their kind, are being disrespected and discounted by the actions of modern humanity.[97]

As I have argued, birders and birding can't escape being implicated in this tragedy, however much we engage in efforts to mitigate it. World birders in particular participate in the kind of over-consumption that is helping to drive the escalating biodiversity crisis. Global tourism, including avian tourism, invariably carries some degree of threat due to the fragility of many places that are labelled 'must visit'. While there are significant benefits to wildlife from the birding industry, the stronger the incentives to bird in the remaining accessible hotspot locations, the more likely it is that mass birding will result in growing levels of intrusion and disturbance to the birdlife. Meanwhile, no nook or cranny of the world's diverse but diminishing wilderness habitats will remain unexplored by intrepid birders as they pursue and capture their trophies. The harder the birds get to see, the more they will be sought after. In the process, the risks of over-exploitation will grow in these places, as well as in the more accessible ones.

And there is another thing, the elephant in the room – the carbon footprint left by the world birder. I can plausibly argue that responsible ecotourism, and world birding specifically, bring direct and indirect benefits to local conservation efforts, helping in however small a way to arrest biodiversity and habitat loss. It is a different thing to defend

97 Thom van Dooren, *Flight Ways: Life and Loss at the Edge of Extinction*, New York, NY: Columbia University Press, 2014.

World birders in their natural habitat, Kota Kupang, Indonesia

my frequent-flying in the face of growing evidence of its impact – however tiny on an individual level – to greenhouse gas emissions. This is not the place to engage with the scientific debates about human-made climate change. I accept the overwhelming scientific consensus that recent, rapid global warming is due to human-induced greenhouse gas emissions and could be slowed or reversed by reducing them. For the globetrotting birder, this growing realization has presented an increasingly stark dilemma. World birders are among the champions of air-miles accumulation; the contribution of greenhouse gas emissions from commercial aircraft to global warming is significant; and global warming is going to impact bird populations and their habitats significantly and almost certainly detrimentally.

There have to date been no effective measures to limit the carbon emissions of the airline industry to levels that are consistent with reaching the bare minimum of safe global warming targets. Everywhere, countries and cities are investing billions in building new airports and runways. Middle classes in both developed and developing countries have come to expect air travel to be cheap and readily available. So, too, have birders. The pandemic has temporarily almost halted business (both of air travel and of avian tourism), but nearly everyone is clamouring to get it going again. Technological changes that might make air transport carbon-neutral are at the moment pie-in-the-sky and (even if they work) too far away to make a significant impact before it is too late.[98] Increased fuel efficiency may slow the pace of growth of emissions, but this is not nearly enough. Efforts to reach international agreements have moved at a snail's pace. Until they speed up and produce results, less flying is the only answer.

But as to world birders' airline travel, I have a somewhat heterodox position when seen from my starting point as a nature lover. I don't think that the solution lies in voluntarily reducing our air miles. Over the years, I have done what I can, short of stopping flying altogether, to mitigate my contributions to greenhouse gases. One obvious way was to buy

98 Umair Irfan, 'Air travel is surging. that's a huge problem for the climate', *Vox Media*, 13 January 2019.

carbon offsets, which in some shape or form compensated for my carbon emissions by reducing someone else's or by promoting carbon storage (such as tree planting). But these, at a macro-level, have generally not succeeded. So why didn't I stop flying and end my world birding adventures?

This kind of self-denial may be worthy and satisfy an itching conscience, but it somehow misses the main point. Going down the personal responsibility path buys into a false narrative, gleefully latched onto by climate change deniers, that seeks to discredit us for our hypocrisy, when the overwhelming burden of blame clearly lies elsewhere. Their argument is trolling, pure and simple. Our hypocrisy can be measured against our concern; their cynicism reflects a lack of it.[99]

This is a problem that can only be solved by sustained public policy initiatives among cooperating governments. It is a corrosive fallacy that caring individuals should assume the burden of personal responsibility for matters that are a collective responsibility, involving everybody who travels or who benefits from airfreighted door-to-door deliveries. Effective actions against climate change, including reducing the carbon footprint of the aviation industry, require governments and international organizations to take measures to establish policies and rules that seek to change everyone's behaviour, not just that of the already converted. It will make little difference in the bigger scheme of things for a few tens or hundreds of thousands of birders to think afresh about the possible impacts of what they are doing before they take off on their next international flight, if most of the rest of the population just carries on as before.

Aside from mitigating my carbon emissions I have also been contributing to the environmental movement and I have been voting for political parties that promote a serious programme to reverse global warming and climate change, including taxing and regulating airlines for their carbon emissions. I have no doubt that technology will be a big part of the solution, but in the meantime, governments have to poke and prod corporations to develop and adopt it – and quickly. We can sit and wait for the pie-in-the-sky technology to arrive and magically solve the problem for us at no cost; or we can support measures, such as carbon taxes, green energy initiatives and decarbonization of infrastructure investment through subsidies and direct investments, that would accelerate this process. Under these conditions, I would willingly pay more for my air travel and, because my pockets aren't bottomless, as a result fly less.

In any case, perhaps it's time to slow down a bit and place more emphasis on the basic value underlying why we are birders: our love of nature and birds, wherever and however many. What motivates too many world birders is the same thing that urges on every high-end consumer: a desire to own the most prestigious status goods and to receive more and more acclaim and admiration – not to mention self-congratulation – for the achievement. In our case, it is the longest list and the shiniest birding trophies.

The tension between my pursuit of pleasure as a birder and my finding so much happening before my eyes that at the same time prompts unease or dismay has been the underlying theme of this book. But the unhappiness I have felt is also dispelled by the hope that the birders of today and in the future can provide a counterweight, a small but significant corrective to the gloomy narrative. At the very least, birders can provide an exemplar as first and foremost nature lovers rather than bean counters and trophy collectors, and by conveying their joy and wonder to their friends and loved ones.

99 George Monbiot, 'I'd rather be a hypocrite than a cynic…', *The Guardian*, 6 August 2008.

The joy experienced by birders when they encounter a magical slice of wildlife is, taking the optimistic view, something that is near universal among all humans. There is evidence for this. Darryl Jones in his book *Birds at My Table*, estimates that between one-third and one-half of all households in countries in parts of Europe, North America and Australia enjoy feeding birds on their balconies or in their gardens. All this suggests there is a deep well of appreciation and sympathy for nature (and for birds in particular) lurking within the human species. Labelled 'biophilia', this is an idea widely attributed to biologist Edward O. Wilson, who wrote a book of the same name in 1984.[100] Let's hope he was right.

But the hope that individual sentiments of this kind will result in everyone 'seeing the light' and changing their behaviour is unrealistic. Like individual international flyers, individual nature lovers will look around them and see everyone else carrying on as before – and so they will as well. Collective and organized action is required, not only from governments but also from communities and associations, such as those formed by bird lovers. The size and potential power of these communities has grown in recent years. The pandemic has accelerated this trend, especially as people have looked for some relief from indoor monotony during lockdowns. The birding community must think hard about what exemplars to offer newcomers, and how they can lead the way in emphasizing the values embedded in appreciating birds for what they are, rather than for what individual ambitions they can satisfy.

In this book, I have tried to convey some of the magic and wonder of birding as one among many possible expressions of a love of nature. This has certainly been my overwhelming experience, although it has been tinged and tainted by my observations of habitat loss and of species decline, and by my participation in forms of birding that I have grown increasingly uncomfortable with. Reflecting on all of this, I now spend more time slow birding on my local patch. COVID-19 and the lockdowns have encouraged, indeed, necessitated this. And, admittedly, advancing age has also made it more congenial. I have rediscovered the delights of being a backyard birder: in my Canberra garden, the twittering Yellow-rumped Thornbills and Silvereyes picking greenfly off the roses; the antics of the Willie Wagtails; the tail-upping and squeaking of the Superb Fairywrens; the dawn and evening melodies of the Common Blackbirds in spring (invaders though they may be here Down Under); and the brazenness of the cockatoos wantonly gorging on the seeds and nuts in my trees. I look out of my window, knowing the species names mean less and less – especially as, in one or two cases, I have begun to know the individuals.

So, I now place less emphasis on the life list and more on the pure enjoyment of watching birds as they go about their daily lives. I shall no doubt do a few more long-distance trips during the coming years, while I still can (and pandemics allowing). But I feel the urgency waning. I have come to appreciate the benefits of slow birding more than I expected. I chase less; and I sit, watch and listen more. I get a thrill out of occasionally coming across Superb Parrots in my local nature reserve and (who knows?) one day I might spot a much rarer Swift Parrot. Slow birding needn't drain the excitement out of looking for special birds. And there are still a few species not far removed from where I live that I have never seen, or only rarely, and I shall keep listening and looking in case they turn up. Indeed, I saw one the other day – the Australian Painted-Snipe.[101] But just as rewarding was a nesting pair of

100 Edward O. Wilson, *Biophilia*, Cambridge, MA: Harvard University Press, 1984.

101 Martin Painter, '2020 Was Not That Bad After All', *anthropocenebirder.com*, January 4, 2021

Hello, Cocky

familiar White-winged Trillers, which I stood and watched for twenty minutes' from under a nearby tree.

Seeing new birds is less and less the main thing. I am recovering something more fundamental about birdwatching that got me started in the first place, namely just a love for birds, while winding back on some of the more peripheral, secondary and mundane elements of being a birder. My bird-loving exemplars these days are not so much Ludlow Griscom and the Bronx birders striding through Central Park with bins at the ready, on the lookout for rarities, trying to be the first to spot them and recording it all on their lists. Rather, they are more John Keats, reclining under his plum tree and just listening; and John Clare, observing his Yellowhammers with curiosity, wonder and sympathy.

INDEX